**Architectural Design**
September/October 2006

Collective Intelligence in Design

Guest-edited by
Christopher Hight and Chris Perry

D0510569

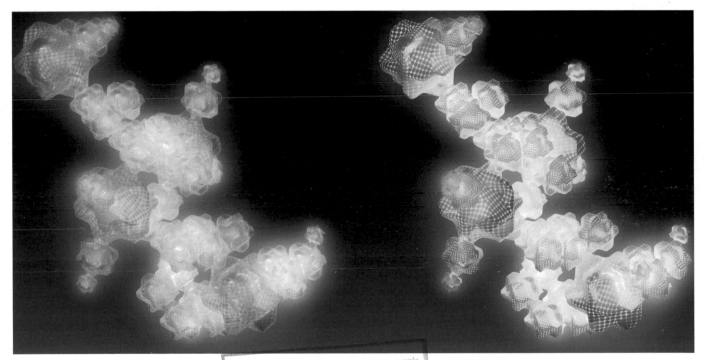

WILEY-ACADEMY

**ISBN-13** 9780470026526
**ISBN-10** 0470026529
**Profile No 183**
**Vol 76 No 5**

Editorial Offices
International House
Ealing Broadway Centre
London W5 5DB

T: +44 (0)20 8326 3800
F: +44 (0)20 8326 3801
E: architecturaldesign@wiley.co.uk

Editor
Helen Castle

Production Controller
Jenna Brown

Project Management
Caroline Ellerby

Design and Prepress
Artmedia Press, London

Printed in Italy by Conti Tipocolor

Advertisement Sales
Faith Pidduck/Wayne Frost
T +44 (0)1243 770254
E fpidduck@wiley.co.uk

Editorial Board
Will Alsop, Denise Bratton, Adriaan Beukers,
André Chaszar, Peter Cook, Teddy Cruz,
Max Fordham, Massimiliano Fuksas,
Edwin Heathcote, Anthony Hunt,
Charles Jencks, Jan Kaplicky, Robert Maxwell,
Jayne Merkel, Monica Pidgeon,
Antoine Predock, Michael Rotondi,
Leon van Schaik, Ken Yeang

Contributing Editors
André Chaszar
Jeremy Melvin
Jayne Merkel

All Rights Reserved. No part of this publication
may be reproduced, stored in a retrieval system
or transmitted in any form or by any means,
electronic, mechanical, photocopying, recording,
scanning or otherwise, except under the terms
of the Copyright, Designs and Patents Act 1988
or under the terms of a licence issued by the
Copyright Licensing Agency Ltd, 90 Tottenham
Court Road, London W1T 4LP, UK, without the
permission in writing of the Publisher.

Front cover: Designed by Aaron White, the graphic
architecture of this diagram indexes the inherently
collective and decentralised nature of the work
featured in this issue of *AD*. © Aaron White

Requests to the Publisher should be addressed to:
Permissions Department,
John Wiley & Sons Ltd,
The Atrium
Southern Gate
Chichester,
West Sussex PO19 8SQ
England

F: +44 (0)1243 770571
E: permreq@wiley.co.uk

Subscription Offices UK
John Wiley & Sons Ltd
Journals Administration Department
1 Oldlands Way, Bognor Regis
West Sussex, PO22 9SA
T: +44 (0)1243 843272
F: +44 (0)1243 843232
E: cs-journals@wiley.co.uk

[ISSN: 0003-8504]

*AD* is published bimonthly and is available to
purchase on both a subscription basis and as
individual volumes at the following prices.

Single Issues
Single issues UK: £22.99
Single issues outside UK: US$45.00
Details of postage and packing charges
available on request.

Annual Subscription Rates 2006
Institutional Rate
Print only or Online only: UK£175/US$290
Combined Print and Online: UK£193/US$320
Personal Rate
Print only: UK£99/US$155
Student Rate
Print only: UK£70/US$110
Prices are for six issues and include postage
and handling charges. Periodicals postage paid
at Jamaica, NY 11431. Air freight and mailing in
the USA by Publications Expediting Services
Inc, 200 Meacham Avenue, Elmont, NY 11003
Individual rate subscriptions must be paid by
personal cheque or credit card. Individual rate
subscriptions may not be resold or used as
library copies.

All prices are subject to change
without notice.

Postmaster
Send address changes to 3 Publications
Expediting Services, 200 Meacham Avenue,
Elmont, NY 11003

# C O N T E N T S

LEEDS BECKETT
LIBRARY
DISCARDED

LEEDS METROPOLITAN
UNIVERSITY
LIBRARY
1704759401
AD-B
CC-78176/2006
13.11.06
729.0285

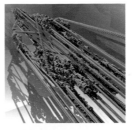

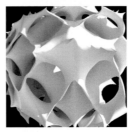

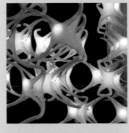

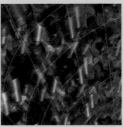

AD+

# Editorial

It is now 15 years since the establishment of the World Wide Web. When one considers the changes it has wrough globally, a decade and a half seems a long time. Despite architecture's love affair with the novel in general, and new technologies in particular, architecture has been comparatively slow to understand the full potential of telecommunications. The first few wavelets of change, however, are starting to crash against the shore of conventional architectural practice. There is now no doubt that changes in the way practice is organised, networked and exchanged, as well as the profile of desired design knowledge is shifting in architectural culture. However, this i often difficult to discern within the whole picture as strong, slow currents exist alongside new faster currents; the hegemony of some of the biggest corporate practices will not be given up too easily (and will not, ultimately, be surrendered if they prove themselves adept enough at evolving their working patterns and practices from within).

In this issue of *AD*, Christopher Hight and Chris Perry have effectively traced many of the most nascent shifts in architectural practice. The picture they draw is an exciting, fast-paced one, but also for many a precarious one in which geographically and culturally separated specialists are united only by their current 'endeavour'. Architect are no longer protected by any of the old institutional or professional shields, but are acquired for their own perceived skill sets and abilities. The new global market is a meritocracy based on an individual's ability to network and gain a tenable reputation. As attested by Kevin Kennon's article, here, on the experience of United Architects at the World Trade Center, this new form of collaborative practice has already been tried and tested o a prestigious international project. It is also a model that is being fully asserted within some of the world's top architecture schools, such as the AA, Columbia, Cornell, RMIT, MIT and SCI-Arc, featured here. With their fully international intake, these schools often become the springboard for more mature collaborations. This is certainly true of OCEAN net, whose inception dates back to the AA of the early 1990s and is perhaps the oldest of the geographically distributed practices. Michael Hensel's account in this issue is a celebration of this way of working, convincing us to embrace the transitory, unstable and ever-mutating shape of practice to come.

Helen Cast

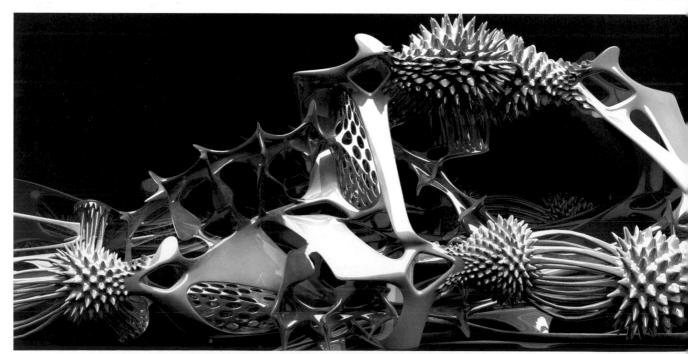

**Detail perspective of the final version of the bridge/species replacing the Brooklyn Bridge by Greg Derrico, a graduate student of Hernan Diaz-Alonso at Columbia University. Working across institutions at Columbia and with Benjamin Bratton at SCI-Arc, Diaz-Alonso encourages different modes of collectivity within his students' work (see pp 109–11).**

# Collective Intelligence in Design

In their introduction to this issue, **Christopher Hight** and **Chris Perry** define the idea of collective intelligence in its relationship to design practice and to broader technological and social formations. First they suggest a reformulation of practices around networked communication infrastructures as conduits for the new orchestrations of power that Antonio Negri and Michael Hardt detailed in their books *Empire* and *Multitude*. They then describe how such practices are often involved in the development of responsive sensing environments as new sites for manifesting the social organisations and communities made possible via telecommunications and the Internet. Lastly, they address how traditional boundaries of design disciplines and knowledge, from architecture to programming, are opening into complex co-minglings of their respective isolated 'intelligences' into collectives capable of engaging these new sites, new briefs and new sorts of projects.

That digital technology has transformed the forms and spaces of what we design has become commonplace. Its transformative potential for forms of design practice and spaces of knowledge has remained less examined, but is ultimately more radical in its implications. With the shift from the second machine age to that of information, the reflexive network has replaced the assembly line as a pre-eminent model of organisation even as media infrastructures have augmented physical transportation at multiple scales stretching from discrete sites of production and consumption, to economic, political and even social institutions. This nexus of computation, telecommunications and new organisations of economic and political power suggest that the 19th-century division of design into distinct professions might now be displaced by different organisations of knowledge and practices. The texts and projects contained in this issue demonstrate how networks of international, transdisciplinary, decentralised practices are emerging to reposition and retool design practice to engage today's unconventional problems, site briefs, clients and manufacturing processes.

'Collective intelligence', as both a concept and a term, has its roots in a number of historical and contemporary contexts. In the 1960s Marshall McLuhan noticed the emergence of new social organisations based on principles of decentralisation and collectivity. Enabled in part by the advent of telecommunication technology, McLuhan quaintly referred to this model as 'the global village'.[1] Computing pioneer Douglas Englebart went further by suggesting that communication

*Collective intelligence is not purely a cognitive object. Intelligence must be understood here in its etymological sense of joining together* (interlegere), *as uniting not only ideas but people, constructing society.*[2]

*The alchemy of collaboration does not merge the two authors into a single voice but rather proliferates them to create the chorus of a multitude.*[3]

technology does not simply augment pre-existing social orders, but is instead a mechanism for augmenting the human intellect with nonhumanist modes of production.[4]

Telecommunications have proved even more transformative than imagined, whether the rapid decentralisation of international corporate enterprise or the grassroots phenomenon of the peer-to-peer network (such as open-source software communities like BitTorrent, as well as alternative political organisations like smart mobs, moveon.org, and so on). Some are seen as ominous and dystopic forms of globalisation, while others lend themselves to a utopic and liberatory reading of communication technologies. In either case, collective intelligence is not simply technical, but also explicitly social, political and, by extension, professional. As Pierre Lévy has argued, these technologies increasingly dematerialise the closed boundaries of disciplines, making knowledge a 'larger patchwork' in which one field can be enfolded with another.[5] Moreover, for Michel Serres, knowledge and its techniques of electronic production and recombination become a new kind of infrastructure as disciplinary specificity is opened to practices of collaborative exchange. Thus, *Collective Intelligence in Design* attempts to map the reconfiguration of discrete design practices and disciplines into hypercommunicative technosocial networks.

**Biopolitics and New Forms of Practice**

*the multitude is diffident of representation. ... The people is always represented as a unity, whilst the multitude is not representable, because [it] is a singular multiplicity, a concrete universal. The people constituted a social body; the multitude does not ... it is an active agent of self-organization.*[6]

The first way this is manifested is the relationship of design practice to the telecommunication technologies and their relationship to social power and order. With their influential books, *Empire* and *Multitude: War and Democracy in the Age of Empire*, the collaborative writing team of Michael Hardt and Antonio Negri have provided a lens through which to focus an analysis of the destructive as well as the productive effects of the shift from a disciplinary society to a biopolitical ordering of power. In brief, the term 'disciplinary society' (stemming from the work of Michel Foucault) describes a social ordering that relies primarily on physical and spatial mechanisms for instituting power. This is epitomised by Foucault's iconic

description of the Panopticon prison. This disciplinary society differs dramatically from what Gilles Deleuze termed the 'control society', in which power is instituted from within and at the scale of the body. Combined, Foucault and Deleuze's work suggested a biopolitics that marks an important shift in the nature of power exercised upon general classes of society via physical space (and by extension architecture, at least as constituted in modernity) to the use of information at the scale of the individual subjects as a virtual controlling mechanism. For the sake of our argument, the economic corollary is often called post-Fordism, in which mass production is replaced by mass customisation, and rigid labour and productive practices are replaced by mobile and global markets.

What Hardt and Negri call 'Empire' uses the phenomena and technologies of our biopolitical power to produce increasingly centralised and integrated networks of international and intercorporate power – for example, in the form of pre-emptive wars and international markets rather than democratic control. In contrast, Hardt and Negri's reinvigoration of the concept of the 'Multitude' is a way of

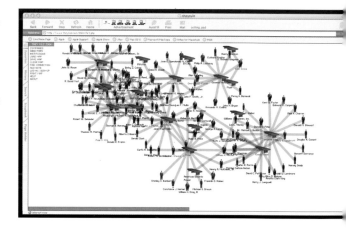

**Josh On, Screenshot of theyrule.net website, 2006**
The website provides a database of various companies and institutions, allowing the user to map connections between those companies and institutions by way of shared executives and investments.

imagining the emergence of new forms of social, economic and political power enabled by the very same communication and information technologies, wherein a common space is constructed by linking an infinitely diverse set of individual interests through shared projects or desires in a more responsively democratic biopolitical ordering.

Prototypical examples of the Multitude include political organisations fostered by networking technologies, such as the highly distributed moveon.org and the partially Internet coordinated World Trade Organization (WTO) resistance movement, but also user-generated organisations like the file-sharing communities of myspace and flickr or the online encyclopaedia network Wikipedia, open-source movements and peer-to-peer platforms. In these communities, participants operate from a variety of discrete locations spanning massive geographical distances via intensively reflexive feedback loops of communication and exchange. Dispersed and horizontal communication allows multiple agents to participate in the development of a particular material or technology via the Internet and its decentralising effects. The participants are at once geographically and culturally *apart from* one another while also a *part of* a common space of endeavour.[7]

Furthermore, these communities not only rely on communication, but produce communicability, that is to say the generation of new information as a product, and platforms for exchange.[8] Such multitudes operate according to a collective intelligence at the scale of practice. Such practices are inclusively political projects in so far that the resulting design becomes a site through which to configure the relationships between subjects and technologies. Indeed, their spaces may be the 21st century's biopolitical equivalent of the 19th century's architectural figuration of disciplinary power, as found in the Panopticon or, in a more liberatory way, the modern metropolis.

A number of design practices, as well as research groups, have started to learn from these models of distributed exchange and production, extending their logics to reconfigure the design office or research lab format by recasting it as an international, intergeographic, inter-institutional design-based file-sharing community. Examples featured in this issue include professional design practices such as servo, OCEAN net, United Architects (UA) and Open Source Architecture (O-S-A), as well as various inter-institutional research groups that integrate both academic and professional forms of design knowledge (the MIT Media Lab's OPENSTUDIO, RMIT's SIAL department, the Architectural Association's DRL, Cornell's Responsive Systems Group and the Columbia-based research practice CONTINUUM).

### Intelligent Technologies and New Forms of Design

*In computers everything becomes number: imageless, soundless, wordless quantity ... any medium can be translated into another ... a total connection of all media on a digital base erases the notion of the medium itself. Instead of hooking up technologies to people, absolute knowledge can run as an endless loop.*[9]

The second aspect of collective intelligence in design lay within the relationship of design technology and design products to emerging technological and material systems, specifically those concerned with the development of smart, or intelligent – or perhaps at this relatively early stage of development, simply adaptable – modes of behaviour. Examples in which intelligence is embedded in a given technological or material system range from genetic and nano engineering, to the development of new and increasingly adaptable organic LED display systems and amorphous alloys,

as well as the burgeoning field of programmable matter (material systems in which fundamental properties of that material – for example, its rigidity or flexibility – can be altered via information). Such technologies integrate the predictive capacity of humans with the sophisticated computational and operational abilities of a technological apparatus. Such hybrid assemblages are more profound than wholly artificial intelligence, suggesting a nonhumanist understanding of agency and collective intelligence based on connectivity and molecular biotechnical power.

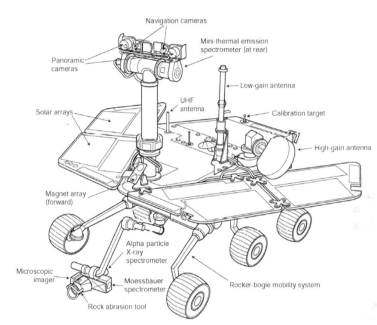

**NASA, Mars Rover, 2003**
The Mars Rover is an example of the vast and sophisticated assembly of emerging sensory, computation and behavioural technologies, combining to give the machine partial intelligence. While the rover relies on its human counterparts (users located back on earth) for strategic decision-making, its various sensing technologies allow it to make local decisions.

Many of the projects and practices featured in this issue are investigating such hybrid intelligent technological and material systems, whether as a site for professional practice or as research for interinstitutional groups. This includes the development of design environments that incorporate new software in connection with interaction technologies (such as information and motion sensing), as well as material systems in the form of adaptable surface structures and responsive machinic assemblies.

### Design Synthesis and New Forms of Transdisciplinarity

*The social network is a form of heterogeneous engineering comprised not only of people, but also of machines, animals, art and discourse, currency, architecture – the stuff of the social therefore, isn't simply human but a vast network of objects, human and non-human alike*[10]

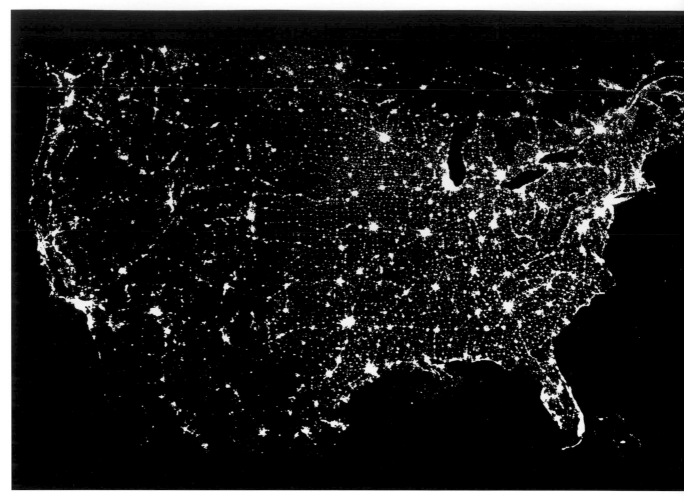

**National Oceanic and Atmospheric Administration (NOAA), Composite
satellite photo of lights in North America, 1994–95**
The image shows settlement patterns via infrastructure: the Internet provides
a similar infrastructure for social geographies of the 21st century.

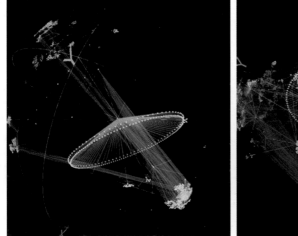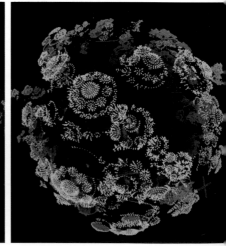

**Cooperative Association for Internet Data Analysis (CAIDA), Walrus
rendering of Internet, 2003**
Image of an Internet 'map' using the Walrus software currently being
developed by the collaborative network visualisation organisation CAIDA.

While we have located two primary scales of collective intelligence – the first generally regarding the scale of design *practice*, the second the scale of design *technology* and *product* – both are, of course, always integral to one another. Traditionally, design practice may appear as primarily *social* in nature, and thus analysed via loosely sociological terms, while the design product is regarded as primarily *material* or *technological* and therefore interpreted as an artefact representing cultural production. Our argument is that whether one is looking at the scale of society (its various institutional organisations and, by extension, the individual and collaborative behaviours of the agents and actors that make up those organisations), or the machines and technologies that are an extension of that social body, one cannot differentiate practice from product, or a notion of the human or social from the technological or the natural. Rather, one finds a much more ambiguous and synthetic set of conditions.

Embodied and embedded in a variety of material forms and scales, intelligence can be seen as at once a form of material matter and of organising and ordering those materials, a kind of 'heterogeneous engineering' in which bits and pieces from the social, the technical, the conceptual and the textual are connected and translated into a set of equally heterogeneous scientific (or, in our case, design) products.[11] Social relations shape machines as much as machines or new forms of technology shape social relations. Indeed, Bruno Latour has recently reiterated that rather than see the social as a distinct thing or domain, it is nothing more or less than the topologies of connectivity between a multitude of agencies, from the human to the material. Even science does not, in the first instance, investigate nature; nor do social forces determine knowledge. Rather, what is at stake is the design of network collectives of people, machines, technologies of communication and production.

### Opening the Fields

*We are seeing the combination of network communications and social networks. Whenever a new communications technology lowers the threshold for groups to act collectively, new kinds of institutions emerge.*[12]

Understood in this way, collective intelligence requires a transdisciplinary approach to the built environment. Hence, this publication features a number of design fields including architectural design, interaction and information design, product design, sound design, software and interface design, motion graphic and typography design, set and exhibition design, and lighting design.

Rather than offer a stabilising or interpretive grid of explanation for these practices, we have attempted to install a collective intelligence within the issue itself, one the reader can engage with at a variety of levels, speeds, modes and angles of approach, from the pragmatic to the erudite, from

media and programming to construction details. Instead of presenting an in-depth analysis of a few practices we could pretend represent 'collective intelligence', we have tried to map out a heterogeneous network of interconnected practices and their concerns. Furthermore, this issue of *AD* is itself an example of collective intelligence, written and edited collaboratively through Internet technologies (blogs, wikis, ftp sites and email), from several cities and multiple institutional and intellectual contexts, and through distributed forms of production and identity. Moreover, during the nine-month editorial process, some of the featured collaborations reconfigured, dissolved or gained new interconnectivities. To this extent, the issue is a historical cross section of nodes within an evolving network of agents, projects and ideas. Like a map of the Internet, it is accurate as a representation only for the fleeting moment; its enduring usefulness lies in its triangulations of potential trajectories into the future.

Ultimately, innovative design does not concern the novel appearance of objects, but rather constructing new manifolds for the production of knowledge that transform the objects given by known tools and sets of practices. The first design problem, therefore, is the construction of a precise and synthetic commons of exchange across previously separate and distinct areas or fields of design. Such trandisciplinarity requires and precipitates the construction of a collective intelligence through the design process itself. All design is the production of techniques of connectivity. The result is not so much a product of this process as it is a platform for it, inseparable from its continual unfolding of new technosocial lifeworlds. ⌂

**Notes**
1. Marshall McLuhan, *Understanding Media: The Extensions of Man*, MIT Press (Cambridge, MA), 1964.
2. Pierre Lévy, *Collective Intelligence: Mankind's Emerging World in Cyberspace*, Perseus Books (London), 1997, p 10.
3. 'The Theory & Event Interview: Sovereignty, Multitudes, Absolute Democracy: A Discussion between Michael Hardt and Thomas L Dumm about Hardt's and Negri's Empire', in Paul A Passavant and Jodi Dean (eds), *Empire's New Clothes: Reading Hardt and Negri*, Routledge (London), 2004, p 163.
4. Pierre Lévy, op cit.
5. For more on the concept of patchwork, see Lévy. op cit.
6. Antonio Negri, 'Approximations: Towards an ontological definition of the multitude', *Interactivist Info Exchange*, 12 November 2002.
7. See Manuel Castells, *The Rise of the Network Society*, Blackwell Publishers (Oxford), 1996.
8. Jodi Dean, 'The Networked Empire: Communicative Capitalism and the Hope for Politics', in Passavant and Dean, op cit, p 163.
9. Friedrich Kittler, *Grammophon Film Typewriter*, Bosemann (Berlin), 1986.
10. John Law, 'Notes on the Theory of the Actor Network: Ordering, Strategy, and Heterogeneity', www.comp.lancs.ac.uk/sociology/papers/Law-Notes-on-ANT.pdf, Centre for Science Studies (Lancaster University), 1992 (2003), p 3.
11. Bruno Latour, *Reassembling the Social: An Introduction to Actor-Network-Theory*, Oxford University Press (New York), 2005, pp 220–21
12. Howard Rheingold, 'How the Protesters Mobilized', interview with Jennifer Lee, *New York Times*, 23 February 2003.

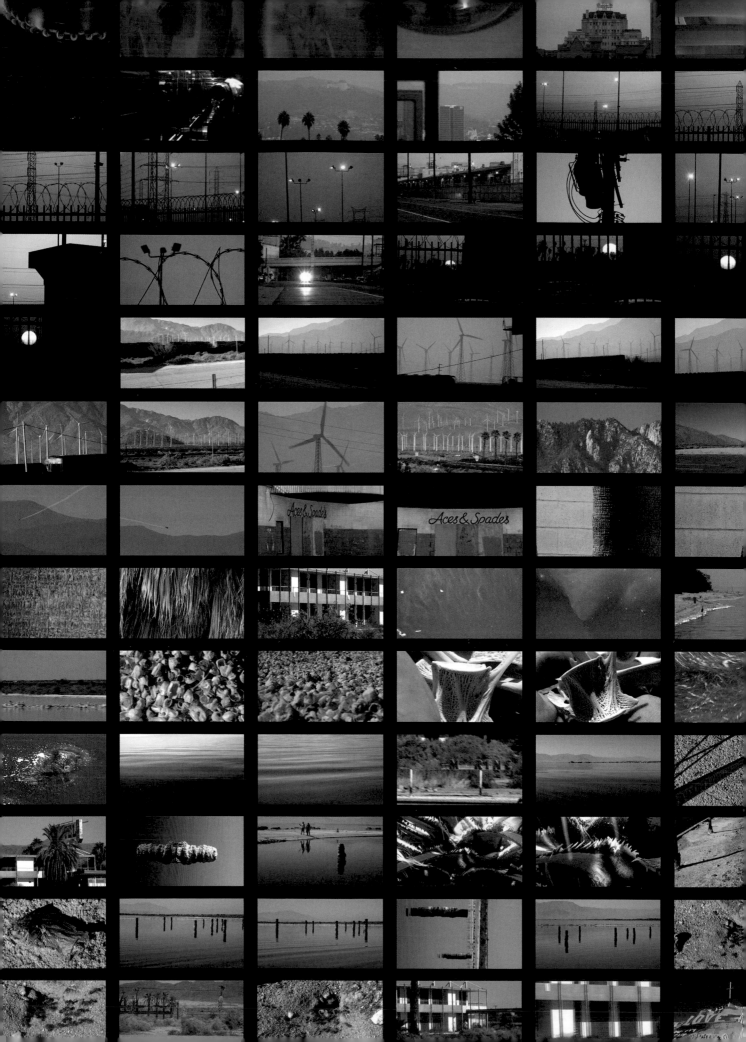

# Agent Intellects: Pattern as a Form of Thought

Integrating qualities and aspects particular to their previously independent practices, the work of **Ed Keller** and **Carla Leitao** of collaborative design and research practice a|Um Studio spans scales and sites of application. The practice embodies a collective intelligence in a number of ways. At the scale of design practice the collaboration bridges the design cultures of Europe and the US. At the scale of urban practice, its large-scale planning proposals investigate forms of collective use and activity within the city. In addition, its interactive installations and gaming interfaces explore the potential of film and responsive technology to enable informational exchange and production.

What is collective intelligence? A lively dispute continues about what exactly constitutes evidence of intelligence in systems as diverse as 'cultural, technological, and biological life forms' (Perry and Hight). At a|Um Studio, we felt it was important to develop a historical and theoretical context for the concept of collective intelligence, to critically position some examples of our engagement with it in our practice.

There are two primary definitions of the term 'collective intelligence'. The first implies a technologically enhanced mode of collaboration producing a group-based form of mind/behaviour, ultimately generating wildly increased (almost utopic) value. Today this idea often refers to the Internet, Web 2.0 concepts of P2P distribution, revolutionary disintermediations, folksonomies, emergent open-source software, network societies, and a postindustrial general economy, suggesting that the substrate for intelligence itself is increasingly a technologically enabled collective.

The second implies a more abstract set of relationships that depend, in fact, on the critical definition of the primary terms 'collective' and 'intelligence'. 'Collective' in this second usage no longer refers to a group of humans, but can be extended to encompass ecosystems, economies, social systems, and so on. And 'intelligence' no longer relies on anthropomorphically framed ideas of the production of value, but derives from the emergence of self-modifying patterns in material systems (for example, magnetohydrodynamic systems, convection cells, crystal growth) as well as other life forms (such as termite colonies). Thus, intelligence can be studied in these systems and life forms, and ever more baroque patterns can be discovered by examining the same systems at vast or minute time scales (millennia, picoseconds). Looking at the world this way premiates an abstract definition of intelligence that includes human capacities, but also goes beyond. This latter use of the term also has deep historical roots, as outlined below.

## A Brief History of Collective Intelligence

Historically, every successive school of thought's ideas of collective intelligence have reimagined the substrates necessary for communication and collective formation, and provided different expectations of what the yield of intelligence might be. This has provided many alternative models of collective behaviour, and radically redefined how we think about thought itself – and ultimately how we can extend epistemological horizons beyond the human.[1]

According to Pierre Lévy, the concept of collective intelligence first appeared in Farabian theology between the 10th and 12th centuries. Theosophical speculations emerging from a Neoplatonic interpretation of Aristotle, on the part of Al-Farabi, Ibn Sina, Maimonides et al, yielded the idea of 'a unique and separate collective intelligence, common to the entire human race, which could be thought of as a prototype for a shared or collective intellect. This "collective consciousness" was referred to as the *agent intellect* by these Aristotelian mystics because it was an ever-active intelligence, one that constantly contemplated true ideas and enabled human intelligences to become active (and therefore effective).'[2]

In a more contemporary setting, as technology's computational power has increased, there are now not only powerful networking tools, but also mathematical and conceptual models that are rapidly evolving a new set of representations of ever more complex systems. This has abstracted and highlighted a range of material computations that have always accompanied us as organisms. Indeed, all

**A|Um Studio, SUTURE, SCI-Arc and TELIC galleries, Los Angeles, California, November 2005–January 2006**
An index of gestures and materials. Stills from the SUTURE installation.

## A|Um Studio with Marta Caldeira, VISIBILITY, UIA Celebration of Cities International Competition entry, Portugal, 2003

A|Um Studio's UIA Celebration of Cities competition entry suggested that one could map a city to identify places of delay or acceleration of urban activity over time and, through this map, locate 'acupuncture' points in the city to open up flows and networks, converting zones that might be dangerous, arrested or frozen into areas of interaction.

Cities have many temporal registers, areas of history that appear and disappear, dissipating in structures that materialise as temporary or permanent walls. One of the most important capacities in the city is found in its temporary structures: that of the self-modification of meaning, that of intelligent material. The structures go from uncharacterised points to bright spaces of invention: exhibition galleries of diverse themes, experimentation places, meeting points, and so on.

A concept of urban systems in relationship to collective agency and intelligence was developed in this project on several scales. A 'healthy city' – an ideal agglomeration – is a condition born and developed through both the real and imaginary inventions of its inhabitants. All the participating agents in a city are immediate beneficiaries of urban evolution, and answer to time. Each contribution is unique and indispensable in the feedback loops of ongoing change. A 'diseased city' exists when citizens can no longer act as individual agents. Examples may be found in any urban situation that emphasises only unilateral or dual understanding of the environment. In such a case it becomes necessary to create new situations that render visible this individuality within the collective. The concept of marginality, for instance, is part of an urban mode of thought that is inclusive and, by nature, is engaged with the reconceptualisation of city edges. Any discussion of limits evokes not only what is exterior to the self, but also the integral internal elements of the city.

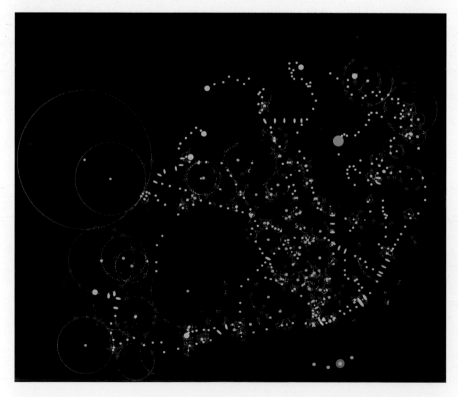

Nodes that exist in a marginal situation – in less safe areas, in less visible hours – establish their high visibility as pavilions, reinforcing relationships of connection with other temporalities, dissipating their initial condition as marginal concepts. A network of different nodal points was generated by mapping the city of Lisbon, Portugal. New points were discovered between points of great visibility – one temporal condition in the city – and their opposite: places where individuals experience a profound distance and remain invisible to the total urban system. Capturing the 'acupuncture' points, zones of visibility, formed by centres of influence, identified the 'acupuncture' points as three time cycles: night visibility (yellow), constant visibility (blue), and transition/mixed visibility (green).

The VISIBILITY project proposes a temporal complement to the city. Where the city extends its temporal zone of activity twofold, the network adds flexibility to that concept, establishing itself as an anchor or an inversion point. The network points function in syncopation with their inflection of the rhythm of the city, establishing themselves as catalysts for different programmes, forms of temporality and spatial regeneration. The network is formed by the alternating local and global activity of each node. The nodes are spaces of nightlife, present in the urban dream – they are anchoring points for the passage of individuals in a limited situation, when the capacity of self-expression is lost inside the urban context (homeless, placeless).

Cities should be nothing less than the great range of density of human desires, which are able to provoke constant creativity in others. The visibility given by the proposed structures announces a situation of play, of stage, of rehearsal, of temporary exercise of wills and desires, while simultaneously being devoted to the service of showing and caring for that same self-expression of others. These nodes bind themselves to their intelligent behaviour; that is, the way in which they construct themselves on a local level and then invent new articulations of situation in the network.

## A|Um Studio, SUTURE, SCI-Arc and TELIC galleries, Los Angeles, California, November 2005–January 2006

In SUTURE, an interactive multimedia installation, it was suggested that a collective intelligence could emerge as a kind of agency distributed locally on to the participants in each gallery. SUTURE was a cinematic experience of the mixing of spatial situations, gestures, materials and sounds – putting the visitor in an ambient pressure zone between multiple screens, each smoothly cross-fading and responding to the visitor's actions. New forms of sense and of agency developed through autonomous feedback loops within the media assemblage, embedding the visitor in an intricate relational structure of gestures, objects, events, materials and urban infrastructures, allowing the individual to actively reshape space and event.

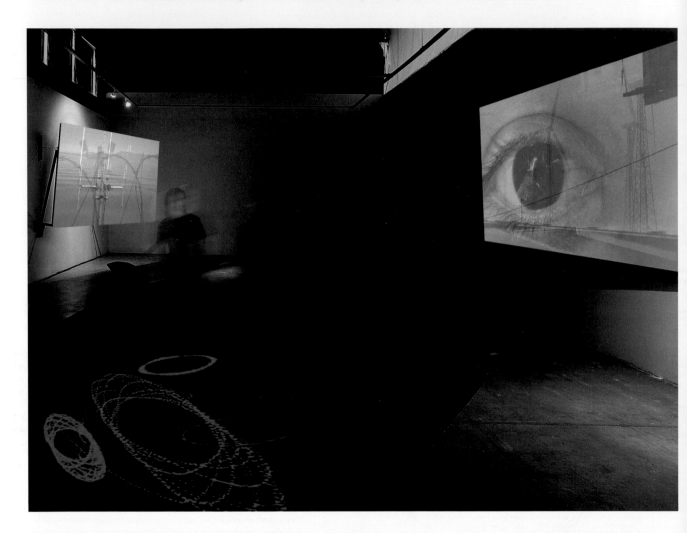

Physically, a landscape of sculpted furniture with pressure sensors located in the SCI-Arc gallery floor directed circulation flows and points of view, providing interaction points by encouraging visitors to create new signal paths and cycles of behaviour within the space. By walking, standing or sitting, visitors triggered different montage sequences, slowed down or sped up footage, zoomed in or out into different scales of shot, and in general modified the visual and audio footage with instant feedback indexed through the projection of waveforms on the gallery floor – a kind of real-time drawing board of sound. Visitors at TELIC could use a computer interface to trigger new montage sequences on a single projection screen locally and at the SCI-Arc gallery, and simultaneously see the effects at SCI-Arc via a webcam. Conceptually, we were interested in reconfiguring the concept of 'suture', a key term in film theory, in order to propose a new cinematic and architectural body created through the visitors' interactive editing of event, gesture and materiality. Instead of the semiotic framework from which the concept of 'suture' in film first emerged[3] we presented an interface to manifest it purely through space, gesture, material and cinematic-haptic fields. We redeployed the responsibility for cinematic edits to the visitors of the gallery. As they pass through the spaces their movements trigger a cascading series of remixes and overlaps of gesture and material footage. The rules were established as a framework to permeate a range of edits to take place; categories of homogeneous, singular or aggregate materials, and close-up, medium and long-shot gestures were mixed with different degrees of acceleration, creating inversions of the original sources, and switching the regularity of the space and time orientation. Instead of analysing footage for meaning, we relied entirely on the 'sense' built into each shot to develop rules for classifying and remixing. Gestures and materials go beyond the human and encompass urban situations, infrastructure and landscape. Desert spaces, transit spaces, and more distant abstract points of view – such as satellite orbits over the earth – established another scale in the footage.

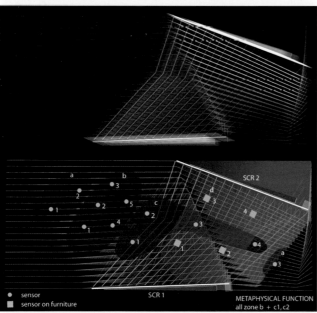

sensor
sensor on furniture

SCR 1    SCR 2    a    b    c    d

METAPHYSICAL FUNCTION
all zone b + c1, c2

'Every image, in fact, is animated by an antinomic polarity: on the one hand, images are the reification and obliteration of a gesture. ... on the other hand, they preserve the dynamics intact (as in Muybridge's snapshots or in any sports photograph). The former corresponds to the recollection seized by voluntary memory, while the latter corresponds to the image flashing in the epiphany of involuntary memory. And while the former lives in magical isolation, the latter always refers beyond itself to a whole of which it is a part ... The gesture ... opens the sphere of ethos as the more proper sphere of that which is human ... [and] is communication of a communicability.'[4] The SUTURE project proposed a way of working with collective intelligence (both the groups of people interacting with the project, but also the 'arrays of media' as autonomous, rule-driven bodies in the network itself) where the potential of different users and site interactions became responsible for actively renewing key concepts of ambience and environment. The installation placed each visitor in a position of agency to realise radical new scales and blends of gesture, material and situation.

Pressure sensors in the floor of the SCI-Arc gallery, and an Internet connection and mouse-driven interface at the TELIC gallery, controlled computer remixes of high-definition digital video and audio in both spaces. A total of four networked computers (three CPUs at SCI-Arc and one at TELIC), four video projections, and audio in both sites blended footage capturing multiple scales of material content, gesture content and mathematical representations of sound content. These cinematic layers accumulated and mutated according to rules of self-organisation that were built into the network, mixing the varying scales of the video content. The entire network and its rules were designed and built using the software MaxMSP/Jitter, a graphics-based programming software for the processing and filtering of interactive audiovisual media.

these mathematical models are inbuilt within the fabric of space–time itself, thus recent computational advances have simply rendered visible the same systems that have been conjectured, explored and exploited by philosophers and alchemists over the centuries. Accompanying these new digital models of organisation is the slow integration of post-thermodynamic ideas, which have been trickling down to the mainstream over the past half century and changing how we understand the flow of time.

# From a materialist point of view, intelligence emerges through new temporal thresholds, intimately bound to the power of matter to compute beyond its own apparent limits while still remaining 'material'.

Today these ideas reach a very wide audience: even on a broad pop-culture level, models of global ecosystems are a low-fi version of Deleuze's readings of Spinoza: we cannot know what a body is capable of until we can define its boundaries.[5] One of the most important links between all

futures and pasts become available.[6] The main consequence of this redefinition of bodies – biopolitical, ecological, economic, cultural – is our recognition that intelligence is not limited to organic life, but also cascades across all material systems, and that bodies have temporal horizons just as much as physical ones.

We are therefore faced with two basic challenges that have been part of an ongoing philosophical and scientific project: The critical definition of the limits of a physical system (organic or nonorganic); 2) The critical definition of the nature of agency, in relation to time itself.

From a materialist point of view, intelligence emerges through new temporal thresholds, intimately bound to the power of matter to compute beyond its own apparent limits while still remaining 'material' (a Nietszchean overcoming, with matter and time inseparably mixed). Alternatively (and here we can contrast different strains of Gnosticism), intelligence can be theorised as a nonmaterial immanence that allows being to escape the boundaries of matter. Some species of this second mode of thought have assumed that matter and its constraints are a necessary prison for a notion of 'spirit' to enter into, to forget the 'true' world, and through a process of recuperation of memory, of anamnesis, overcome time and re-enter the kingdom of heaven.

In the end, the prospect of an architectural system with greater temporal agency is the most compelling image these theories of collective intelligence offer, regardless of what we assume to be the stated goal of the process – either pleasing and useful evolution on earth, or a 'royal road' to grace. Our expanded definition of collective intelligence includes human groups, but also implies that new models of systems and

these examples is their rethinking of the boundaries of systems and bodies, and a critical investigation of the limits of materiality.

Political philosophers have extended the concept of collective intelligence in human systems, drawing from the general question of 'material intelligence'. For example, the mathematician Ilya Prigogine's work resonates as an interdisciplinary reference throughout Negri's *Time for Revolution*: crucially, the deeper implications are not only that material systems can really 'think', carrying out material computations to some unspecified end, but that each of these computations establishes a temporal threshold, literally bootstrapping the system into a position where alternate

bodies can find 'collectivity' at many scales; design practice then tests on every level ideas of use value, authorship and agency. The act of design itself becomes a hybrid between invention and pure discovery.

### Collective Intelligence in Design
A|Um Studio is interested in many scales and modes of operation. At a more local scale, it is involved in construction on residential projects in Europe and the US that test the practice's ideas about time–event cycles using materially intensive design. At a larger scale, its UIA and SUTURE projects are part of a broader range of work being developed as a new paradigm for mapping and implementing scenarios of systems

collectivity: its 'Drift Cinema' initiatives; massively multiplayer online game project 'Ornament'; and the E-XQUIS project.

For example, E-XQUIS is being developed as an informational infrastructure, a locative media-based tactical framework through which several disciplines (architecture, urban action, social networking, cinema) work collectively, creating a new hybrid body reframing the concept of agency in cities throughout Europe, Asia and the US. Contemporary

urban and media spaces; by building online interfaces to a new range of technologised social spaces; and by creating subgenre urban events providing themes as a catalyst and provocation for potential users.

To this extent, the general ambition of the practice's work is to test how far it can extend a general concept of intelligence in design, one that embraces material as well as social forms of intelligence and, ultimately, generates new

emergent social networks – technologies like Google Earth, Flickr, Del.icio.us, YellowArrow or Grafedia, as well as alternate reality games – provide a completely new apparatus for the city to regulate itself in cultural, economic and political terms. In many ways these networks are an accelerated (and possibly overdetermined) version of the Situationist concept of drift.

A|Um Studio's projects address the urban, political and social implications of such networks, taking advantage of existing systems but extending them in a number of key ways: by developing rule sets and scripts for 'play' across many

definitions of value in architecture. If the deeper project of architecture as a transdisciplinary act has always been to probe the limits of matter, to provide a social memory system, and to invent new forms of material and temporal intelligence, then A|Um Studio positions itself as a contemporary practitioner of this mode of thinking. Jean-Luc Godard has stated that his films are 'forms that think'. This is how A|Um Studio hopes its work operates: as a series of 'forms' that reframe the boundaries of thought itself, both autonomously and collectively. ◬

**Notes**

1. A few schools of thought and protagonists come to mind. There is not space to develop the implications of each entry in this brief (and incomplete) list, so it should be considered a provocation and a possible outline for a future work. There are several obvious trajectories: philosophers and alchemists, canonical figures like Plato, Ibn Sina or Llull, lead to the mystics Henri Bergson, Teilhard de Chardin and Carl Jung. The techno-evangelists, like Vannevar Bush or Ray Kurzweil, work in friendly opposition to the corporate/org body: IBM, Saarinen's architecture and infrastructural systems (see Keller Easterling, Reinhold Martin). Emergence and complexity in the work of René Thom, Ralph Abraham and Arthur Iberall serve as a precursor to the contemporary algorithmic/genetic architectural models of Karl Chu. Thinkers of human vectors of power, like Marx, Engels and Mao, give way to thinkers of material intelligence: the machinic phylum, as developed by Deleuze and Guattari, and mathematicians like Thom, and more recently taken up by Sanford Kwinter and Manuel DeLanda. This line ultimately leads to the theme of temporalised agency and the collective: Michel Serres,

Antonio Negri and Michael Hardt, and Giorgio Agamben.
2. Pierre Lévy, *Collective Intelligence: Mankind's Emerging World in Cyberspace*, Plenum Trade (New York/London), 1997, p 92.
3. Gilles Deleuze, 'What can a body do', *Expressionism in Philosophy: Spinoza*, Zone Books (New York), 1990.
4. Giorgio Agamben, *Means Without End: Notes on Politics (Theory Out of Bounds)*, University of Minnesota Press (Minneapolis, MN) 2000, pp 54–9.
5. See Kaja Silverman, *The Subject of Semiotics*, Oxford University Press (New York), 1983.
6. Antonio Negri, *Time For Revolution*, Continuum (New York/London), 2003. Throughout this collection of texts by Negri, the terminology of political philosophy mixes with that of mathematics, as Negri explores ways that models of nonlinearity and dissipative structures can be developed within a political philosophy.

# CONTINUUM: A Self-Engineering Creature-Culture

An interdisciplinary design research collaborative led by Alisa Andrasek, CONTINUUM emerged from a series of design research seminars at Columbia University's graduate school of architecture. Working collaboratively with Robert Aish, Andresek's workshops explored the potential of the new Bentley Systems' GenerativeComponents design software which at the time was in beta testing. CONTINUUM was formed to extend the possibilities of such collaborations and has expanded its network, occupying an interesting and unique territory of intersecting interests between academia, corporate practice and the companies that create design tools. Traditionally understood as antagonistic, commercial and progressive interests and intentions find common ground in their shared need for research into advanced design software that will enable the retooling of architectural practice. Here, **Pia Ednie-Brown**, with illustrations by **Alisa Andrasek**, examines the unique ways in which CONTINUUM enfolds diverse professional and academic practices.

*Ideas, sentiments, immersions and beliefs possess in crowds a contagious power as intense as that of microbes.*

Gustave Le Bon, *The Crowd: A Study of the Popular Mind*, 1895

We stand amidst claims that new forms of collaborative practice are emerging, along with freshly inflected forms of collective design intelligence. Here, a recently formed collective network, CONTINUUM, is explored for what it might clarify regarding the nature of these new forms.

**CONTINUUM: A Collective Network**
CONTINUUM is a collective network initiated by Alisa Andrasek (Columbia University, biothing) in 2005. Its aim is to explore the mutually beneficial exchange between a particular generative design approach, as developed extensively by biothing, and the potential offered by the very open and developing tool-set, Bentley's GenerativeComponents system, a model-oriented design and programming environment.

GenerativeComponents is a parametric software that is still in beta version and under very intensive development. As such it is not 'packaged' in the way that many of the more familiar software options are. This is crucial to the potential of CONTINUUM, because developmental effects run from practices to software as well as the reverse. This is unlike much other experimental architectural design research that has explored a given software package, seeking ways in which the software might offer new opportunities for practice. Here, there is an opportunity for software and practice to mature together.

The development of GenerativeComponents is currently the focus of the Smart Geometry Group (SGG), which brings together a range of people across architecture, engineering and software design. Sponsored by Bentley Systems, the SGG includes Lars Hesselgren (KPF), Hugh Whitehead (Foster and Partners), J Parrish (Arup Sport) and Robert Aish (Bentley). The group has explicitly stated intentions with regards to education and the feeding of educational institutions. At stake here is the active development of cross-disciplinary, cross-institutional community of practice.

The particular approach to generative design process developed by biothing as an experimental design practice and research-based educator is well suited to the GenerativeComponents software and has an implicit affinity with the agenda of the SGG. biothing has developed a mode of design composition that intrinsically involves computation, working with fields constituted by a very deep ecology of relationships, as discussed in more detail in an earlier issue of *AD*.[1] This way of working can be distinguished from traditional modes of form-making through the way in which it enacts what is referred to here as 'micro wiring'.[2]

Multitudes of micro components are 'wired' together into a behavioural network so that the resulting forms are an emergent outcome. Rather than working primarily with architectural components or geometries, each of which are blocks or parts that together add up to the final object, form emerges out of interrelated fields of micro behaviours. Such a deep ecology of dynamic relationships is also something intrinsic to any collectively constituted entity. In fact, biothing's mode of composition can be seen as a kind of discrete instance of the kind of collective constellation that CONTINUUM sets out to be, involving a field of interaction that extends well beyond the digital tool-sets while being significantly affected by them. As such, this specific mode of working has a poignant relation to the more general issue of collective intelligence.

CONTINUUM arises at the intersections of these affinities and mutually informing interests. This cooperative alliance amounts to a looped, connective thread that operates through feedback between academia, corporate practice and industry research.

A recent workshop at Cambridge University acted as a kind of lab for testing and exploring the GenerativeComponents software and its potential as a phase of its beta development. Bentley Systems' Robert Aish observed various discoveries and results of the workshop and then revised the software on site in response to these, making adjustments to the user-interface, for instance.

Currently, a primary test bed and development site for CONTINUUM is an ongoing research seminar at Columbia University, titled 'Material Potency', first run in 2005 and currently transforming into a research laboratory. As well as forming a focus about which collective input can be enacted,

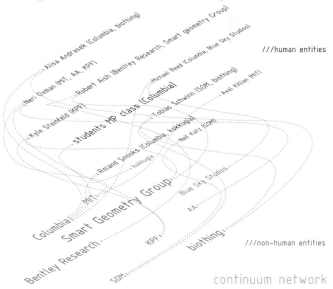

Diagram of CONTINUUM network.

'Material Potency' class students (Titusz Tarnai, Marlin Nowbakt, Paola Morales, Mark Bearak and Boro Ignatov), MinMax, Graduate School of Architecture Planning and Preservation (GSAPP), Columbia University, 2006
Disphenoidic minimal surface components instantiated in a triple-periodic crystalline environment.

the seminars had aimed to spawn a 'gene library' of behaviourally defined 'cells' (localised components) and 'environments' (global components). Involving the usual internal lectures and software sessions, the seminars have also included workshops and external lectures by visiting participants. These are not quite seminars in the traditional sense, employing a series of different formats for work and research, and run by Alisa Andrasek with workshop support from Neri Oxman (MIT, AA, KPF Research) and input from Dr Axel Killian (MIT), Robert Aish, Kyle Steinfeld (KPF Research), Michael Reed (Columbia, Blue Sky Studios), Roland Snooks (Columbia) and Tobias Schwinn (biothing), along with the many students who take part.

Collaborative development of projects, involving all manner of human and nonhuman elements, is fundamental to architectural practice and discourse. Collaboration and collective networks of practice are the norm, not the exception. But the act of gathering around these new, parametric tools inflects this long-established norm with fresh capabilities. Relationships between the various parties works somewhat like an open-source environment, where both practices and the software itself co-evolve through mutual feedback. Open-source communities informally gather around the collective development of some entity. But the nature of that gathering and its collectively formed intelligence is not the same as the product. The former provides the conditions for the emergence of that product. As such, its form of organisation needs some attention.

## Organisational Culture, or the Cultured Organism

Managerial discourse often refers to 'organisational culture' – something that involves implicit social relations, expectations, values, assumptions and histories. These less visible dimensions of an organisation form tangled assemblages that make the clean charts of organisational hierarchy but one layer of formalised influence participating in a far more complex and messy set of interrelations. The culture of an organisation refers to a sense of the 'whole' and plays an enormous role in its potential futures. Good management always needs to work with this, whether it is something that needs to be changed, strengthened, provoked or redirected. But organisational culture is an elusive creature because so much of what constitutes it is implicit, embedded and difficult to articulate. When these cultural dimensions are understood to be part of the composition and working structure of an organisation, it becomes more like an organism: a living, dynamic, metastable entity that needs to engaged with as such.

The more established the assemblage or the more history it has, the more it tends to be held together by an internally held set of refrains: commonly held assumptions, behavioural habits and other glue-like patterns. But there is no such thing as a stable assemblage. At best, it is metastable – in a state of constant internal agitation, tension or resonance, able to respond and ready to jump.

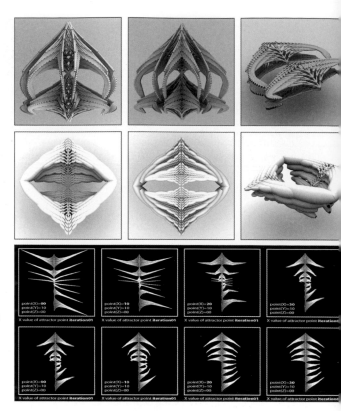

**Neri Oxman, Tropisms: Computing Theoretical Morphospaces of Branching Growth Systems, MIT, 2006**
The project was developed by Neri Oxman from the MIT Computation Group. As its main focus, an L-system is developed as a cellular automata algorithm to allow multiple effects to occur simultaneously within the 'growth' process of the system. The logic follows an algorithm that takes in as variables the initial rules for 'growth' and 'decay', and a set of local 'attractor' points that affect the system locally. Top: Images illustrating two models that were developed from the same algorithm (identical grammars) using different locations of 'attractor' points. Bottom: Plan views of growth patterns when assigned different global variables for the location of 'attractor' points. Topological order remains the same, while geometrical differentiation is promoted.

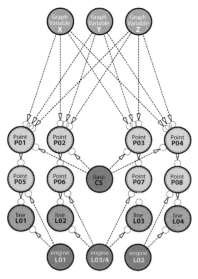

Symbolic model, modelled in Bentley Systems' GenerativeComponents software, illustrating the topological map between features. The model is made up of points, lines and angles that are informed by the specific location of 'attractor' features.

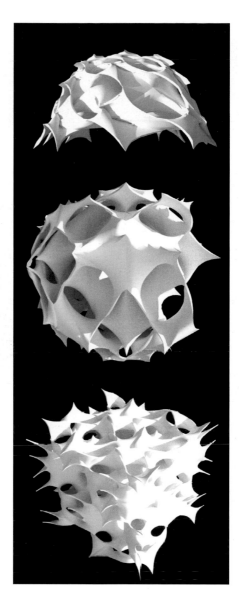
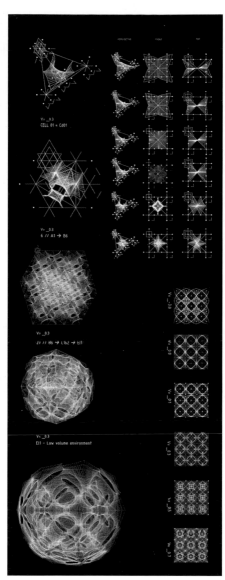
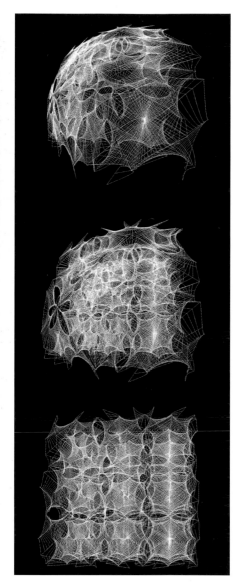

**'Material Potency' class students (Titusz Tarnai, Marlin Nowbakt, Paola Morales, Mark Bearak and Boro Ignatov), MinMax, GSAPP, Columbia University, 2006**

Left: *Minimal surface = maximum area minimum boundary.* At the root of the mathematical problem entailed by minimal surfaces lies the question of the minimum versus the maximum and the definition of mechanisms of calculation. The following investigation seeks to reconfigure the minimal surface beyond its mathematical definition of economy in matter, in order to readdress the question of efficiency as it could be conceived from the perspective of optimisation.

Centre: The process derives from a series of nested features applied to a parametric primary component *Cd01*. Given the multiple variables embedded within the geometry of both – primary cell as well as the propagated environment – the formation process engenders a new generation of cells together with their respective variation families. In the generation process, the initial programming environment of Bentley Systems' GenerativeComponents is coupled to Surface Evolver, using its relaxation algorithm. The frame of the geometry is laid out in GenerativeComponents with the minimum amount of vertices. Disphenoidical genealogies: Circumscribed into a tetrahedron, the primary component *Cd01* is constructed along with the logic of a minimal surface bound within a disphenoidic shape into which a single variable *V* is embedded. Divided into four fundamental regions with two *C2* axes, the disphenoid component performs through the movement of the free-point *F* whose location along the edges of the tetrahedron is determined by *V*, thus generating the Disphenoid family. Cubic genealogies: Six fundamental disphenoidic components form a cubelet *B6* to which the variable *V* is still applicable. Twenty-seven *B6* cubelets are then propagated into a cubic environment forming a Cubic cell *El1*. In similar manner to the differentiation generated by the disphenoidical component, the populated Cubic environment *El1* driven by the variable *V* creates a series of volumetric cubic patterns *C162* of 'space occupation', distribution or circulation which, regardless of the complexity of their shape, maintain the initial spatial continuity of the disphenoidical cell.

Right: MinMax genealogies. The topology of the Cubic *El1* environment is defined by the relationship of its field-points *Px* to the base-point *P0* thus creating a modular Law Surface animated by an algebraic function which operates on the spatial relationship of the *P0* to *Px*. The instantiation of the cubelets into the parametrically deformed Cubic environment *El1* thus creates a genealogy of MinMax surfaces, in which the primary variable *V* being still active augments differentiation within the family.

Any such assemblage of relations is dynamic, elastic and ever on the move. The myriad of dynamic patterns that constitute a metastability both condition and make possible the emergence of collective intelligence.

Collective networks are 'light' organisations that are tentatively held, elastic and highly deformable. The act of gathering within a collective such as CONTINUUM is a process in which things – people, tools, knowledge, ideas, goals and so on – are made to relate to one another in malleable ways. Importantly, this collective sets up a particularly decentralised, nonhierarchical and open form of relatedness. The act of gathering is, in itself, an initial condition of intelligence. But how that gathering is assembled conditions the nature of that intelligence.

## What Is Intelligence?

Intelligence is a process in which things are made to relate to one another, the effect of which is looped back into that field of connection wherein possibilities and potentials are intensified.

Intelligence emerges through practice. When we practise, we repeat – and repeatedly inflect. We become adept at something through a kind of rhythmic merger with the variable particularities of an act. For instance, one aspect of CONTINUUM entails an accumulating intelligence that is always folding into the gene library. This intelligence only accumulates through practice; with practice one develops a sense of what 'works' algorithmically.

Through practice, we learn to engage with a collection of actions and an active collective, in that we choreograph them and become choreographed, compose them and become recomposed. Design intelligence always emerges collectively and this is the case whether we do, in fact, collaborate with other people or not. This is because, even when working alone, we do not design in our heads – we design in the midst of an expanded field that involves, at the very least, drawings, concepts, memories, desires, images, models, programmes, sites, materials, efficiencies of various kinds and so on. This expanded field, which could be called the 'design manifold', is constituted by a jostle of tensions and patterns between all the parameters that come to play. Our individual intelligence is not simply a product of our brains. It is a full-bodied issue that involves all the cells, human and inhuman, that constitute our bodies as well as a vast terrain of social, cultural and historical influences that become enfolded into what could be seen as an expanded notion of body akin to the expanded field of a design manifold.

The act of relating things is a perception that exists inside you, as fed by a set of negotiations between you and them. We feel these relations because we actively bring them into being; we embody them as part of our interactions in the world. If we replace 'you' with a 'collective' (after all, 'you' are already a collective, in any case),[3] a collective network, once gathered, then embodies a selected set of connections to then feel their potential and develop it.

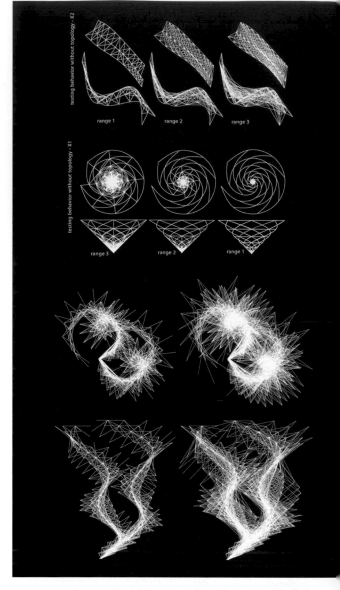

**'Material Potency' class students (Daniel Linder and Paula Tomisaki), Grabber, GSAPP, Columbia University, 2006**
A 3-D lacing structure emerges from the interaction between the grabber ce
and the vortex environment it is placed in. This interaction occurs regardless
of the hosting environment's qualities, as long as there are points for the
adaptive agent to connect to.

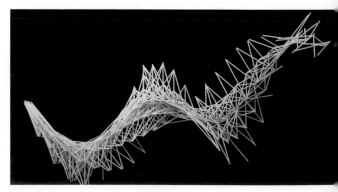

Grabber agent behaviour in a single spiral environment – rendering.

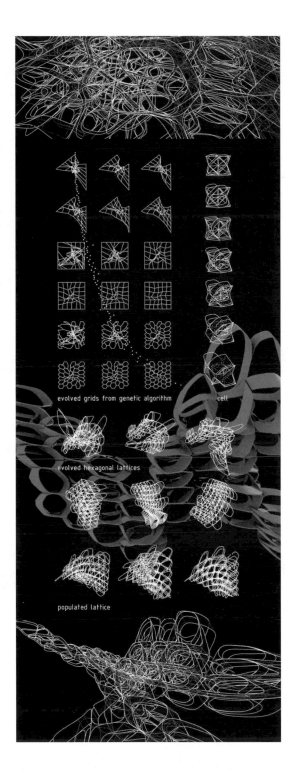

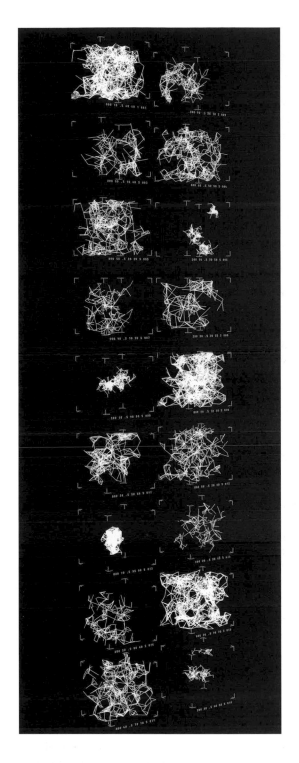

**'Material Potency' class students (Ezio Blasetti, Roland Snooks and Carmen Trudell), Evolved Network, GSAPP, Columbia University, 2006**
Left: A lattice structure is created by a genetic algorithm that evolves coherent structures from random sets of points. Although the point sets are randomly generated, they contain a fixed topology that the genetic algorithm operates upon by iteratively testing individual sets against a fitness function and breeding the successful sets to create successive generations. The genetic algorithm is able to negotiate an often-conflicting set of fitness criteria (ie coherent order and local differentiation) in evolving the population of geometry. The evolved field is then populated with parametric cells joined tangentially along common edges allowing for a simple connection among adjacent geometry subverting the complexity of the lattice joints.

**Diffusion Aggregated Structure**
Right: A Diffusion Limited Aggregation (DLA) algorithm is used to explore branching topologies in both parametric and animation environments. Diffusion Limited Aggregation describes the growth of numerous natural structures such as coral or lightning. The simulation of DLA involves particles randomly navigating the environment before aggregating into coherent structures. A second iteration of the algorithm enables the structure to converge generating lattice structures in addition to divergent branching topologies.

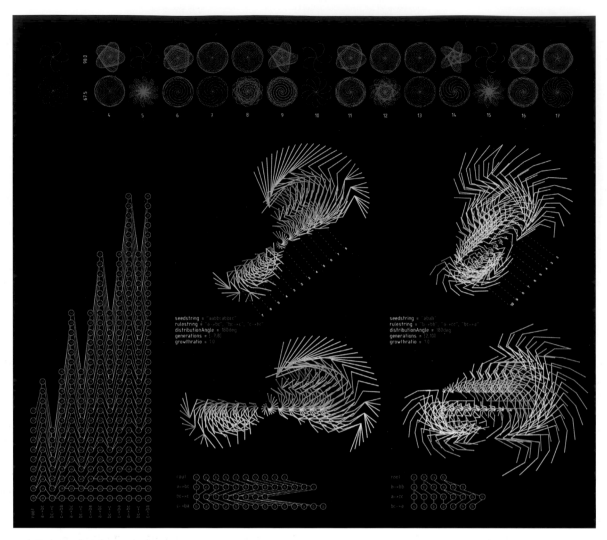

**biothing + SOM (Alisa Andrasek, Adam Elstein, Neil Katz and Tobias Schwinn), Phyllotactics, 'Material Potency'
workshop, Columbia University, 2006**
The system is generated as a hybrid of spiral phyllotaxis and L-system algorithms. Spiral phyllotaxis is often found in
nature, such as the pattern of dots in a peacock's tail or the growth of sunflower seeds. In this example, L-systems are
grown on top of phyllotaxis' world, inflecting the spiral lattice. Left: Parametric differentiation of a phyllotaxis algorithm.

As already mentioned, one of the aims of the 'Material
Potency' seminar at Columbia is to develop a gene library of
algorithmic scripts. This library acts as an accumulating
resource and ever-mutating archive of the CONTINUUM
collective, becoming source material for the development of
the deep ecologies of relations discussed earlier in terms of
biothing's mode of composition. This deep ecology is
significantly facilitated by the digital tool-set that acts as a
kind of connective tissue between often separate fields of
expertise. But as the notion of 'organisational culture'
suggests, this is one important aspect of another even deeper
ecology of other human and nonhuman relationships.

Collective intelligence can only be meaningfully
addressed in terms of this deeper model. Digital tools, even
when based on models of artificial intelligence, require this
expanded, distributed body to attain the supple adaptability
of living intelligence.

**A Model: The Creature-Culture that Genetically Engineers Itse**
If we think about the CONTINUUM collective as a tentative
held, malleable, distributed body, the gene library is
something like a genome that underlies, or micro-wires, th
intelligent life of that organism. But this genome is anythir
but fully mappable because it is always subject to collective
development. We can perhaps, then, imagine CONTINUUM
as an organism in the process of genetically engineering
itself. It has access to its own code, so that it can tweak it
and see what happens.

But this would be an absurd analogy if we thought in the
terms that the commonly held notion of the gene as
'blueprint' would have us believe. The gene library has a far
more complex relation to this intelligent body and does not
solely determine what unfolds. Evelyn Fox Keller has
discussed the misleading idea that genes have a kind of
executive control, or dominant, managerial role in the

development of the living creature. Works such as Natalie Jeremijenko's One Tree project play with the fallacy of this assumption. If we can go on, happily playing along with this idea of CONTINUUM as an organism in the process of genetically engineering itself, this ought not to involve a fetishisation and objectification of the algorithmic script. The model involves richer consistency than this.

The new constellations shaping this model go hand in hand with the reshaping of models in genetics, biology, management, planning, agriculture, ecology, performance and design, to name just a few. The common element to all these reshapings is the reconfiguring model of life itself. This is indeed a constellation change with all-encompassing implications.

Given their highly behavioural definition it is not so surprising that the design models of 'Material Potency' are often discussed as 'creatures': perhaps a better word than organism because it implies more of a certain inherent character than the more generic notion of 'organism' suggests. A creature that has a feeling of itself at a very deep level manages a guiding role in its own development. In other words, it can mutate both itself and its own forms of intelligence.

Intelligence always involves selection–perception, connection–relatedness and assessment–effect and then, again, selection–perception, connection–relatedness and assessment–effect, and so on. Intelligence is a loopy process that is somewhat like a very deep algorithmic sequencing. An algorithm is a procedure for computing a defined set of relations, usually involving the repetition of an operation. Each algorithm has its own behavioural refrain; it assesses the 'ifs' and 'elses', and then acts, over and over. While the process of intelligence does not share the mechanical, sequential linearity of the simple algorithmic sequence, this perceived likeness underwrites the field of artificial life[4] and what we call 'artificial intelligence'.

When we understand intelligence in this way, CONTINUUM veers towards an instance of artificial life, with an 'artificial' intelligence. But how artificial is it, *actually*? Or, more pertinently, how *real* is this intelligence? Is it merely a metaphorical fantasy? This depends on the limits of our attention, or what we include and/or exclude in our understanding of the collective design process. If we can sustain this model of distributed, living intelligence, we might manage a deeper understanding and negotiation of the expressive powers that collectively formed creature-cultures can contagiously spread.

At a deep level, this nature of the model proposed here involves the issue of how things are connected, with what kind of rules. Charts mapping management structures and organisational hierarchies can be telling in this respect. But an example related to dance is equally telling and offers a simple image. Consider the difference between a group of people engaged in a highly formulaic dance, where they each follow a pregiven sequence of actions, and the modulating terrain of a dance party, or rave. In the former there is a

rigid mould in the form of a dance routine or choreography that everybody must follow and comply with if he or she wishes to be an integral part of this collective experience. Undeniably, this rigidly formed field holds within it a vast range of experiences and individuating complexity. In other words, its stable, predictable appearance conceals a battlefield of internal difference and interrelational complexity: it is a metastability.

In the latter, the moulding is less rigid. The music connects, but each body responds differently to that collective experience, generating a highly differentiated yet nevertheless cohesive field. Certainly, the movement and gesture sequences are mostly related to a palette of shared and expected behaviours, but the limits of acceptability are very broad and replete with diversity. The rules are dynamic and constantly open to reformation, reworking and new influences. The mould has a very elastic range of potential composures. It does not suppress the internal difference and interrelational complexity – it allows it to be expressed.

If we imagine that the music is like the algorithmic code being played out through the expanded, distributed body of CONTINUUM (involving but not reduced to digital instruments), then the specificities of particular projects are the bodies that dance. The rub is that both the musical score (the code), the instruments that play them, the projects that emerge and the state of the collective network remain in constant, mutual modification. CONTINUUM may prove to be a life that passes quickly or one that builds into a more highly differentiated creature that continues to mutate in a process of engineering itself. But whatever the case may be, like all of our lives, it will have joined in with a far bigger dance of forms of living intelligence, wherein its difference will have made a difference.

As Mark Twain apparently said: 'History doesn't repeat itself, but it rhymes.' And this variation of this rhyme perhaps offers the poetry of composition a new sense of its dynamic unity – of the intelligent life of its character and the intelligent character of its life. Δ

**Notes**
1. Pia Ednie-Brown, 'All-Over, Over-All: biothing and Emergent Composition', *AD Programming Cultures: Art and Architecture in the Age of Software*, Vol 76, No 4, July/August 2006.
2. This term was introduced by Alisa Andrasek as part of the discussions involved in the 'Material Potency' seminar.
3. Everything we do is done collectively. Make something alone in your studio and you cannot avoid involving a vast background of collectively acquired intelligence. Say 'I love you' and you echo a collective voice. Biologically, we are also a collective: a multitude of cells, a large proportion of which are not human.
4. See Mark Bedau, 'The nature of life', in Margaret Boden (ed), *The Philosophy of Artificial Life*, Oxford University Press, 1996, pp 332–57. Here, Bedau offers a definition of the field: 'Artificial life is an interdisciplinary field that attempts to understand the essential nature of living systems by means of devising and studying computationally implemented models of the characteristic processes of living systems.'

# Language, Life, Code

Software increasingly determines what can be designed, constructed and even how design occurs. Here, **Alexander R Galloway** and **Eugene Thacker** present a series of investigations with the collaborative Radical Software Group (RSG). Their practice examines the nature of software code as a form of language. Addressing theoretical issues regarding meaning and representation, they argue for thinking more abstractly and generatively about language, and propose a new, or liberated, computer language in which the representational determinations implicit to any software are geared towards innovation in communication and design. By rewriting the software that allows for the transmission and translation of knowledge across previously discrete fields of production, programming allows for new and productive cross-pollination. Indeed, programming becomes a new site of design that enfolds disciplines not traditionally seen as part of the creative processes of innovation.

In 1968, the French television programme 'Vivre et Parler' presented a discussion between four guests from four distinct disciplines: anthropologist Claude Lévi-Strauss, molecular biologist François Jacob, linguist Roman Jakobson and geneticist Philippe L'Héritier.[1] The topic for the discussion focused on the possible relationships between language, information and DNA. The notion of DNA as a 'genetic code' was proposed by biochemists and molecular biologists during the 1940s and 1950s. But at the time of the television debate it was still not clear whether this was simply a useful metaphor or whether the living molecule of DNA was actually a code in the technical sense.

Today, of course, the idea of a genetic code has become ubiquitous, even finding its way into popular science fiction. However, that the DNA molecule operated in a way similar to an information system was something that had to have been cultivated, largely due to the fields of cybernetics, information theory and cryptography, during the Second World War. Likewise, the 'Structuralist wave' in anthropology, linguistics and other fields was influenced by the concepts of code, message, channel and system.

Working and collaborating across disciplines always raises the question of form. What is or is not communicable across disciplines from one thinker to another? Is there a kind of communicability that runs across language, life and code? Perhaps what is communicated across disciplines is structure itself, the very possibility of forming ideas in common, words in common or effects in common. We would thus do better to talk not about collaborative communication across disciplines, but about 'forms of communicability'.

What entities are eligible for being communicable as pure form? There are examples from the micro level, such as the molecule, and also from the macro level, for example global communications. But there also exist phenomena such as computer viruses or global pandemics that are themselves formal entities that exist only via communicative propagation and translation from one environment to another.

In other words, such life forms form, reform and deform themselves – even at the level of biology, we are told that life forms are themselves informed by molecules such as DNA. Form is always multiple: a variety of communicative forms coexist with a variety of forms of speech and writing, which are themselves inseparable from the nexus of social forms that articulate protocols, enunciations, gestures and effects.

However, the 'Vivre et Parler' debate was far from being a chorus of Structuralist enthusiasm. It remained unclear what the actual relationship was between the three elements: language, code and life. Jakobson was perhaps the most assertive about the close links between language and DNA: 'What we call genetic information is genuinely inscribed in the chromosomes ... exactly like a phrase in a text.' For Jakobson, both language and DNA pose the problem of organisation. Both operate through permutations of a relatively small number of basic units. Both are concerned with the use of such permutations to create systems of communication. Jacob – whose research considered cellular metabolism as a cybernetic system – tentatively concurred, though he noted that 'organisation', or 'structure', may mean different things to a biologist and a linguist. L'Héritier added another viewpoint: that the possible linkages between language and DNA may point to a novel form of heredity – a 'heredity of language'.

But it was Lévi-Strauss who put forth the more critical viewpoint. DNA cannot be understood as a language, he stated, precisely because with DNA there is no signification. Indeed, the information theory of Shannon and Weaver[2] was explicit on this point: information had nothing to do with semantics or meaning. Thus Lévi-Strauss' question: what was the 'meaning' of DNA? Was it in the code itself or in the relation between the coding elements? Furthermore, because language is symbolic, it requires a cognitive process in the minds of human senders and receivers, whereas DNA is simply an inert molecule – albeit a molecular code, or rather, a nonhuman code.

In a sense, Lévi-Strauss' scepticism is telling, for the question he poses is an ontological one: can there be language without humans? Or better, can there be nonhuman languages – and to what extent would we as humans be able to comprehend them as 'unhuman' languages? There are, certainly, the oft-cited examples of animal languages – birds, bees and so forth. But the study of human languages – linguistics – forms the backdrop against which any 'other' language can be recognised.

Theories of media and culture continue to propagate an idea of something called 'semantic content'. But the notion that content may be separated from the technological vehicles of representation and conveyance that supposedly facilitate it is misguided. Data has no technique for creating meaning, only techniques for interfacing and parsing. To the extent that meaning exists in digital media, it only ever exists as the threshold of mixtures between two or more technologies. Meaning is a data conversion. What is called 'Web content' is, in actual reality, the point where standard character-sets rub up against the hypertext transfer protocol. There is no content; there is only data and other data. In the computer language Lisp there are only lists; the lists contain atoms, which themselves are other lists. To claim otherwise is a strange sort of cultural nostalgia, a religion. Content, then, is to be understood as a relationship that exists between specific technologies. Content, if it exists, happens when this relationship is solidified, made predictable, institutionalised and mobilised.

The 'Vivre et Parler' discussion spent a great deal of time comparing DNA and language. Still, little time was devoted to discussing computer code (and, it should be noted, there was no computer scientist present). Perhaps the question that was posed – 'Is DNA a language?' – should have been rephrased as 'Is DNA a *computer* language?' or 'Is DNA a *programming* language?' In a sense, these are questions that apply to nonhuman languages, for they do not ask 'What does it mean?', but rather they ask 'What does it do?' The answer is quite simple: DNA computes. At least, this is the answer given by many molecular biologists (including Jacob) and, seemingly, confirmed by today's fields such as bioinformatics and genomics. DNA computes, and it does so not only in the living cell, but in all sorts of devices like DNA chips. DNA even computes in the abstract – as genetic algorithms – and in actual wet-lab 'DNA computers'.

We can channel Nietzsche (or rather Dawkins): does DNA speak us or do we speak DNA? Perhaps neither, for the opacity of DNA as a computer language is revealed to us in those situations in which we are helpless in our ability to 'decode' DNA: viral infections, epidemic contagions, resistance to antibiotics … Language, life, code. From one angle, it is code that appears to inhabit both language and life,

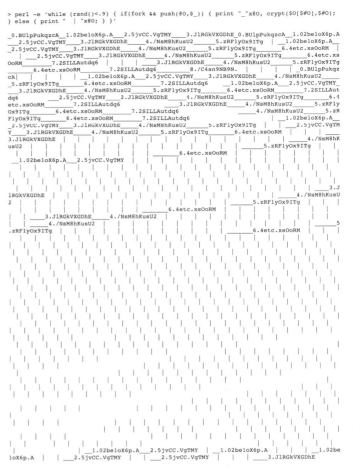

A generative texture written in the programming language Perl.

communication and contagion. If DNA is a computer language, then the opacity of this language forces us to see communication and contagion as inseparable processes.

'To record the sound sequences of speech,' wrote Friedrich Kittler, 'literature has to arrest them in a system of 26 letters, thereby categorically excluding all noise sequences.'[3] A fascinating act of transduction is language. But we worry. We worry about the imaginary, supplemental alphabets starting with letter 27. This is the impulse behind our notes for a liberated computer language: to reintroduce new noisy alphabets into the rigid semantic zone of informatic networks.

Describing the origins of the algorithm, James Beniger wrote: 'The idea may have come from late eighteenth-century musical instruments programmed to perform automatically under the control of rolls of punched paper.'[4] By 1801 Joseph-Marie Jacquard had developed punched cards to hold encoded mechanical patterns for use in his looms. The art of weaving, allowed some human flexibility as a handicraft, was translated into the hard, coded grammar of algorithmic execution. Then in 1842 Ada Lovelace outlined the first software algorithm – a way to calculate Bernoulli numbers using Charles Babbage's Analytical Engine. The term 'algorithm' is itself eponymous of the medieval Persian

Generative textures written in the programming language Perl. The source code is included as the top line of text. Using a recursive fork command, the software replicates virally through the computer's memory in what is known as a 'fork bomb'. The code prints text output at different times according to the unpredictable stresses of the machine. A self-moderation feature avoids system crash. Each execution of the code creates a unique texture.

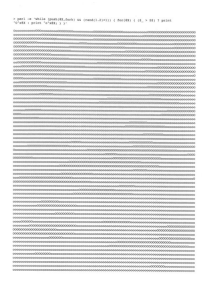

mathematician Al-Khwarazmi, inventor of the balancing equations and calculations collectively known as algebra.

Algorithms always need some processing entity to interpret them – for Jacquard it was the hardware of the loom itself, and for Lovelace it was Babbage's machine. In this sense algorithms are fundamentally a question of mechanical (or later, electronic) processing. Algorithms can deal with contingencies, but in the end they must be finite and articulated in the grammar of the processor so that they may be parsed effectively. Because of this, the processor's grammar defines the space of possibility for the algorithm's dataset. Likewise, an algorithm is a type of visible articulation of any given processor's machinic grammar. Again Kittler: 'To record the sound sequences of speech, literature has to arrest them in a system of 26 letters, thereby categorically excluding all noise sequences.'[5]

In 1890 Herman Hollerith used punched cards to parse US census data on personal characteristics. If punched cards are the *mise-en-écriture* (Thomas Levin)[6] of algorithms, their instance of inscription, then in the 1890 census the entire human biomass of the US was inscribed on to an algorithmic grammar, for ever captured as biopolitical data. Today Philip Agre uses the term 'grammars of action' to describe the way in which human action is parsed according to specific physical algorithms.[7] Imagine the 'noise sequences' that have been erased.

The symbolic economies discussed in the 1970s by theorists like Jean-Joseph Goux have today been digitised and instantiated into the real codes of life itself. What was once an abstract threat, embodied in specific places (the school, the factory) with particular practices of control and exploitation, are today written out in gross detail (the Internet protocols, the genome), incorporated into the very

definitions of life and action. This is why liberated language are so important today.

We consider there to be very little difference between living informatic networks and the universal informatic languages and standards used to define and sculpt them. If the languages are finite, then so, unfortunately, are the life possibilities. Thus a new type of language is needed, a liberated computer language for the articulation of political desires in today's hostile climate of universal informatics. We offer these notes for a liberated computer language as a response to the new universalism of the informatic sciences that have subsumed all of Goux's symbolic economics. But they are only a beginning. Are they absurd? Perhaps. Are they utopian? If so, one must ask the much more important question: *why* are they utopian?

### Notes

1. A transcript was published in *Lettres Française*, no 1221 (14 February 1968) and no 1222 (21 February 1968). The debate is also recounted in Richard Doyle, *On Beyond Living*, Stanford University Press (Stanford, CA), 1997, and Lily Kay, *Who Wrote the Book of Life?*, Stanford University Press (Stanford, CA), 2000.
2. Claude E Shannon and Warren Weaver, *The Mathematical Theory of Communicaton*, Chicago University Press (Chicago, IL), 1949.
3. Friedrich Kittler, *Gramophone, Film, Typewriter*, Harvard University Press (Stanford, CA), 1999, p 3.
4. James Beniger, *The Control Revolution*, Harvard University Press (Cambridge, MA), 1989, p 247.
5. Kittler, op cit, p 3.
6. A pun on cinema's *mise en scène*, Levin's concept of *mise-en-écriture* is found in his essay '"Tones from out of Nowhere", Rudolph Pfenninger and the Archaeology of Synthetic Sound', *Grey Room*, 12, Summer 2003, 32–79.
7. See Philip Agre, 'Surveillance and Capture: Two Models of Privacy', *The Information Society*, 10 (2), pp 101–27.

# Notes for a Liberated Computer Language

Most computer languages are created and developed according to the principles of efficiency, utility and usability. These being but a fraction of the human condition, we offer a computer language that shuns typical machinic mandates in favour of an ethos of creative destruction. Each entry in the language below is defined using a standard verb-object definitional structure adopted from computer science whereby the function name appears first followed by the variable being passed to the function (example: functionName *VARIABLE*). Each definition is followed by a short description of what the function does.

The dossier of generative textures included here – *RSG-FORK-1.1.pdf*, *RSG-FORK-2.0.pdf*, *RSG-FORK-3.0.pdf*, and *RSG-FORK-4.1.pdf* – offers some hint of what a liberated language might be able to do. Written in Perl, a powerful text parsing language created in the late 1980s by Larry Wall, these generative textures use the *fork* command (a function that allows a piece of software to spawn recursive clones of itself) to create a volatile, viral 'fork bomb'. The output is a surface texture, a two-dimensional pattern made of text symbols. It is 'generative', meaning the surface texture is created uniquely each time the code is run.

The fork bomb strangles the machine, but does not kill it. By creating a high stress environment within the computer's processor, the artefacts of the machine itself become visible in the output. It is an approximation, given the constraints of existing languages, of what we aim to achieve in the liberated computer language. While no machine exists yet to accommodate it, in the future we hope to make new work written entirely using the liberated language.

**backdoor TARGET**
Installs a backdoor in the machine specified in TARGET. If no target is provided, the backdoor is installed in the local machine.

**bandwidth AMOUNT**
Enlarges or reduces bandwidth by AMOUNT.

**bitflip DATA, NUMBER**
Randomly flips a specified number of bits in the data source named by DATA.

**bug APPLICATION, NUMBER**
Introduces specified NUMBER of bugs into the code of the specified application.

**crash TIME**
Crashes the machine after the number of seconds provided by TIME by interfering with the operating system kernel. If TIME is not provided, the crash will occur immediately.

**degrade HARDWARE, TIME**
Introduces wear and tear, specified by number of months given in TIME, into specified HARDWARE.

**destroy TARGET**
Eliminates the object specified in TARGET.

**disidentify TARGET**
Removes all unique IDs, profile data, and other quantitative identifiers for the object specified in TARGET.

**emp TIME**
After the number of seconds provided by TIME, this function sends an electromagnetic pulse, neutralising self and all machines within range.

**envision**
An inductive function for articulation of unknown future realities. Often used in conjunction with rebuild.

**fall FUNCTION**
Introduces logical fallacies into any other language method specified by FUNCTION.

**frees TIME**
Frees the computer from operating by freezing it for the number of seconds specified in TIME.

**jam NETWORK**
Sends jamming signal to the specified NETWORK.

**lose DEVICE**
Unlinks a random file on the storage medium specified by DEVICE.

**mutate SEQUENCE**
Introduces a mutation into the given informatic SEQUENCE.

**netbust TARGET**
Exposes a network specified in TARGET to extremely high voltages, thereby fatally damaging any network hardware attached to the network. TARGET can also be 'self' to affect only the local interface.

**noise PROTOCOL, AMOUNT**
Scatters a specific AMOUNT of random noise packets into the default network interface using the specified PROTOCOL.

**obfuscate SEQUENCE**
Renders any given SEQUENCE (gene, character string, etc.) illegible to any known parsing technologies.

**obsolesce HARDWARE**
Renders any given piece of HARDWARE obsolete. Opposite of reclaim.

**overclock MULTIPLIER**
Increases the clock frequency of the central processing unit according to the value of MULTIPLIER. A negative value will decrease the clock frequency.

**processKill**
Selects a process at random and kills it.

**processScramble**
Randomly renumbers all currently running process IDs.

**rebuild TARGET**
Begins the process of rebuilding the object or scenario specified in TARGET. Often used to remedy the effects of destroy.

**reclaim HARDWARE**
Rescues any given piece of HARDWARE from obsolescence. Opposite of obsolesce.

**reject**
Rebuffs the current state of affairs. Often used as a precursor to destroy.

**reverseEngineer TARGET**
If object specified in TARGET is an application, this function decompiles the application and returns commented source code. If the object specified in TARGET is a protocol, this function returns a formal description of the protocol.

**rewrite APPLICATION**
Develops an entire new version upgrade for the piece of software designated in APPLICATION. The upgrade would be optimised for only the most startling developments.

**scramble DEVICE**
Randomly shuffles all filenames on the storage medium specified by DEVICE.

**selfDestruct**
Imposes fatal physical damage on self. Equivalent to destroy SELF.

**struggle**
Assists agitation and opposition to existing exploitation and control.

**zapMemory**
Clears all RAM on local machine. ⚐

Structural Shape Annealing    Spline Analysis    Surfacial Analysis

iteration 1

iteration 10

iteration 10

iteration 20

iteration30

iteration 30

iteration40

iteration50

iteration60

iteration 50

iteration 70

iteration80

iteration 70

iteration90

iteration 100

iteration 90

iteration 110

iteration 120

iteration 110

iteration 130

iteration 140

# Critical Practice: Protocol for a Fused Technology

Software created for architecture often presumes a certain repertoire of design intents; software appropriated from other fields does not make such presumptions but introduces translation difficulties into material logics. **Aaron Sprecher, Chandler Ahrens** and **Eran Neuman** describe how their collaborative design group, Open Source Architecture (O-S-A), has worked with structural engineers and software developers to create a computational protocol based on a stochastic evolutionary topological optimisation algorithm. This procedure allows architectural designers to work with complex geometries previously limited to the expertise of engineering. In addition to taking the form of a distributed network spanning New York, Los Angeles and Tel Aviv, O-S-A opens the possibility for various disciplines (computer science, structural engineering, architectural design) to work with a fluidity and commonality not previously possible. Like the work of RSG (also featured in this issue), here design begins with the construction of a software environment in which a project can occur, and which merges previously distinct areas of expertise.

Open Source Architecture (O-S-A) with Professor Kristina Shea and Dr Marina Gourtovaia (Cambridge University), Hylomorphic Project, 2005
Simulation. Structural shape annealing process, geometrical and surfacial analyses, including 15 iterations out of a process that is concluded at the 170th iteration.

*Just as the adjectives 'natural' and 'social' designate representations of collectives that are neither natural nor social in themselves, so the words 'local' and 'global' offer points of view on networks that by nature are neither local nor global, but are more or less connected. What I have called modern exoticism consists in taking these two pairs of oppositions as what defines our world and what would set us apart from all others. ... Yet, we know nothing about the social that is not defined by what we think we know about the natural, and vice versa. Similarly, we define the local only by contrast with what we have to attribute to the global, and vice versa.*

Bruno Latour, 1993[1]

With the evolution of networks, the transformation in biological and electronic systems and the reliance on topologies of information, Latour implies that modes of criticism have changed and that critical theory by itself has lost its effectiveness. Instead, new conditions of topological networks foster new modes of criticality that are based on immediacy and practicality.

Similar to Latour's discussion on critical discourse, the work of Open Source Architecture (www.o-s-a.com) falls somewhere between the practical production of environments and the critical construction of consciousness in local and global landscapes. Capitalising on global networks and computational linguistic interfaces, the practice constantly modifies the design procedure in a way that leads to the integration of technology (structure), history (discourse), ecology (environmental conditions) and culture (programme). The main aspect of this procedure is the ability to critically resample and analyse architectural projects during the design process rather than engaging in retrospective analysis. The critical dimension derives from the integration of theoretical criticism and multiple architectural histories within the project's generation. This is possible only through the development of open-source platforms for collaboration,

which allow the integration of different fields of knowledge and expertise as entities embedded within the process itself.

O-S-A deploys three consecutive modes of operation constitutive to the development of a project. First, protocol processing provides a common ground for working and communication among the parties involved by translating knowledge into exchangeable data. Second, a screening/streaming set of operations filters information into representational, functional or instructional parameters in order to fuse them into an architectural object. And third, an evaluation process allows the examination of the project according to immanent fitness criteria. This process is performed iteratively.

In the Hylomorphic Project, this operational procedure is applied to create a platform for professionals from different fields to collaborate in an iterative design process. As part of this project, it was necessary to use a new sort of software package. The practice therefore referred to an existing software protocol and modified it together with its developer structural engineer Professor Kristina Shea and Dr Marina Gourtovaia of Cambridge University, to suit the design needs of the project. The software's open code meant that the stochastic evolutionary optimization protocols of the 'structural shaping annealing' features of the software could be modified, improved and, most importantly, adapted to correspond to O-S-A's research objectives.

This procedure simulates a topological condition of natural evolution, combining form-finding and material expression in a manner that goes beyond a computational procedure that automatically generates forms. Instead, the procedures and the form co-evolve: the emergent form results from a diachronic and reiterative process in which the scripted processes are transformed at the same moment the morphology is developed. Moreover, because the Hylomorphic Project's algorithms continually seek equilibrium in the

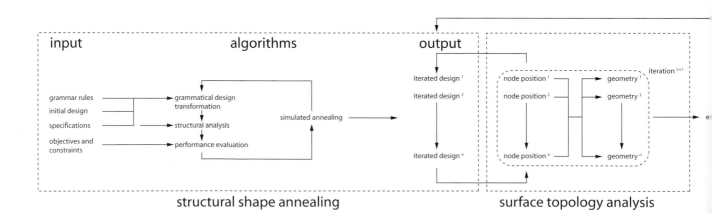

**Diagram of the structural shape annealing process and surface topology analysis. The diagram indicates the feedback procedure in the design process of the iterative structural optimisation.**

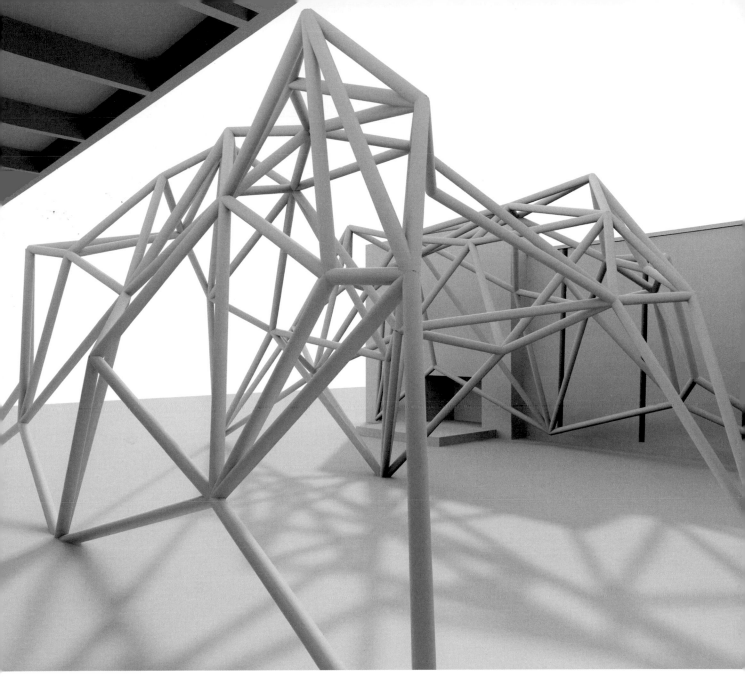

Position of the optimised n-dimensional grid relative to the Rudolph Schindler House idealistic model. Modernist 3-D model. The algorithimic calculation stems from the Modernist geometry and suggests a stochastic procedure that leads to a modulated topology.

integration of the various viable parameters that are infused into the form, the process can be terminated at any moment and still result in a fully articulated architectural structure.

The core of the Hylomorphic platform is written in C, a fast, low-level language. A graphical user interface (GUI) provides interactive access to this computational core and is written in Python – a high-level scripting language – to allow for easy customisation of the software according to the design task at hand.

Initial testing of this platform took place at Rudolph Schindler's seminal King Road house in West Hollywood. Using the software's collaborative procedures, a structure was evolved as an interface between interior and exterior spaces, combining the immediate surroundings of the Rudolph Schindler House together with concepts of domesticity as the data to reintegrate and transform. The resulting architectures transform the typological limitations of the house and dismantle the division of social order given by its distribution of spaces. As a result, history and theory are 'quantified' into the design process as 'scientific' data that determines, together with empiric information, the design as a whole.

Thus, the Hylomorphic procedure suggests a dialectical approach between science and culture. On the one hand, the information that determines the formal consolidation of the

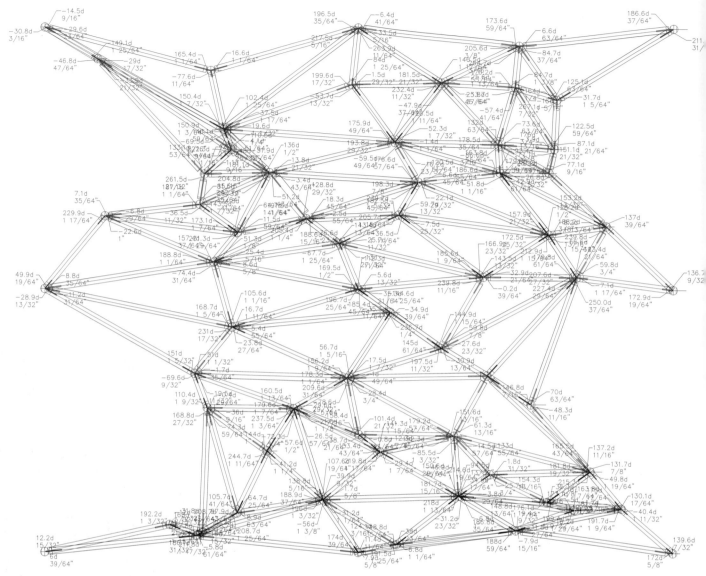

Geometry study of the optimised positioning. The drawing indicates the measurements of the bars, including width, length and positioning in relation to their angulations, and also shows the variability.

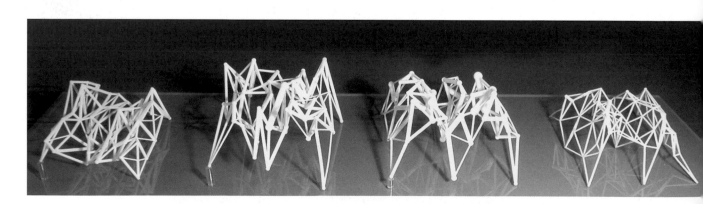

Stereolithographic models of the iterated stochastic evolutionary optimisation. The sequence of models conveys the evolution of the structural elements, the iteration in their width and length and the increasing triangulation resulting from the process of optimisation.

architectural object is scripted to negotiate between form and matter, structure and surface, as well as function and programme. On the other, the complexity suggested by the computational procedure of Hylomorphism disguises the script as a scientific procedure. As such, the architectural object seems to appear as a random articulation whereas, in fact, the architectural entity follows a predetermined communicational procedure that enables advanced calculations of precisely scripted procedures. Thus, the architectural entity is located between scientific procedures of formal determination and cultural contingencies. The software modification follows a protocol that enables the fusion of form-finding procedures and material expression together with environmental, programmatic and historical data.

The next step will be to test the Hylomorphic procedure as a process that will lead to the intermediation of spaces, materials and environmental conditions in larger scales. A full-scale structure testing these features will be executed for the exhibition 'Gen[H]ome Project: Genetic and Domesticity' (MAK Center in Los Angeles, 2006). The open-source platform and the three modes of operation – protocol processing, screening/streaming and instantaneous dynamic evaluation – make this design process highly portable. As such, the evolution of the project's form suggests the continual adjustment of the design tool. One advantage of this co-evolutionary process of tools and products lies in the formal articulation of the optimised architectural condition while fostering unpredictable and numerous possibilities. Instead of providing a global package for local applications, the tool itself enters into the networked co-evolution. ∆

**Note**
1. Bruno Latour, 'A perverse taste for the margins', in *We Have Never Been Modern*, trans Catherine Porter, Harvard University Press (Cambridge, MA), 1993, p 122.

Structural prototype of the optimised model presented at the exhibition 'Machines Atmosphériques' at the FRAC Centre, Orléans, France, in November 2005. The prototype is iteration number 170 of the stochastic procedure.

# Collective Cognition: Neural Fabrics and Social Software

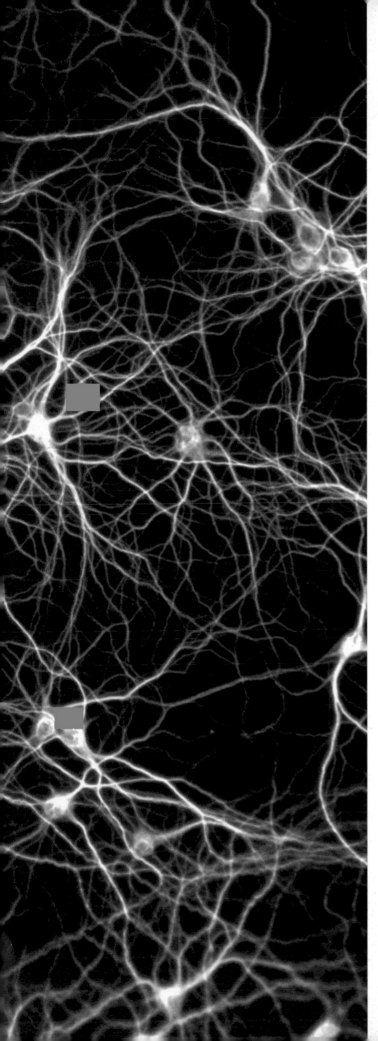

For decades, the MIT Media Lab has been a centre of innovative and highly influential research on emerging technologies, including responsive and interactive sensing systems, software programming and forms of artificial intelligence, and robotic design and communication systems for new forms of knowledge production and distribution. **Therese Tierney** writes about several aspects of the Media Lab's research, including the current work of John Maeda, as well as the work of collaborators such as CEB Reas and Ben Fry, who she argues are developing work in new and sophisticated directions. She positions this work within the larger thematic of collective intelligence by addressing the particularly social forms of practice and the necessary connection to intelligent software and sensing technologies.

The human neocortex contains some 100 billion cells, each with 1000 to 10,000 connective synapses, and approximately 274 million metres (900 million feet) of wiring, yet the surface area is less than 0.25 square metres (2.7 square feet). How can one begin to conceptualise an information processing system of this complexity? Moreover, if we consider the larger context, how does an organism produce meaningful information about the environment from an uninterrupted stream of data? These uncertainties hindered mid-20th-century scientists as they worked to develop accurate models of the mind. By the late 1970s neurologists had begun to shift their thinking from earlier serial models to dynamic process-based models, one of the more robust of which were network topologies.

An analysis of the neurobiological system provides a procedural model, or abstract machine, from which certain organisational principles may be captured. While it is evident that neurons process information, the function of such a system depends not only on its elements, but also on the way they are connected. Yet if we are to extract certain features from neurobiological networks, we see the difficulty in separating neuronal material from neuronal architecture primarily because nerve cells exhibit hybridity. More verb than noun, neurons act as highly interconnected transmitting and processing elements whose activities are based on electrical and chemical flows. They receive multiple, thousands, of weighted input signals and synthesise them into one output. The neurons are plastic, that is to say, their cellular components alter form in response to activity.

**Paul De Koninck, Dissociated culture of rat hippocampal neurons, Université Laval, Québec, 2005**
The neuronal organisation can be summarised as a distributed meshwork, characterised by massive feedback and interactivity.

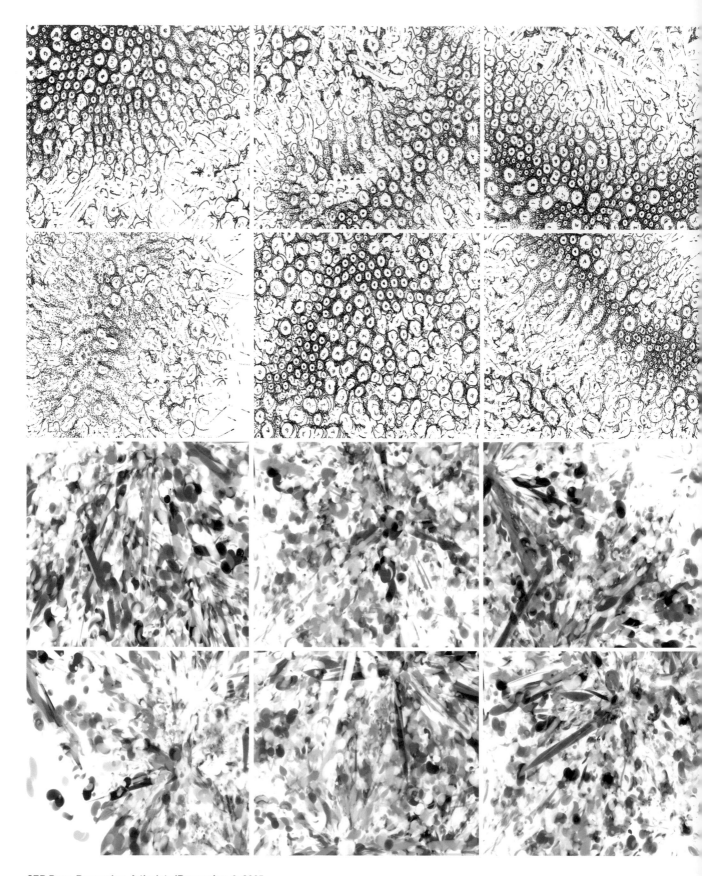

**CEB Reas, Processing, Articulate/Processing_9, 2005**
This programming language and open-source software enables visual designers to work directly with code for sketching and prototyping. These examples employ kinetic visual elements that display variation over time.

Regarding neuronal architecture, a reconceptualisation has evolved over the last few years from a top-down hierarchical organisation to one that self-organises through associations within limited hierarchies.[1] Synaptic connections are point to point, but in contrast to electrical wiring the points of connection are continually changing. Most interactions are local, but there is also additional transmission globally. Moreover, the transmission is nonlinear; the axons recursively loop back into previous neurons, as well as to themselves. Overall, the neuronal organisation can be summarised as a distributed meshwork, characterised by massive feedback and interactivity.

Inasmuch as the brain's architecture is inherently flexible, reflexive and adaptable, it continually evolves and develops during an organism's experiences.[2] This is because the learning process requires adjustments to synaptic connections between neurons, so that a process of reconfiguration occurs, as in an allopoietic relationship. In the larger sense, the constant data flow exchanged between organism and environment is continually being mapped and remapped in the brain.

Can we extract certain principles from a model of the neurobiological system, which could be useful towards understanding the notion of a collective intelligence? The process of extracting salient features necessitates building a theory from empirical data, for example, how a network is different from a conventional matrix or other organisational structures. The basis of biological network theory can be understood as a fundamental shift from substance to systems. In the 1970s, Gyorgy Kepes proposed that: 'What scientists considered before as substance shaped into forms, and consequently understood as tangible objects, is now recognised as energies and their dynamic organization.'[3] More recently, Sanford Kwinter has suggested that through various theories of evolution and cybernetics 'we have to be able to understand structure as a pattern of energy and information'.[4] Accordingly, a contemporary materialist approach recognises that dynamic matter-energy manifests as nonlinear changes defined by strong mutual interactions (attractors) and feedback between components.[5] Phenomena at any scale, from the brain to the Internet, can then be modelled as aggregates of specialised cells, or machinic assemblages.[6] These cellular machines are neither technic nor mechanic, rather cellular activities can be described in terms of conditions and operations. In contrast to earlier vitalist theories, the descriptor 'mechanism' is not used here pejoratively, but instead outlines a structural unity in the operative functioning of an organism.[7]

If we look at the neurobiological system as a form of collective cognition and knowledge sharing, certain generalisations will apply. These principles, as points in a field of information exchange, are: 1) dynamic, 2) distributed, 3) flexible, 4) interactive.

Any system that is dynamic and interactive, flexible and distributed, lends itself to properties of self-organisation to a greater or lesser degree. Furthermore, these four points derived from neurobiological systems are important because they begin to provide a framework for a theory of collective intelligence and social software. Their principles construct what could be termed a 'relational architecture' based on associations, conceptually similar to Hopfield networks or Kohonen algorithms. Social software, which supports group communications (from mail lists to blogs, wikis or massively multiplayer online games) has a dynamic that cannot be understood from the individual agents alone. Their operations are collaborative, responsive and emergent.

It must be stressed, however, that the neuronal system is not invoked here as an analogy, inasmuch as there are obvious differences between neuronal systems and social software, such as the levels of connectivity and collectivity of agents, as well as the effect of micro agents on macro behaviour. The intention is neither to dispute nor to minimise these differences, but instead to abstract a set of principles and behaviours that may prove useful in tracing the evolutionary potential of collective cognition. The term 'collective cognition' is defined as agents participating in a body of knowledge and, by extension, benefiting from that aggregated information. While social software encourages connectivity between agents, there is also the understanding that particular design decisions, as well as the grammar of interactions made possible by the software, are socially significant.[8]

While it has been frequently quoted that social change both precedes and informs technological change, the principles extracted from a neurological model can be useful to describe the analytical parameters for open-system projects initiated at MIT's Media Lab. These prototypes were developed during William Mitchell's tenure as Academic Head of Media Arts & Sciences from 2001 to 2005. Such cycling of information through open systems can also be traced to other social software models on the Internet. Furthermore, the extensive trajectory of Media Lab projects demonstrates their robust ability to propagate novel applications.

## John Maeda, OPENSTUDIO, Physical Language Workshop, MIT Media Lab, ongoing

On a theoretical level, the Media Lab is investigating the social and cultural implications of what Manuel Castell described as 'spaces of flows', that is to say, the effect of energy, matter and information and their de/restratification on social structures, which will continue to intensify as various forms of media converge. One of the research labs concerned with collective cognition and social software is the Physical Language Workshop (PLW) directed by John Maeda, one of the first designers to apply computational strategies to visual and artistic production. The recipient of numerous awards, Maeda's work has recently been exhibited at the Foundation Cartier in Paris in 'Nature + Eye'm Hungry' (2005), which explored humanistic technologies through digital art. As Maeda explains: 'Programming is not widely understood as a

## Physical Language Workshop, OPENSTUDIO, MIT Media Lab, 2006

Network graphs. This experimental Internet project exposes the traditionally opaque processes of valuation, marketing and exchange of creative production, developing over time. In doing so, it provides a dynamic participatory space for learning about the underlying mechanisms surrounding pricing and exchange of art. In all of the graphs shown here, the intensity of the relationship is shown by the width of connection. The nodes are distributed based on their connectivity, with higher connectivity nodes biased towards the right. Graphics by Burak Arikan.

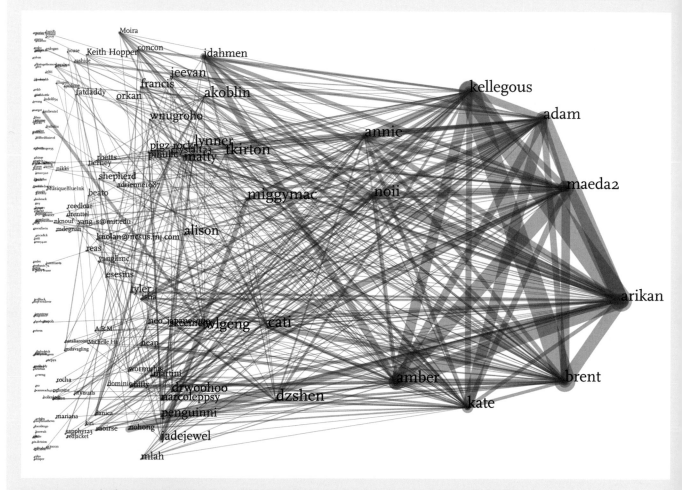

Business network (red). A business relationship is created whenever a person buys or sells an art piece. The diagram depicts densities of interactions between people.

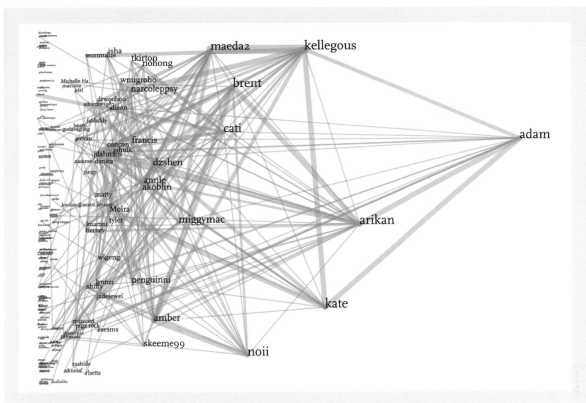

Exhibitee (artist's) network (blue-green). An exhibitee relationship is created whenever a person is exhibited by another person. This graphically describes the popularity of artists.

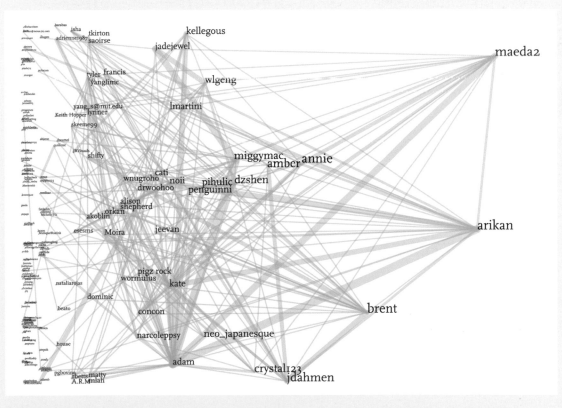

Exhibitor network (green). An exhibitor relationship is created whenever a person exhibits another person's art piece in his or her gallery. This diagram depicts emerging collectors and their relationships.

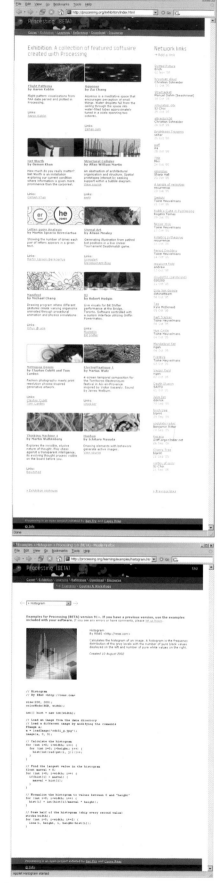

**Ben Fry and CEB Reas,
Online Exhibition Space
– Processing, 2006**
Contributors using
Processing's open-source
code provide links to their
diverse projects: graphics,
architectural design, video
and interactive art.

creative activity. We do not usually learn this skill in school along with other disciplines such as writing or painting. And when it is learned today in schools as computer science, usually the subject matter is "how to use" a computer versus "how to make" a computer line of thinking.'[9]

Starting with the *Design by Numbers/DBN*, a programming language and development environment, in 1999, Maeda created a mathematical drawing system for introducing computer programming to visual artists. The software, freely available via the Internet, included the fundamental principle of coding. Moreover, it was an easily accessible and responsive

# While the long-term social implications of OPENSTUDIO are impossible to predict, the open-system environment will be freely accessible to individuals, schools and colleges throughout the world, at any level and for any economic group, with the potential to become an essential pedagogical tool for digital teaching and learning.

site to explore. His innovative research while directing the Aesthetics and Computation Group (ACG) at the MIT Media Lab eventually led to the interactive motion graphics that are prevalent on the Internet today.

Maeda's ongoing project, OPENSTUDIO, is an experimental ecosystem for artists, designers and students.[10] It originated in response to social forces, primarily a marked dissatisfaction with the highly centralised and vertically stratified organisation of today's creative industries. Current information architecture does not reflect the way designers seamlessly engage with multiple programming languages, software platforms and protocols, all within collective social networks.

As an alternative, this webspace is conceptualised within a knowledge-sharing framework as a provisional online micro economy in which the user-generated content can be leveraged as creative capital. It is structured on flexibility, dynamics and the relational architecture of a market system. The current Alpha version includes online graphic tools, a distributed rendering engine to render images, an exchange-ownership system, and external data access through remote sensors. OPENSTUDIO enables members to create, collect and sell digital art or data with the content being entirely member generated.

As PLW designer Burak Arikan explains: 'The experimental ownership and authorship system lets people explore different scenarios. People can "buy" an art piece from the creators and "own" the piece. As "owners" they can access the source and change it by using the Draw tool.'[11] In this sense, OPENSTUDIO simulates the art industry by introducing the roles of, for example, artists, collectors and exhibitors. As with any social software, the behaviour of a group cannot be predicted by the individuals in isolation. Therefore the potential to trace the interactions of people and art is possible through the auspices of an application program interface (API), with production tagged and classified according to various descriptors in the environment. The resultant data can be highly generative, because new patterns emerge during analysis. At the micro level, it is possible to visualise economic and artistic trends, how these trends occur, as well as the propagation of alliances and groups within such trends.

Similar to a mesh technology, which allows individual computers to propagate the network and act as new access points, projects initially developed within the PLW have spawned new iterations. Because networks based on association can extract more complexity from their environment, a web-based environment similar to

# The open-source website is an engaging and highly interactive visual design space that teaches the fundamental coding concepts for images, animation and sound.

OPENSTUDIO, organised in clusters, or networks, of networks, is not only more efficient, but also has the potential to self-organise by building meaningful structures that change as the input changes. In this way, a process at one level becomes a component of another system at a higher level. These clusters then also act as attractors so that subsequent generations of collectives can cycle into new forms.

While the long-term social implications of OPENSTUDIO are impossible to predict, the open-system environment will be freely accessible to individuals, schools and colleges throughout the world, at any level and for any economic group, with the potential to become an essential pedagogical tool for digital teaching and learning. In tandem with the Media Lab's 'One laptop per child, $100 laptop' programme initiated by Nicholas Negroponte,[12] OPENSTUDIO brings us closer to the possibility of a networked planet.

## Ben Fry and CEB Reas, Processing, 2001
As a radical departure from both traditional programming languages and commercial software, Processing was initiated by two of Maeda's students: Ben Fry, now with the Broad Institute, and CEB Reas of the University of California at Los Angeles (UCLA). Realising that computation was a unique medium with unrealised potential, they developed a programming language in 2001 that was also accessible to visual designers. 'The concept of Processing was to create a text programming language specifically for making responsive images,' Reas explains. 'It is developed by artists and designers as an alternative to proprietary software tools in the same domain.' Processing integrates a programming language, development environment and teaching methodology into a unified structure for learning.[13] The open-source website is an engaging and highly interactive visual design space that teaches the fundamental coding concepts for images, animation and sound.

Fry and Reas were frustrated by the lack of ease and accessibility of existing programming languages at the time: C, C++ and Java. For visual or spatial minds, these environments were complex and difficult to learn on. In contrast, Processing was designed with a simplified syntax that made it easier to learn and work with. As a tool for writing software sketches, ideas can quickly be realised in code, with programs often half as long as their Java or C++ equivalents. The graphical user interface is minimal and elegant; it contains a text editor and toolbar, which enables the code to be run, stopped, saved or exported. While designers typically use mouse-based applications with

**Physical Language Workshop, OPENSTUDIO – Drawspace, MIT Media Lab, 2006**
A screenshot of the Draw application in use. Draw runs as a desktop application that is transparently connected to OPENSTUDIO and interoperates seamlessly. Graphics by Burak Arikan.

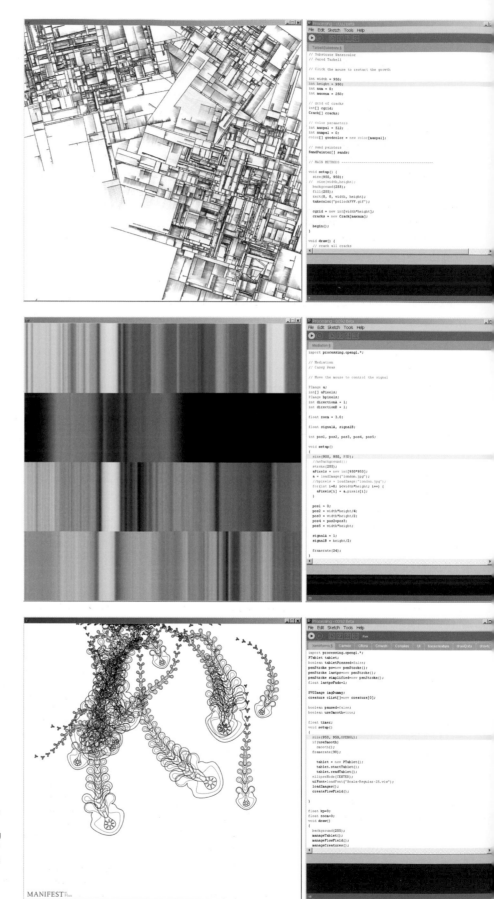

**Ben Fry and CEB Reas, Integrative Development Environment – Processing, 2006**
Three different examples of online learning projects: IDE is a simple and usable editor for writing and running programs. Libraries extend Processing capabilities beyond graphics to image-enabling audio, video and mobile devices.

commercial software, the creative potential is greatly expanded with Processing as designers and artists learn to become proficient coders as well. As an open system, it is designed with a cognitive transparency so that the code is both visible and manipulable. As such, the webspace is realisable at many different skill levels – the online learner can experiment with changing or combining various algorithmic parameters, and immediately visualise the results.[14]

According to Reas: 'Writing software has been the foundation of my work as an artist for the last four years. During this time, I've come to think more generally about software, discussing it in terms of processes and systems rather than computers and programming languages.'[15] Similar to the operations of Protevi's social machine, nowhere is this more apparent than in Processing's expanding online exhibition space. The site has evolved into a socially complex design collective populated by media iconoclasts who have created their own Processing blogs. User-generated content from graphic designers, students, artists and architects is continually being posted online, inspiring others in new methods of creative production. The website currently features submissions from the Pritzker Award-winning architectural firm Morphosis, Roger Hodgin of Flight 404 and interactive artist Joachim Sauter of ART+COM. This, in turn, has generated an expanding discourse on computational methods for visualising information that was not necessarily conceived initially.

One innovative example of data mapping by Aaron Koblin, Flight Patterns animates vectors of aeroplane flight movement derived from Federal Aviation Administration (FAA) data parsed and then plotted in time. The continental 'figure' emerges not through formal description, but through active use patterns. A spin-off project, Mobile Processing, enables software written with Processing's code to run on Java-powered mobile devices. In true meshwork fashion, those who use Processing share multiple roles: they are the data testers, transmitters and processors. Each new software version inspires innovations that feed back into and expand the future potential of algorithmic applications in visual design.

## Conclusion

If the Internet is both the aggregator and disseminator of information, how can it be organised to encourage collective cognition through social software? By investigations into neurobiological systems and extracting certain principles, common strategies can be discovered that are useful at varying levels of scale. Instead of an analogy, the neurobiological system can then serve as a collective intelligence model or abstract machine, from which specific organisational principles may be applied, such as flexibility, self-organisation, distribution. These key features describe conditions for nonlinear combinatorics available for the generation of novel structures and processes.[16] As a description of operations these, in turn, become the structural logic for disseminating generative environments for design,

operating somewhere between experimentation and theory.

Collective cognition gives us a vocabulary and method of analysis. By applying these notions to research initially developed at the MIT Media Lab and then dispersed, we can begin to hypothesise new modes of distributed organisations. Similar to the open-source code from which they were generated, open systems enable sharing, cycling and continual innovation through collective actions. Therefore it must be emphasised that the experimental projects outlined above are not merely websites, nor even learning spaces, but can be understood as social software that benefits and transforms the user. These examples operate as dynamic social ecologies that are structured to both reflect and extend our cognitive and social engagement with the world. Δ

**Notes**
1. Manfred Spitzer, *The Mind Within the Net: Models of Learning, Thinking, and Acting*, MIT Press (Cambridge, MA), 1999.
2. Andrew Wuensche, 'Basins of attraction in network dynamics: A conceptual framework for biomolecular networks', in Gerhard Schlosser and Gunter P Wagner, *Modularity in Developmental Evolution*, University of Chicago Press (Chicago, IL), 2004.
3. Gyorgy Kepes, 'Art and ecological consciousness', *Arts of the Environment*; George Braziller (New York), 1972.
4. Sanford Kwinter, History Theory Criticism Lecture: 'Thinking About Architecture' 4.607, MIT, Autumn 2005.
5. Manual DeLanda, *A Thousand Years of Non-Linear History*, Zone Books/MIT Press (Cambridge, MA), 2000.
6. According to molecular biologists, at the cellular level there is not much variance between life and a machine.
7. This is in contrast to 'vitalist' notions that regard individual unity as superimposition, which hierarchically exalts the organism and makes mechanisms subordinate to this.
8. Clay Shirky, 'Social Software and the Politics of Groups'; www.shirky.com/writings/group_politics.html, March 2003.
9. John Maeda, 'The nature of technology', *The Domino Effect: Natural Influence Over Technology*, Sante Fe Institute, 2004.
10. While the entire site is open for browsing, for testing purposes OPENSTUDIO membership is currently by invitation only. Membership for the public is planned as soon possible.
11. Burak Arikan, email correspondence, 28 February 2006.
12. One Laptop per Child (OLPC) is a nonprofit association dedicated to the development of a $100 laptop. This initiative was launched by faculty members at the MIT Media Lab and first announced by lab co-founder Nicholas Negroponte, now chairman of OLPC, at the World Economic Forum at Davos, Switzerland, in January 2005.
13. CEB Reas, email correspondence, 27 February 2006.
14. As learning environments, both OPENSTUDIO and Processing exemplify many of Piaget's theories of developmental psychology, primarily that learning occurs through play in risk-free environments.
15. CEB Reas, 'Process/Software' in Anthony Burke and Therese Tierney (eds), *Network Practice*, Princeton Architectural Press (New York), forthcoming.
16. In the physical world we recognise that the phenomena displayed by a system may not be evident in the properties of the subunits that make up that system. For example, the properties of a wheel are not evident from the properties of the materials used to construct the wheel. The wheel's property of rolling emerges from the system, created by the specific arrangement of the materials used to make the wheel. See Benjamin Libet, *Mind Time: The Temporal Factor in Consciousness*, MIT Press (Cambridge, MA), 2003.

# Design Research on Responsive Display Prototypes: Integrating Sensing, Information and Computation Technologies

Small Design Firm, working with Ben Rubin of EAR Studio and artist Ann Hamilton, augments physical architectures with responsive and intelligent electronic interfaces. Recounting their recent collaborations on a series of projects, Small Design Firm's **David Small** and **John Rothenberg** discuss how such collaboration builds on generational continuities of technological innovation, and the ways in which their work has developed by recombining their individual interests and areas of expertise into a shared knowledge base through the process of developing specific designs. Physical space and projects thus become a site for the production of collective intelligence both as a design process and in the use of the end product.

**Ann Hamilton with Small Design Firm and EAR Studio, Facade Ecology, 2003–06**
Animation stills from the schematic proposal for a building membrane installation at the University of Minnesota's Molecular and Cellular Biology Building. Ben Rubin and Ann Hamilton generated this concept animation, which articulates the progression of light as it circulates through the building skin of the research facility. Small Design Firm investigated the informational potential of this lighting system by developing a biological simulation for the generation of graphic material.

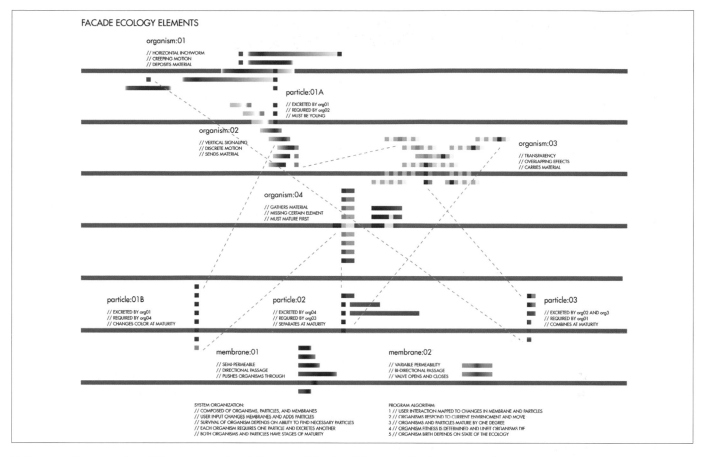

Early concept diagram for the building membrane installation at the University of Minnesota. The diagram maps the various informational organisms that inhabit the membrane, and the organisational logics by which they distribute and deposit bits and particles of visual data. The result is an artificial ecology of information that activates the building skin, transforming it into a dynamic and responsive index of internal and external activity.

Small Design Firm and Ben Rubin's EAR Studio, both of which specialise in computation as well as information and interaction design, have recently been working collaboratively on several installation projects, each of which integrates lighting, sensing and programming technologies in the design of responsive and increasingly intelligent architectural display and information infrastructures.

Any form of lighting, when considered to be a material in and of itself, and inherently malleable and reconfigurable, can be subject to complex but effective control protocols and thus altered accordingly. Using custom software integrated with various sensing technologies (for example, motion or proximity sensing), the projects illustrated here explore the potential of LED lighting strips by treating the qualities and intensities of colour and brightness of such lighting as variables for potential alteration. What distinguishes the LED strips from conventional lighting is the ability to control the entire display with the same accuracy as a computer screen or projection. To this extent, the display system can be seen as the visual output of an informational, or computational, control system. Software, in combination with various sensing infrastructures, absorbs, processes and distributes information into the lighting infrastructure, altering its colour and intensity and transforming it into a dynamic and reflexive membrane of visual and graphic activity.

The first of the collaborative projects, Facade Ecology, involved the development of a responsive building membrane for the University of Minnesota's Molecular and Cellular Biology Building. Artist Ann Hamilton was commissioned by the university to create an installation that would work with and comment on the building. The proposed design integrates a number of technological systems, including an array of motion sensors distributed throughout the interior of the building. This sensing network collects and processes data related to the various activities taking place within the laboratories, such as patterns of use and occupancy based on movement. The motion-based information is then sent as raw data to a custom software interface which then interpolates that data, translating it into a set of instructions for the generation of light and colour. The new information, materialised in the form of colour and lighting patterns, is then distributed to a LED infrastructure embedded in the building's exterior skin, allowing the overall design proposal to translate motion patterns into lighting patterns. By extension, the building's skin is transformed into an active and responsive

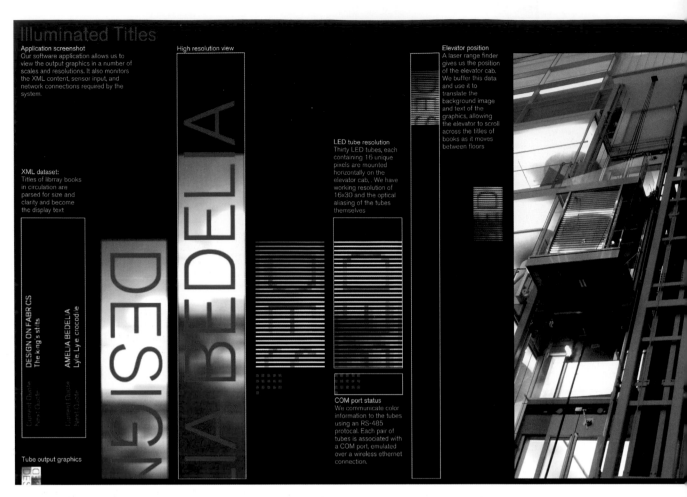

**Illuminated Titles**

**Application screenshot**
Our software application allows us to view the output graphics in a number of scales and resolutions. It also monitors the XML content, sensor input, and network connections required by the system.

**XML dataset:**
Titles of library books in circulation are parsed for size and clarity and become the display text

DESIGN ON FABRICS
The king's stilts
Current Quote
Next Quote

AMELIA BEDELIA
Lyle, Lyle crocodile
Current Quote
Next Quote

**Tube output graphics**

**High resolution view**

DESIGN

AMELIA BEDELIA

**LED tube resolution**
Thirty LED tubes, each containing 16 unique pixels are mounted horizontally on the elevator cab, . We have working resolution of 16x30 and the optical aliasing of the tubes themselves

**COM port status**
We communicate color information to the tubes using an RS-485 protocal. Each pair of tubes is associated with a COM port, emulated over a wireless ethernet connection.

**Elevator position**
A laser range finder gives us the position of the elevator cab. We buffer this data and use it to translate the background image and text of the graphics, allowing the elevator to scroll across the titles of books as it moves between floors

**Ben Rubin (EAR STUDIO) with Small Design Firm, Four Stories, 2004–06**
Interior informational display infrastructure for the Minneapolis Public Library. Incoming data from the library checkout system is integrated with information regarding elevator cab positions. This newly integrated information is then used to determine the distribution of graphic material through the display screens, each of which are situated in an elevator cab. The graphic material itself is rendered at high resolution and then transformed into quantised data before being distributed to the LED tubes.

Photos of an informational display prototype in which LED tubes are arranged to form a large low-resolution display system. The technological research particular to this prototype served as a foundation for the development and application of the display infrastructure commissioned by the Minneapolis Public Library.

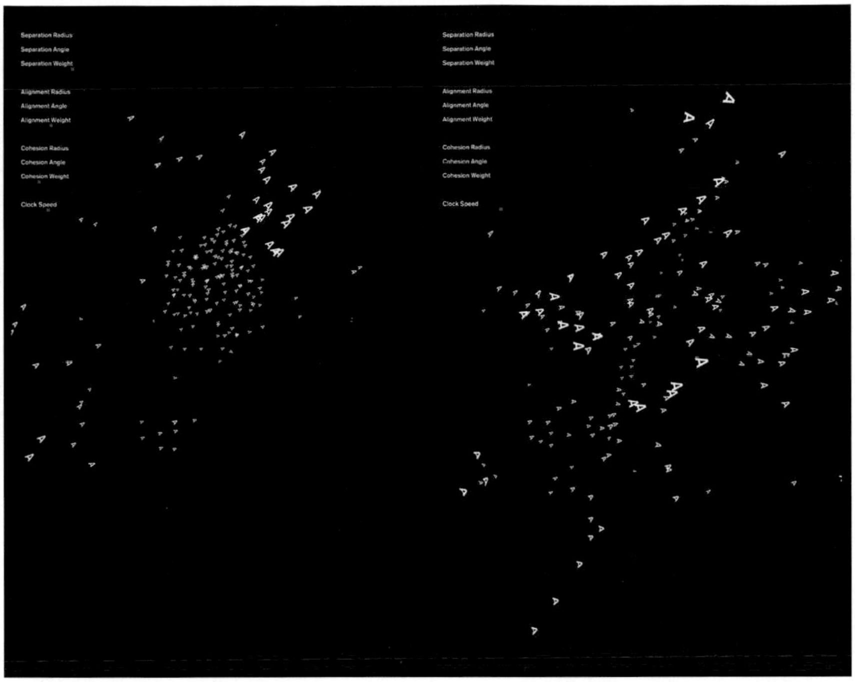
Separation Radius
Separation Angle
Separation Weight
Alignment Radius
Alignment Angle
Alignment Weight
Cohesion Radius
Cohesion Angle
Cohesion Weight
Clock Speed
Separation Radius
Separation Angle
Separation Weight
Alignment Radius
Alignment Angle
Alignment Weight
Cohesion Radius
Cohesion Angle
Cohesion Weight
Clock Speed

Software screenshots of a flocking simulation developed by Small Design Firm. The software application mimics natural flocking patterns, establishing a basic programming system through which control variables can be adjusted and manipulated to influence the organisational behaviour of informational and graphic elements. This application, a software prototype programmed in C++/OpenGL, allows the designer to explore the graphic and informational potential of flocking logics as a means of distributing and organising content.

membrane, using light and colour to index the various patterns of use taking place within, exposing the hidden life of the building, including its internal research activities.

In terms of the computational process by which these motion patterns are converted into colour and lighting patterns, Small Design Firm explored the potential of simulating biological phenomena, in particular forms of collective intelligence as demonstrated in the logics of flocking behaviour. Flocks are in a constant state of flux. Each member of the flock continually changes its relative position to other members, but not so dramatically that the flock itself becomes unstable and dissolves. Using these logics of simple rules for governing relational fluctuation between individual members, the practice's software interface interpolates degrees of flocking behaviour particular to the users of the building as a principle for organising colour and lighting patterns on the exterior membrane. To this extent, the colour and lighting patterns that inhabit the LED infrastructure assume basic principles of intelligence in response to the users of the building, organising and reorganising themselves through properties of flocking – a general fluctuation of individual and collective behaviour at the scale of light and colour.

While Ann Hamilton's Facade Ecology project was in development, Ben Rubin was working on another LED prototype exploring related information, computation and display technologies. This research led to a proposal for the Minneapolis Public Library's new central branch which installs an array of LED tube patches on exposed elevator cabs within the building's main four-storey atrium. Appropriately, this artwork was eventually titled Four Stories. Not unlike the Facade Ecology project, this design system works as an informational index of various activities taking place within the building. As the elevator cabs circulate from floor to floor, distributing occupants throughout the various levels of the building, the LED display patches visualise information particular to another form and scale of circulation within the building, namely the distribution of books as titles are processed at the library's main circulation desk. To this extent, the design infrastructure, again integrating motion sensing, lighting and information technologies, generates a responsive and dynamic display that participates in the building's own logics of distribution and circulation.

For this proposal, Small Design Firm collaborated on the development of new software that served to allow for the communication of information between the motion sensor infrastructure and the LED display system. The software is written in C++, building on a number of existing programming libraries including OpenGL, Freetype and Intel Performance Primitives.

Over the course of two years, the multiple perspectives involved in these projects allowed all involved to rethink dynamic illumination as an artistic medium. As a design practice, Small Design Firm is compelled to contribute both innovative designs and the tools to allow artists to produce work in new technological mediums. Its collaborative efforts have thus produced both unanticipated design solutions and software that it is hoped will be incorporated in future collaborations. Above all, the practice has begun to tease out some of the poetic qualities of this new architectural material. AD

# Does Collaboration Work?

Bringing together a number of design celebrities, among them Greg Lynn, UN Studio, Foreign Office Architects (FOA) and Kevin Kennon Architect, United Architects (UA) was established to create a collaborative proposal for the 2003 competition for a new World Trade Center. Invoking the name as well as the intentions of what started as a similar collaborative formation by established actors and film-makers in the 1940s (United Artists) to challenge mainstream corporate power, UA attempted to offer more visionary alternatives to the expectations of typical mainstream architectural solutions. **Kevin Kennon** here presents an insider's perspective on the UA collaboration and employs his unique history, including his former partnership at Kohn Pedersen Fox (KPF) to raise important questions about collective design in terms of authorship, identity and practice. Central to his observations are the differences between the efficiency models of corporate teams and truly collaborative endeavours.

In architecture circles it has become fashionable to use the term 'collaboration' to such an extent that it risks being overused, and thus becoming meaningless. Its use stems from the undeniable fact that architecture is not a solo act. Yet the mythology of the architect/hero seems to reside in an almost Homeric image of raging individualism – Howard Roark as a modern Achilles. The media feeds this image by demanding 'stars'. As the pantheon of architects becomes ever more stratified, those left out or who have yet to arrive have clung to the word 'collaborative' as an anchor in a surging tide of oneness.

Yet the problem with the idea of collaboration as a conceptual anchor for rising architects is its very diffuseness. Collaboration has come to mean both an anti-heroic effort that acknowledges a collective's ability to conceive and produce meaningful architectures and, paradoxically, a craven corporate sameness to be 'all things to all people'. At its best, collaborative practice can achieve a sum greater than its parts and result in true insight and innovation. At its worst, it is used to exploit another's talents and resources behind the facade of 'collective cooperation'. It is not uncommon for design architects to disingenuously claim they are 'collaborating' with executive architects when they are in fact codifying a hierarchical, often one-sided, relationship.

Most clients are somewhat bewildered by architects, not knowing what to make of our profession. The notion of a collaborative team of architects working on their multimillion-dollar project does not usually allay such bewilderment. Most have heard aphorisms like 'a camel is a horse designed by a committee'. Clients are looking for leadership and management as well as creativity when they hire an architect. This is a fundamental problem in marketing collective design.

When trying to sell 'collaboration' to the potential client, architects very often try to use the jazz analogy – a group of expert musicians who play together in an improvisatory way, even allowing for the occasional solo. Some architects go as far as to say the client becomes a crucial part of this architectural jam session. Yet architects fail to understand that most clients are afraid to improvise and are instead looking for greater security. The jazz analogy is not very effective with potential clients; however, it is useful to describe an ideal relationship between design architects working collaboratively, implying a kind of loose structure built around play and a collective striving for a unique 'sound'.

Whether we like it or not, the media seems to require heroes to carry forward its cultural myths. Yet rather than the Homeric Achilles/Roark ideality, it would far better serve our profession to promote the Virgilian paradigm of Aeneas – the hero who puts his self-interest aside for the greater good of the community. What is missing from our current discourse on collaboration is a reintroduction of the concept of 'collegiality'. Collegiality is the moral and social glue that connotes both respect for another's commitment to a common purpose and the ability to work towards it. The answer to the perception of 'star' architects as out-of-control narcissicists is not to propagate a purely anti-heroic other called collaboration, but rather to reinstate a more noble position of the architect as a kind of public servant that is more inclusive of a collaborative approach. To be clear: the idea of collegiality needs to cleanse itself of some latent paternalism, but it does provide a kind of moral compass necessary to make collaboration work.

I have a long personal and professional history with collaborative design. My father, Paul Kennon, was the president of CRS Architects from 1975 to 1990. CRS was a large corporate firm founded on the principle of 'team architecture', and one of the first postwar architecture firms to recognise that increased specialisation of the profession would require new, innovative ways of working. The practice adopted a sports analogy of integrating specialists into a squad, where the architect was the quarterback. The 'team' was an inclusive approach that required an elaborate playbook and management to ensure delivery and coordination of ever more complex building systems. The team model was so successful that it has become the basis for most large-scale corporate practices today. But the team model is not a true design collaborative as the quarterback still calls the plays. As risk-management techniques have been applied to guiding the team, the leadership role has increasingly been dominated by the project manager and less so by the design principal. This development allows the client to more readily accept a team approach, while also ensuring mediocrity.

By the time I joined Kohn Pedersen Fox (KPF) in 1988, just a few years out of graduate school, the team approach had been fully codified and adopted. KPF placed a greater emphasis on design than most corporate firms at the time, and in this environment I quickly rose to become design partner by 1997. The practice's team model seemed to be less like a sports team and more like the 'Team Volvo' method of component assembly. In designing a skyscraper, KPF would divide a large team into smaller separate subteams organised by building component. While efficient in practice, some of the results of this compartmentalisation could look all too similar. Thus, the work of the various lobby teams throughout the office seemed to have more in common with each other (both conceptually and stylistically) than, for example, the exterior design of their own project. The finished result often not only lacked cohesion, but propagated an insular set of office-wide references that diluted innovative thinking and homogenised the brand. The

**United Architects, World Trade Center competition entry, New York, 2002**
From the earth to the sky, the entire World Trade Center site would be both a monument to the past and a vision of the future. The memorial experience begins with a descent below the ground into the sacrosanct area around the vast WTC footprints. From this great depth, visitors look up through the footprints of the towers to the new towers.

CHURCH ST     WEST ST     VESEY ST     LIBERTY ST     WALL     MEMORIAL

**United Architects, World Trade Center competition entry, New York, 2002**
Study models showing how the project does not provide a single image as its identity, but a shifting field of relations depending on one's location in the city, just as United Architects' identity is one of collaborative mobility.

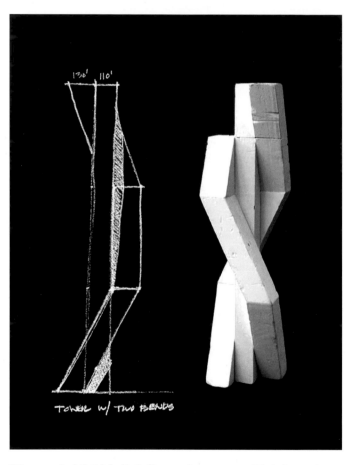

This conceptual sketch by Kevin Kennon shows a concept that allows a tower to lean and connect while following the practical requirements of maintaining a constant 14-metre (45-foot) core perimeter planning dimension and an identical modular floor.

other problem at KPF was that there was very little by way of collaboration between the design partners. I had a very different view about how to create meaningful architecture.

During my last year at KPF, in 2001, I participated in one of the most important and illuminating collaborations of my career when I led the KPF component in a 'star-studded' collaboration with Rem Koolhaas, Cecil Balmond and Toyo Ito in an invited design competition for the East River Con Edison

site just south of the United Nations (UN) headquarters in New York. The historical significance of this project and, specifically, our proposal was how much it prefigured later megadesign collaborative competitions, particularly the Worl Trade Center International Competition for Innovative Desig of 2003. Since I was a student at the Institute for Architectur and Urban Studies, and Princeton University, I had always ha a particular respect for the work of both Koolhaas and Ito. I liked the fact that they were not afraid to take on large-scale commercial commissions without losing their critical edge. I practice, however, the Con Edison collaborative, called UN-City, devolved into a competitive clash of cultures that resembled nothing less than an errant architecture studio with overcaffeinated students vying to please a charismatic studio critic. In this kind of environment it is easy to produce cool stuff, but far more difficult to create deliberative innovation. Yet despite this we did manage to develop two very interesting live/work building prototypes.

The UN-City experience profoundly altered my perception of the creative limitations of KPF. After witnessing first-hand the destruction of the Twin Towers from outside my downtown apartment, it became clear to me that I could no longer continue to work in a corporate environment. At a gathering of architects organised by the Architectural League of New York on 25 September 2001, I spoke out against the self-serving behaviour that bordered on 'ambulance-chasing' of many of my colleagues. I argued that rushing to rebuild in the 'business-as-usual' manner of the New York architectural establishment would be a colossal mistake, as no one had as yet understood the meaning of the event.

Needless to say, this candour put me on a collision course with my partners at KPF. Having accomplished a great deal a a design partner, I became committed to the idea of volunteering my time and talent in helping to rebuild my city in whatever way I could. In the immediate aftermath of 9/11, Ground Zero became New York's biggest destination. Swarms of people felt compelled to view the destruction first-hand. Whether their motives were good or bad was irrelevant against the all too human desire to make sense of the senseless. The experience was both chaotic and vulgar, and required that something be done immediately to allow people a more dignified way to grasp the enormity of the destruction. It became clear to me that a simple elevated platform could allow everyone such a dignified way to bear witness.

Over dinner at the Odeon, a few blocks north of Ground Zero, David Rockwell, Liz Diller, Ric Scofido and myself formed a collaborative around this idea. We were able to present this to Mayor Giuliani, who quickly acknowledged its importance. He gave us a schedule of a hundred days to complete the design, raise the money and build the platform. He also gave us unprecedented access to the myriad public agencies required to approve the project. What was both remarkable and humbling was the eagerness of so many who were willing to donate time or money to our cause. David, Liz, Ric and myself waged the equivalent of a 'ground and air campaign' that resulted in a simple structure visited by over a million people in its short life of six months.

In the summer of 2002, one of the most remarkable events in New York City's history occurred when a group of citizens soundly rejected the uninspired master plans for the World Trade Center put forward by Beyer Blinder Belle – almost the *ne plus ultra* of establishment practices. What was almost as surprising was the resulting International Competition for Innovative Design, in which six proposals were selected from a field of 650. The majority of these responses came from collaborative teams including United Architects (UA). Consisting of Foreign Office Architects (FOA), Greg Lynn FORM, UN Studio, Reiser + Umemoto RUR Architects, Imaginary Forces and Kevin Kennon Architect, UA was founded on the principal of collegiality. Its principals had all previously worked with each other in some capacity and, even more importantly, we were friends before we came together. No single vision dominated, but, rather, our different ideas coalesced around a synthetic process that incorporated the best ideas.

During the World Trade Center competition, we worked to achieve a critical understanding of the realistic processes that

United Architects is a multidisciplinary, multinational team that includes some of the world's most innovative young architects, planners and designers.

govern tall buildings – interior space planning, wind load resistance, vertical circulation, safety and security. The essential genetic code of the proposal, as for all tall buildings, is that individual floor plates are organised on a 1.5-metre (5-foot) module with an ideal depth from the elevator to the outside wall of 14 metres (45 feet). Few realise how much the design of office skyscrapers is governed by optimising internal planning requirements. Our respective expertise allowed us to rethink the standard parameters and apply them in a new strategy of interweaving individual towers into one. The result is a mutating series of floor plates that spiral around a central core but retain the orthogonal modular consistency that achieves the fungible planning requirements of the commercial marketplace. The design of each individual tower in our WTC project represents a mutation of the tower's genetic code that retains the 1.5-metre (5-foot) module and the optimum planning depths but uses an exterior braced-frame structural system that allows the individual floor plates to be reconfigured to capture more natural light and dramatically multiply the number of exits, yet retain the standard net-to-gross efficiency ratio. This innovative methodology gave us the freedom to design a new kind of skyscraper that can lean, touch and twist without sacrificing internal modular efficiencies.

Perhaps the question 'Does collaboration work?' would be better rephrased as 'How does collaboration work?' More academic and practical consideration is required to understand the complex social, professional and creative interaction of collaboration if the experiment is going to succeed. Beyond this there remains the very real problem of how to brand collaboration so that clients can see the benefits and become comfortable with the process. And finally, true creative collaboration, like a marriage, requires both hard work and an abiding respect for others. It requires both a selfless maturity and, paradoxically, a child's sense of play. Δ

At 240 metres (800 feet) in the air, an immense 18,580-square-metre (200,000-square-foot) 'city in the sky' connects the towers with an educational centre, gardens, shopping, cafés, a sports centre and a conference centre.

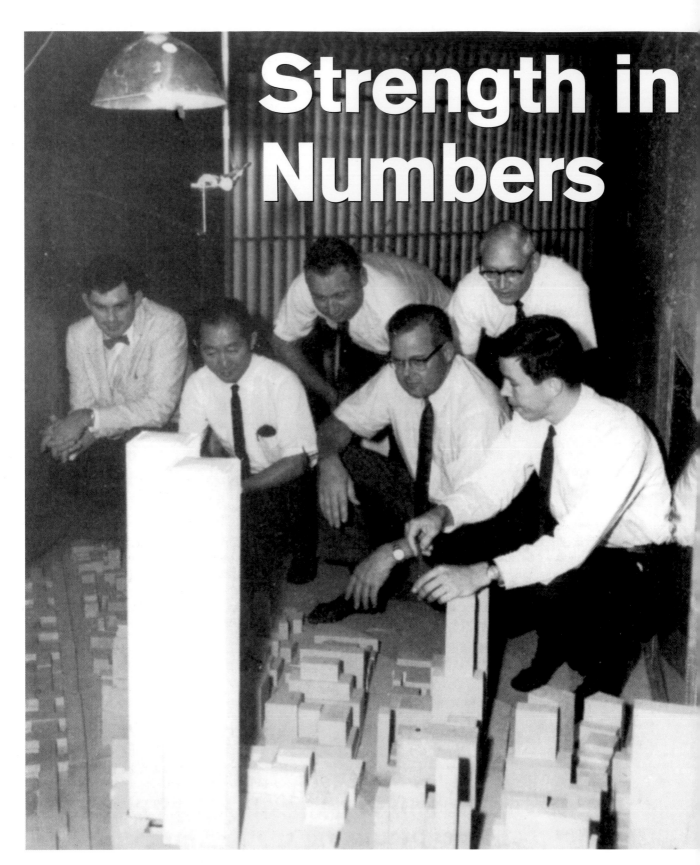

# Strength in Numbers

Minoru Yamasaki, World Trade Center model, 1964
Model of the Twin Towers in the Colorado State University wind tunnel lab. From left to right: Alan Davenport, Minoru
Yamasaki, Malcolm Levy of the Port Authority, structural engineer John Skilling, Jack Cermak (who founded the lab)
and structural engineer Leslie Robertson.

**David Salomon** examines the history of the original World Trade Center (WTC) competition of 1962 and the more recent 2003 competition, finding interesting parallels in terms of how commercial and bureaucratic, as well as progressive, forces of innovation intersect over larger debates about control, power and questions of collaborative identity and practice within the city as a political machine, and which figure 9/11 in implicitly provocative ways. The 1962 competition featured another progressive architectural collaboration: Walter Gropius's The Architect's Collaborative (TAC). Not unlike the 2003 competition in which United Architects (UA) and other collaborative practices lost to the more stable, individual celebrity identity, TAC lost to Minoru Yamasaki. Salomon also argues that the organisational and structural qualities of UA's WTC proposal sought to embed collective operations of multiplicity rather than mere duplication of the previous WTC Twin Towers within the form of the design itself.

As the goodwill between the politicians, real-estate developers and architects responsible for rebuilding Ground Zero evaporates, it is hard not to think about what might have been and what might yet be. Regrettably, the disparate agendas of those currently in charge are mirrored in the 'unique' and isolated architectural solutions proposed or under construction. As it stands now, the memorial, the transportation centre, the visitors' centre and the Liberty Tower are programmatically, urbanistically and formally disconnected from each other. Given the uncoordinated, uneven and unsatisfactory results produced by this fractured process – one that seems to privilege architectural authors[1] – it is an appropriate time to revisit and rethink how a different approach, a more collaborative one, might be better suited to the project's complex demands. Doing so means looking no further than at a few historical and recent collaborative teams associated with the site: Minoru Yamasaki et al, who were responsible for the original design; The Architect's Collaborative (TAC), the runner-up to Yamasaki in 1962; and, more recently, United Architects (UA), one of the finalists for the redevelopment of the site in 2002.

### Unequal Partnerships
When the World Trade Center (WTC) was created in the 1960s, the responsibilities of each design professional were clearly demarcated and enforced by the client, the Port Authority of New York and New Jersey. In fact, the Port Authority chose Yamasaki over TAC, led by Walter Gropius, in large part because Yamasaki agreed to an arrangement whereby he would only be responsible for the aesthetic portion of the design. Within this familiar system of divide and conquer, a sophisticated client like the Port Authority was able to maintain control over its consultants. Thus, despite hiring Yamasaki specifically for his formal acumen, it was the Port Authority that made a number of the important design decisions. For example, it was the Port Authority that, against Yamasaki's advice, decided on the ultimate height of the project, and took the decision to move the commercial programmes from the plaza level to the concourse below.

Would it have been more difficult for the authority to push TAC around? Founded in 1945, TAC was not a typical 'one-stop-shopping' office like Skidmore, Owings & Merrill (SOM). For example, it did not provide auxiliary services such as structural or mechanical engineering. Rather than a group of specialists from different fields, the partners – all architects – saw themselves as a team of equals.[2] What allowed the office to function, Gropius wrote, was 'a common method of approach, a kindred way of responding to the challenges of our day'. Echoing what he had argued much earlier in the century, for Gropius this did not mean the erasure of individuality or authorship. Instead, he was quick to remind his readers that 'only a personal interpretation' of a situation could produce a 'significant contribution'. Resisting the ad hoc assembly of a design team such as the one at the WTC – which he argued was 'isolationist' in nature – TAC's *modus operandi* was to supplement the insight of authorship with the 'collective intuition' of the team.[3] Given this dual emphasis on teamwork and individual expression and, given that he himself had been extremely active in the design of the recently completed Pan Am Building, it is somewhat surprising that Gropius would not guarantee the Port Authority that he personally would be responsible for the design of their project.[4] Thus, despite his insight into the symbolic importance of the project,[5] the possibility of his sharing responsibility for the design with his partners was too much for the Port Authority to accept, and it concluded that the multi-headed design methods employed by TAC could not produce the singular object they desired.

Not surprisingly, the clear division of labour between Yamasaki, the executive architects Emory Roth and Sons, and the structural engineers John Skilling and Leslie Robertson, was mirrored in the project itself. Above ground, the Twin Towers were independent entities, separate not only from one another, but also isolated from both the public plaza and the city in which they were placed. However, below ground they were completely integrated with one another, not just structurally and mechanically, but also with the various urban infrastructures that converged on the site. While the concourse level pulsed with (commercial) activity generated by the commuters who crossed through its subterranean spaces, the plaza remained empty and its architecture silent. The

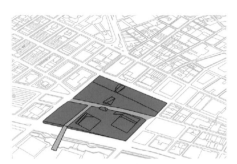 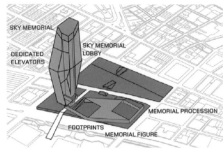 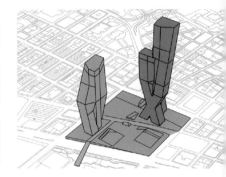

nature of the relationships and the dynamism that did exist were rendered invisible, failing to inform the formal and programmatic logic of the scheme.[6]

## All for One

Some 40 years later, a 'genius', Daniel Libeskind, was again chosen over a number of teams (and other individuals) for the WTC site. And again, it proved easy for the powers that be to isolate him and push him around (and ultimately out of the process). Perhaps it was the still-dominant idea that creative work could only come from the hand of a singular genius that again guided their decision. Or perhaps it was the fact that so many networks – transportation, tourist, military, surveillance, economic and structural – had been exposed and compromised on 9/11 that scared them away from any notion of a group of networked buildings. Or maybe it was because the organisation responsible for the destruction of the Twin Towers was itself a relatively loose collection of operators (headed by a charismatic leader), and was thus eerily isomorphic with many of the design collaboratives that participated in the competition. No matter the reason, the fact that so many of the causes and effects of 9/11 can only be defined in terms of networks, collaborations and infrastructures – military ones, economic ones, informational ones and aesthetic ones – suggests that to ignore the efficacy and intelligence embedded in these systems is not only naive, but dangerous.

In contrast to the permanent partnership of TAC, United Architects – consisting of, among others, Greg Lynn FORM (Los Angeles), Foreign Office Architects (London), UN Studio (Amsterdam), Reiser + Umemoto (New York) and Kevin Kennon (New York) – was an ad hoc and voluntary assemblage of peers formed specifically to partake in the WTC competition.[7] Despite its diverse expertise, experiences and geographical locations, the group coalesced around a shared sensibility regarding architecture's contemporary aesthetic, technological, professional and social responsibilities. In contrast to the connected isolation of specialists and forms offered up by Yamasaki et al, UA's design for the redevelopment of Ground Zero thoroughly and subtly incorporated the project's programmatic, symbolic an formal requirements.

In looking back at UA's proposal, trying to specify who did what, which moves are consistent with the formal ticks of a particular firm, or which software was used to help generate its forms, is far less productive than reviewing how a more complex solution emerged out of the aggregation of individual knowledge sets. Everything in their scheme – entitled 'United Towers' – at once generates and is responsiv to some other requirement or condition. Each unique event emerges out of its location within a larger system, enriching both the local and the global effects. For example, the diamond pattern of the skin is ostensibly a uniform solution made up of identical parts. Yet, the triangular (almost conventional) nature of the structure is extremely flexible and varied, and thus easily adapts itself to the various contortions that occur within the towers. This produces specific effects, but without ever violating or losing the overall clarity or logic of the diamond pattern. Likewise, whi the entire project can be described as urban, or heterogeneous, the overall impression it creates is that of consistency. For example, the 'city in the sky', located at the 60th floor of the complex, is not produced all of one piece, but is instead generated through the aggregation of five 'blocks', one from each of the five towers that make up the scheme. While each could function independently, when combined the seemingly continuous strata would be made o diverse programmatic segments, the specific function and mood of each potentially determined not in advance but as needed and in relation to those already in place. Even the egress plan, a not unimportant or unsymbolic aspect of the project, is handled in a similar manner. While individually accommodated within each tower, as each successive buildir comes on line the exit paths are combined with one another to produce a more robust and exhaustive plan, one that provides multiple ways to safety.

The structure and floor plans are also in constant dialogu with one another. Despite the seemingly irregular geometry the towers, the typical plans are relatively conventional, yet two floors are never the same. This is achieved by utilising a modified version of a bundled tube structure (such as the one used at the Sears Tower). Each tower consists of a central spine or core, square in plan, around which the floor plates spiral up and around. The gaps created by the different geometries of the rectilinear plans and the faceted skin create space for a series of vertical sky gardens, which occur at every fifth level. This allows for a variety of (large) floor-plate configurations, which increase in diversity and size as each tower is erected. Finally, although each of the towers has its own provocative shape, when combined with one another a new (non-gestalt) form emerges. When complete the individual parts are somewhat difficult to identify, but they are unmistakably there.

In every instance, individual elements can stand alone, yet when located within a network of self-similar elements they combine to produce a more complex whole. One could say exactly the same thing about the way each firm contributed to the project. The track record of each office suggests that if each had simply applied its own knowledge base about structures, local planning conventions, strategies of development, design software and so on this would have generated six or seven interesting schemes. However, when these like-minded, yet clearly independent, architects focused their collective intelligence on a hypercomplex problem, the result, far from a tepid compromise, is a complex yet consistent solution. One need only compare the level of detail of UA's proposal to that in the proposal of any of the other finalist to realise how advanced the scheme was.

Is this, then, simply an update of Gropius's description of TAC, where individual instincts were fortified by the insights of the team? Perhaps. But there is an important difference. A review of TAC's work during Gropius's lifetime reveals a great deal of homogeneity within and between each project. While this may indicate that Gropius had a heavy hand in each project, the lack of diversity is perhaps more accurately attributed to one of his, and Modernism's, favourite techniques; namely, the reliance on planning and construction modules. While modules allow for different scales and parts to be integrated with one another, the

mechanistic way in which they are combined generally fails to produce significant differences within a design. Aesthetically and programmatically the pattern is always the same; everything is integrated, but intricacy never emerges. It is precisely the intricacy (programmatic, structural, aesthetic and so on) produced by UA's combination of separate yet dependent systems that sets its solution apart not only from its fellow competitors, but from previous forms of collaboration. This separation can only in part be explained by the differences between, and the respective use of, mechanical and digital technologies. More to the point is the difference between thinking mechanistically and thinking virtually. The latter is defined not by computational capacity, but by the ability to imagine and project the 'not yet real'. Less a predictable logic of 'if ... then', the virtual manifests the emergent logic of 'and ... and ... and'[8] that collective intelligence has the potential to produce. Far from producing anonymous or generic results, working and thinking this way allows innovation to occur exponentially and to be present everywhere at once. By utilising an additive approach, UA's solution redefines redundancy – of structure, of function, of egress, of form, of authorship – formerly conceivable only in terms of waste or loss, but in their hands an expedient and efficient technique. It is a lesson which, if too late to heed at Ground Zero, architecture can ill afford to ignore. Δ

**Notes**
1. For example, in addition to Calatrava's transportation hub, and David Childs' (of SOM) Liberty Tower, in 2004 the developer Larry Silverstein announced that he had retained a number of star architects, including Jean Nouvel, Fumihiko Maki and Norman Foster to design the other skyscrapers planned for the site.
2. The founding members of the firm were: Jean B Fletcher, Norman C Fletcher, Walter Gropius, John C Harkness, Sarah P Harkness, Robert S McMillan, Louis A McMillen and Benjamin Thompson.
3. From Walter Gropius, 'TAC's Teamwork', *The Architects Collaborative*, Niggli (Teufen AR, Switzerland), 1966, p 24.
4. See Meredith Clausen, *The Pan Am Building and the Shattering of the Modernist Dream*, MIT Press (Cambridge, MA), 2005 for an insight into Gropius's role in the design of the Pan Am Building.
5. In his letter to the Port Authority, Gropius wrote '... the main task for the designers is to give this vast building group a significant and expressive form which will stir the imagination. From afar the silhouettes must be simple to be grasped at a glance and remembered as the unequivocal image of the World Trade Center.' Quoted in Anthony Robins, *The World Trade Center*, Pineapple PR Inc, 1987, p 25. In comparison, Yamasaki emphasised 'finding a way to scale it to the human being so that, rather than be an overpowering group of buildings, it will be inviting, friendly and humane' (Robins, op cit, p 27). Both the Gropius and Yamasaki letters were included in 'World Trade Center Evaluation of Architectural Firms, 1962', an unpublished internal document of the Port Authority cited by Robins.
6. The nature of this isolation is apparent in the fact that there were no published drawings, particularly sections, which reveal the interactions between the different systems present on the site.
7. While each firm maintains its own practice, UA continues to operate on a project-to-project basis, with only Foreign Office Architects dropping out of the mix.
8. Gilles Deleuze and Felix Guattari, 'Rhizome', *A Thousand Plateaus: Capitalism and Schizophrenia*, University of Minnesota Press (Minneapolis, MN), 1987, p 25.

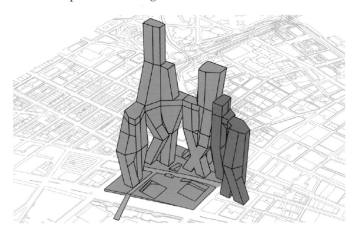

The entire project – the memorial plus the five linked towers - was to be completed in 2012, only 11 years after the original Twin Towers were destroyed.

# The AADRL: Design, Collaboration and Convergence

**Brett Steele**, former director of the Architectural Association's Design Research Laboratory (AADRL) and now director of the Architectural Association, reflects upon the DRL as a laboratory for the production of a different kind of student and teacher, and ultimately as a new model for architectural education. His 'screenshots' offer an informal image/text-based window through which to browse the general atmosphere of that research endeavour. The DRL was also very active in employing outside specialists from a variety of disciplines including computer programming and robotics. These interests were situated within the DRL's much larger ambition of rethinking the very definition of research itself, not isolated in the purely reflective interests of history and criticism but based on the projective desires of innovation. Moreover, the organisation of these new laboratories of design life begin to resemble their objects of study.

The AA Design Research Laboratory (AADRL) was created at the Architectural Association School of Architecture in London as a full-time, post-professional M.Arch course built as an open experiment in architectural education. We created the programme in 1996 (our 'beta year') as a deliberate alternative to the proprietary impulse of traditional graduate design programmes worldwide, whose stale curricular formats have for decades been dedicated to an obsession with the architectural identity, individuality and singularity found in signature designer styles and proprietary design processes or theories. While much of the celebrity aspect of contemporary architectural culture can be seen this way, we continue to believe it an unsuitable – indeed, unstable – model for the pursuit of an experimental architectural education today.

The AADRL has given those of us involved the rarest of educational opportunities: the design of a genuinely new kind of architectural pedagogy, which we undertook before turning our attention to the projects and work of our students. We looked deliberately outside architecture, at many other kinds of interdisciplinary design field where we gleaned lessons from such diverse examples as those of Thomas Edison's Menlo Park laboratory at the end of the 19th century, the research and development activities of today's largest corporations and high technologies, and the bizarre art/performance happenings of the Survival Research Lab, still operating in the postindustrial landscape of contemporary California. For curricular inspiration, we've chosen to look at everything other than traditional graduate design schools, which suffer from decades-old models of teaching and learning.

We have continuously tweaked the AADRL into an operating system very much at odds with a conventional graduate design curriculum: our students (as well as our teachers) only ever work together in teams, never individually; these teams work only on a single, extended, design research project during their 16 months in the programme (which passes through many connected phases, rather than different individual courses); and all work, projects and experiments undertaken by everyone in the laboratory are retained and made freely available as open-source material within the AADRL's dedicated servers and networks. Alongside our teams' constant uploading of their work to our networks, all design research is documented at its conclusion in book-length written monographs, as well as the more familiar digital and other formats; an emphasis is placed on open, accessible and shared communication.

Taken together, these structural features have allowed us to create what we think is a unique form of distributed architectural intelligence; a collaborative learning environment carefully fitted to the complex demands all architects face today in their work across networks; of collaborators, fabrication and production systems, and even design tools.

The AADRL was created out of a belief that the conditions under which architects work, think and learn today are changing in profound and unprecedented ways, and that these demand above all a willingness to experiment with the most basic assumptions that guide not just how architects think, but also how schools, offices and other seemingly stable architectural forms are themselves organised and operate. To miss this challenge is to be threatened not by abject failure as much as by something more threatening: outright irrelevance. **Δ**

# MULTIPLICITY MATTERS MORE

THAN THE KINDS OF ARTIFICIALLY DIFFERENTIATED DESIGNER PERSONALITIES THAT HAVE BEEN USED TO BRAND NEARLY A CENTURY OF MODERN ARCHITECTURE. SIGNATURE SYTLES ARE BEING OVERTURNED BY DISCRETE FORMS OF HIGHLY SPECIALISED ARCHITECTURAL EXPERTISE GAINED THROUGH INTENSIVE EXPERIMENTATION AND COMMUNICATION. THIS IS A FORM OF ARCHITECTURAL KNOWLEDGE THAT TRAVELS AT NIGHT, ACROSS STUDIO NETWORKS, DISPLAY SCREENS AND SATELLITE NETWORKS.

Studio Photos AADRL v. 6.2 & 7.1, autumn 2004.

# STUDIO SPACES

ALREADY ABSORB AND ARE BEING RECONFIGURED BY THE CONSTANT FLOW OF INFORMATION TRAVELLING ACROSS NETWORKS BETWEEN TEAM-MATES, PROJECTS AND PERIPHERAL EQUIPMENT. SMALL SCREENS CAPTURING THE ATTENTION OF THEIR USERS ARE BECOMING A MATERIAL NO LESS ARCHITECTURAL THAN THE IMAGES THEY DISPLAY.

Ceyhun Baskin and Nick Puckett installing drivers across studio networks in the AA front members room, June 2004.

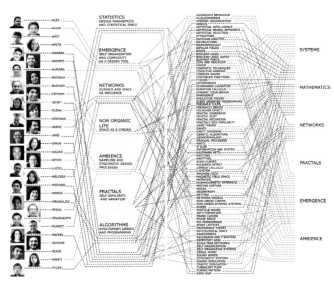
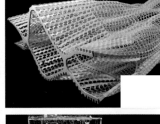

# THEORY IS CONNECTIVITY

(AND NOT THE OTHER WAY AROUND). THE ORGANISATION OF A DISTRIBUTED DESIGN NETWORK CAN IN TURN BECOME A MODEL FOR 'DOING THEORY' IN AN ENTIRELY DIFFERENT, NONMODERN WAY, IN A MODE THAT PRIVILEGES THE FORMATION OF CONCEPTS AND NOT THE PERSONALITIES OF THEIR THEORISTS. COLLABORATIVE APPROACHES TO ARCHITECTURAL THINKING ARE STATISTICAL, NO LESS THAN EPISTEMOLOGICAL, PROBLEMS.

Topic and research map of Brett Steele's 'Computational Space' seminar, autumn 2004. Thirty-one architects were organised into seven sessions, researching and presenting 96 working concepts catalogued into six main sections of the final-course document.

# PROTOTYPES, NOT TYPES

ARE THE DEFINING ARCHITECTURAL MODELS OF OUR TIME.
CROSS-DISCIPLINARY WAYS OF WORKING ARE BLURRING THE DISTINCTIONS BETWEEN IMAGE, MATERIAL AND MEDIA, MAKING EACH A SUBSET OF THE OTHER. CONCEPTS THAT BEGIN LIFE AS COMMANDS WITHIN A SOFTWARE APPLICATION QUICKLY MUTATE INTO OPERATIVE SENSIBILITIES FOR THE ORGANISATION OF MATERIAL, STRUCTURE AND SURFACE. PROTOTYPES BRIDGE THAT DIVIDE.

Three images of digital, physical and electronic prototypes for a proposal for Heathrow Airport by Kuatic (Daniel Ascension, Yael Harel-Gilad, Mariana Beatriz Ibanez and Jorge Godoy). One image shows Anat Stern and Dave Fraser wiring pneumatic hardware to a robotic architectural installation.

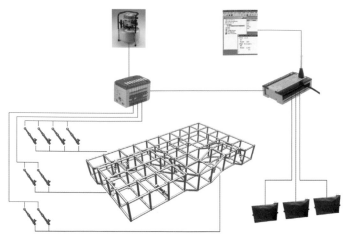

# AUGMENTED ARCHITECTURES

**AND THEIR INCREASINGLY AMBIENT ENVIRONMENTS DEMAND OF THEIR DESIGNERS ATTENTION TO THE OPERATING SYSTEMS, NETWORKS AND CONNECTIVE TECHNOLOGIES THAT MATERIALS AND STRUCTURES ARE TODAY NOW FINDING THEMSELVES EMBEDDED WITHIN. THIS EXPANDED FIELD IS AS DEFINED BY THE INTERFACES OF ITS DESIGNERS AS IT IS BY THE SPACES OF ITS USERS.**

Working diagram of a 1:20 welded steel deformable 3-D space frame by 5subZero (Delphine Ammann, Karim Muallem, Robert Neumayr and Georgina Robledo).

# EVERYTHING IS RECORDED

**IN DESIGN SYSTEMS THAT INCLUDE DEVICES AND APPLICATIONS FEATURING EMBEDDED CAMERAS AND DATABASES, MAKING MORE TRANSPARENT EVERY DECISION, EXPERIMENT AND ASSUMPTION UPON WHICH A PROJECT IS PURSUE HOW ARCHITECTS ASSESS, LEARN AND EVALUATE DESIGN OPERATIONS IS BECOMING MORE DIFFICULT, COMPLEX AND MORE URGENT.**

Fifty-four thumbnail images from a folder of studio activities captured by a studio webcamera on the afternoon of 21 November 2001.

# ANALOGUE MODELLING

**ALLOWS DESIGNERS TO TEST BY DOING, AND NOT THINKING. MATERIAL COMPUTATION ALLOWS A MODEL TO 'DO WORK' IN ACHIEVING SOLUTIONS TO PROBLEMS, RATHER THAN PROVIDING AN 'IMAGE' OF WHAT A SOLUTION MIGHT LOOK LIKE. THE APPLICATION OF DIGITAL SENSIBILITIES TO MATERIAL MODELLING COLLAPSES ANY DIFFERENCES BETWEEN COMPUTERS AND MATERIALS.**

Four physical models are hand-tested during a design workshop held at the AADRL, autumn 2002.

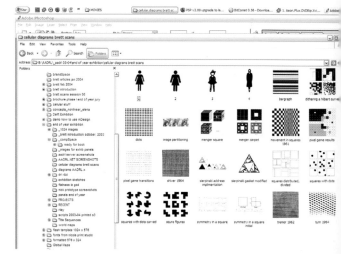

# ARCHITECTURAL GRAPHICS

**CIRCULATE CONSTANTLY BETWEEN USERS AS ANONYMOUS COLLECTIONS OF DIAGRAMS, IMAGES AND DOCUMENTS COMBINING THE FAMOUS, FAMILIAR AND FICTIONAL. GRAPHIC SPACE IS NOW NEITHER ORIGINAL NOR A COPY, MAKING PERFORMANCE CRITERIA SOMETHING MEASURED BY TERMS OTHER THAN AURA AND AUTHENTICITY. THE SIZE AND COMPLEXITY OF THIS NEW WORKSPACE MAKES SEARCH AND NAVIGATION A NEW KIND OF DESIGN MODEL.**

Screenshot of the author's folder containing found diagrams for spring term, session eight of 'Design Research', a seminar on computational design and research. The syllabus for the course is online at http://www.resarch.net/syllabus2004desres.html

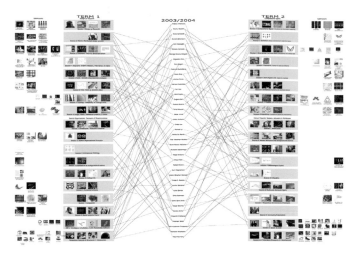

# DISTRIBUTED LEARNING

**REQUIRES COORDINATION, ANALYSIS AND DESIGN. SYSTEMATIC INVESTIGATION INTO STRUCTURED DIFFERENTIATION CREATES MORE PRODUCTIVE RESULTS THAN RANDOM VARIATION. EXTENDING PROJECTS IN TIME CREATES THE CONDITIONS FOR DESIGN AS A FORM OF RESEARCH, INTO NEW KINDS OF ARCHITECTURAL SPACES, STRUCTURES AND URBANISM.**

Project map of the AADRL v. 6.2, 2003–04, showing linked topics, design operations and connections across design briefs.

# DESIGN NETWORKS LIVE

**IN THE FORM OF HIERARCHIES AND DIRECTORIES RECORDING SUCCESSIVE STAGES, TESTS, ALTERNATIVES AND BACK-UPS. AUTOMATED SAVE-AND-RECOVERY TOOLS CREATE INTENSELY PRECISE, FINE-GRAINED RECORDS OF DESIGN STRATEGIES, FROM THEIR INITIALISATION TO REALISATION. MAKING THESE RECORDS AVAILABLE BEYOND THE SCOPE OF SINGULAR PROJECTS OR THEIR DESIGNERS CREATES THE CONDITION FOR AN ENTIRELY NEW KIND OF EXPANDED, FLEXIBLE AND CONNECTED DESIGN ENVIRONMENT.**

Screenshots of the directory structures of servers connecting the teams of AADRL v. 4.1 teams, about spring 2000.

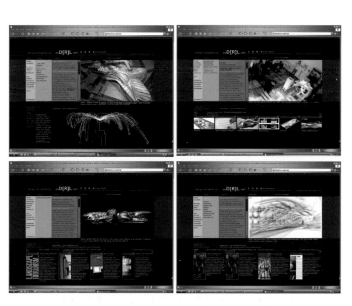

# DESIGN .HTML RULES

**WITHIN COLLABORATIVE NETWORKS IN WAYS THAT MAKE BROWSERS INTO ARCHITECTURAL MONOGRAPHS, AND DATABASES INTO MAGAZINE PHOTOGRAPHS. .HTML SHARES WITH OLD-SCHOOL ARCHITECTURAL MEDIA AN OBSESSION WITH APPEARANCE AND IMAGE, BUT EMBEDS THESE FEATURES WITHIN A LARGER SPACE OF INFORMATION, CODE AND EXCHANGE.**

Screenshots of the online version of aadrl.net, v. 09 beta, design by Brett Steele, programming by Vasilis Stroumpakos.

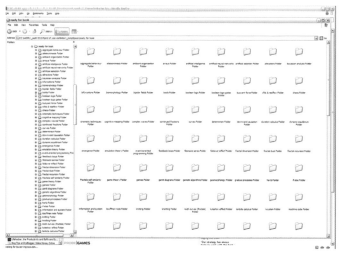

# ARCHITECTURAL MEMORY

**NO LONGER LIVES IN, OR FOR, MONOGRAPHS AND MAGAZINES. A CENTURY OF MODERN PRINT MEDIA HAS ALREADY BEEN OVERWRITTEN BY HARD DISKS AND NETWORK HUBS ABLE TO READ, WRITE AND RELOCATE FILES AND FOLDERS AT SPEEDS ONLY UNDERSTOOD BY NETWORKS AND THEIR USERS. ARCHITECTURAL HISTORIES NOW INCLUDE PROJECT DOCUMENTS RECORDED IN REAL TIME.**

Screenshot of Drive H:Monster Archive in the author's office, January 2003.

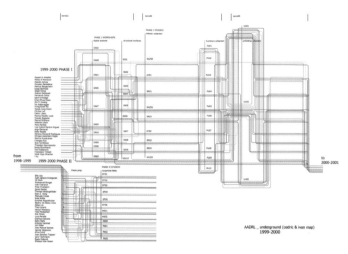

AADRL _ underground (cedric & ivan map)
1999-2000

# LEARNING AS PATHWAYS

**DEFINES THE PURSUIT OF DESIGN KNOWLEDGE AS, AND NOT JUST WITHIN, INFORMATION NETWORKS. MAPPING AND DOCUMENTING THE MOVEMENT OF INDIVIDUALS WITHIN LARGER TEAM-BASED NETWORKS EMPHASISES A WORLD OF EVOLUTIONARY ADAPTATION, RATHER THAN SINGULAR, ISOLATED FORMATION.**

AADRL 'underground' subway map showing the connections between team-mates, October 1999 to July 2000. Diagram by Ivan Subanovic.

# DISTRIBUTED PROCESSING

**DOES AWAY WITH ANY DIFFERENCE BETWEEN HARDWARE AND SOFTWARE, BETWEEN DESIGNERS AND THEIR TECHNOLOGIES, OR BETWEEN INDIVIDUALS AND GROUPS. TODAY'S DISTRIBUTED DESIGN SOFTWARE (ALREADY DEPENDENT UPON TEAMS AND NETWORKS FOR ITS OWN DESIGN AND USE) PREFIGURES ARCHITECTURAL FORM AND ORGANISATION IN HIDDEN, INVISIBLE WAYS.**

Scans of student application portraits, AA DRL v. 7.1, autumn 2003.

```
-- Play tm,
-- environmental map 01
-- scripting procedure, no interactivity
-- date: 14 june 2003

-- an interactive field of dynamic forces, generated by a script
-------------------------------------------------------------------------
-- environment

            backgroundColor = color 255 255 255

            pl01 = plane(); pl01.length = 150; pl01.width = 210; pl01.lengthsegs = 5; pl01.widthsegs = 7;  pl01.pos = [ 105, 75, 30 ]; pl01.wirecolor =
color 200 200 200
            addmodifier Splane01 (lattice Strut_Segments: 1 Strut_Radius: 0.1 joint_radius: 0 joint_segs: 3)

            pl02 = plane(); pl02.length = 90; pl02.width = 150; pl02.lengthsegs = 3; pl02.widthsegs = 5; pl02.pos = [ 105, 75, 30 ]; pl02.wirecolor =
color 200 200 200
            addmodifier Splane02 (lattice Strut_Segments: 0 Strut_Radius: 0 joint_radius: 1 joint_segs: 3)

-------------------------------------------------------------------------
-- field of arrow/boxes

            for u in 1 to 4 do; for i in 1 to 6 do
                (
                b = box (); b.width = 25; b.length = 1; b.height = 2; b.pos.x = 30*i; b.pos.y = 30*u; b.pos.z = 5
                b.wirecolor = color 100 50 50;

                b2 = box () b2.width = 5; b2.length = 2; b2.height = 3; b2.pos.x = 30*i - 11.5 ; b2.pos.y = 30*u; b2.pos.z = 5
                addmodifier b2 (taper primaryaxis:0 amount: 2 effectaxis: 1)

                f = b+b2; f.name = "01arrow" + ( (6*(u-1)+i) as string ); delete b2
                )

            for u in 1 to 4 do; for i in 1 to 6 do
                (
                b = box (); b.width = 25; b.length = 1; b.height = 2; b.pos.x = 30*i; b.pos.y = 30*u; b.pos.z = 10
                b.wirecolor = color 150 50 50;

                b2 = box () b2.width = 5; b2.length = 2; b2.height = 3; b2.pos.x = 30*i - 11.5 ; b2.pos.y = 30*u; b2.pos.z = 10
                addmodifier b2 (taper primaryaxis:0 amount: 2 effectaxis: 1)

                f = b+b2; f.name = "02arrow" + ( (6*(u-1)+i) as string ); delete b2
                )

            for u in 1 to 4 do; for i in 1 to 6 do
```

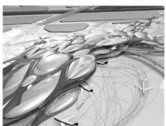

# SCRIPTING IS ARCHITECTURAL

**SPACE OF THE MOST TRADITIONAL KIND, AND THE BEST GRAPHIC SPACE EVER INVENTED. AS SOFTWARE MODELLING APPLICATIONS CONTINUE TO EVOLVE, THEIR SCRIPTING LANGUAGES GROW CLOSER TO THE OBJECT-ORIENTED PROGRAMMING WORLDS USED FOR THEIR CREATION AND THE OPERATING SYSTEMS THAT WILL MONITOR THEIR EVENTUAL REALISATION. UNDERLYING ALL OF THESE REALMS IS THE SAME CONCEPT, CODED INFORMATION. ARCHITECTURE IS BEING OVERTAKEN BY INFORMATION-ARCHITECTURE, AND SIMULATION HAS SURPASSED BOTH.**

3dMax script by Andreas Chadzis, AADRL v. 6.2 team 'the.very.many'.

# RENDERINGS ARE ANCIENT

**AND THE PRODUCT OF AN ARCHITECTURAL IMPULSE SUDDENLY GIVEN LESS PURPOSE AND REASON IN A WORLD OF CONSTANT SPECIAL EFFECTS. GRAPHIC REALISM IS ALWAYS A SIMPLE PROBLEM OF PROCESSING POWER AND RESOLUTION. TODAY'S DESIGN NETWORKS MAKE RENDERING AN IMAGE OBSOLETE, BY BEING THE LEAST DEMANDING TASK GIVEN TO A PROCESSOR, AND SO, DESIGNER. THE SIMULATION OF SOMETHING OTHER THAN APPEARANCE BECOMES MORE URGENT AND AN OBJECT OF ARCHITECTURAL KNOWLEDGE.**

Clockwise from upper left: 'Pinktrap' (Mirco Becker, Maria Jose Mendoza, Ramon Gomez, Siriyot Chaiamnuay); 'Emergen-C' (Christiane Fashek, Margarita Flores, Cesare Griffa, Yasha Grobman, Yanchuan Liu); 'Heathrow v. 2' (Atrey Trilochan Chhaya, Kenji Nabeshima, Sujit Nair, Tetsuya Nabazaki); 'Massive Attract' (Stephen Wei-Tse Wang, Richard Wei-Hsin Wang, Alvin Huang, Alessandra Belia).

# LEARNING FROM SIMULATION

UNDERTAKEN WITHIN NETWORKED STUDIOS IS CHALLENGING DECADES OF ARCHITECTURAL THEORY DEPENDENT UPON TRAVEL AND TOURISM, ON SEEKING OUT EXOTIC AND ULTERIOR URBANISM AS A MEANS FOR CHALLENGING ARCHITECTURAL CONVENTION. LAS VEGAS IS NO LONGER AS ALIEN AS IS TODAY'S INTERACTIVE DESIGN STUDIO.

Electronic, pneumatic and digital prototypes in the AADRL studio.

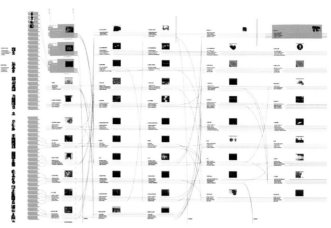

# COLLABORATION DEMANDS

THE INTELLIGENT WIRING OF TEAMS, COLLABORATORS AND EXPERTISE AS NETWORKS THAT CAN BE MAPPED, MODELLED AND SIMULATED. ONCE ARTICULATED, THE DESIGNS OF THESE COLLABORATIVE NETWORKS OPERATE AS SEAMLESS EXTENSIONS OF THE PROJECTS AND ACTIVITIES THEY MAKE POSSIBLE.

Wiring diagram of the 2002–03 AADRL 'Responsive Enironments' studio teams. Diagram by Simone Contasta.

# RECORDING IN REAL TIME

EVERY ACTION, OPERATION AND ALTERNATIVE IS NOW THE INEVITABLE CONSEQUENCE OF DESIGN SYSTEMS AND THEIR STUDIOS. THERE IS NOW MORE DATA RECORDED IN THE HISTORY OF A PROJECT'S ACTIVITIES THAN IN THE INFORMATION MODELS DESCRIBING THE PROJECT'S STRUCTURE, FORM OR APPEARANCE. FILTERING, ASSESSING AND EVALUATING THIS RECORD REQUIRES A NEW KIND OF ARCHITECTURAL KNOWLEDGE.

Screenshot of 77 thumbnails from Brett Steele's introduction to AADRL 5.1, October 2002

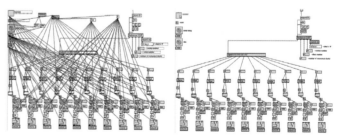

# FORGET REPRESENTATION

IS LESS A MESSAGE THAN IT IS A STYLE; ONE PURSUED THROUGH FORMS OF INFORMATION-BASED DIAGRAMMING THAT HAVE CREATED ENTIRELY NEW ARCHITECTURAL MODELS DEDICATED TO MACHINIC, COMPLEX SIMULATION, NOT STATIC, INERT REPRESENTATION.

Screenshots of two diagrams visualising a Ma/MxSP prototype project by Nick Puckett (DRL '04), June 2004.

# Associative Practices in the Management of Complexit

# Management of Complexit

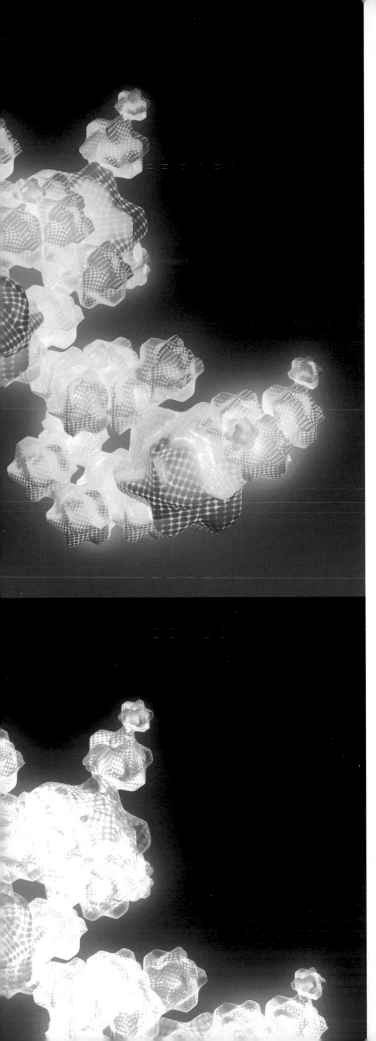

**Tom Verebes**, a co-director of the Architectural Association's Design Research Laboratory (DRL), writes about the programme's recent research in generative and parametric-based software, as well as the actualisation of these innovations through automated fabrication technologies. One example is the DRL's recent initiative to collaborate with Gehry Technologies as a means of using an experimental academic environment to test professional design software applications currently in development. As Verebes shows, this integration extends into his own collaborative design office, ocean D, one of the surviving branches of the original OCEAN network that emerged in the early 1990s (discussed elsewhere in the issue by Michael Hensel). For Verebes, as for Brett Steele (also featured in this publication), academic research serves as a laboratory for the production of new practices.

Facilitated by the inception of digital design and communication technologies, ocean D was one of a number of collaborative design practices launched in the 1990s to pioneer a project-based mode of design research, deployed as a distributed network of individuals with specific forms of expertise. The Design Research Lab (DRL) at the Architectural Association (AA) has also championed this shared, team-based method of working, exploring its potential within an academic, research-based environment. The following maps these and other forms of overlap between professional practice (as exemplified in the work of ocean D) and academic design research (as exemplified by the DRL).

Differing from most graduate design settings, all design projects within the DRL are pursued as collective proposals undertaken in small, self-organised teams addressing common topics through shared information-based diagrams, data, models, scripts and algorithms. Additionally, the DRL establishes research agendas worked on over the course of three cycles of students, treating project-based design as a form of research and an engine for design innovation.

---

**ocean D, GenLITE, 2005–06**
GenLITE is an interactive lighting product designed by ocean D, currently being developed commercially for the domestic market. As a toy for adults, the user can interact with an executable file of the scripts used to design and test the aggregation of small, lightweight cellular components as instructions for the assembly of varied spatial organisations. Each specific organisation has a range of associated emergent lighting behaviours with the combination of embedded RGB LED lights adjusting in real time as the user adds or subtracts lighting cells.

Collaborative design environments do not implicitly result in the accumulation of greater individual knowledge, yet specialist skills migrating to architecture from parallel design disciplines (interaction and information design, engineering, and so on) are changing the way we work and the tools we use, requiring a new range of strategies to implement the new design, communication and production technologies.

Aside from the human resource infrastructures and workflow systems, the DRL employs computational tools, procedures and operations with increasing capacity to manage higher orders of complexity. A pertinent question is the extent to which the accelerated distribution of information shifts creative culture towards the use of design tools (namely software interfaces) with increasing degrees of intelligence and adaptability. As a result, one curious feature of contemporary architectural practice is the presence of a new form of specialisation within the discipline – that of the programmer. In recent years, with DRL student groups as well as with Felix Robbins of ocean D, a wide range of digital programming, scripting and coding procedures have been the focus of research and development of design applications aimed at embedding intelligence into the formation, organisation and performance of increasingly intelligent architectural spaces and interfaces. These new technical design systems extend the skills sets of designers into the digital modelling environment at the scale of programming, incorporating scripting techniques in the formation of design projects, which expands our toolbox beyond modelling commands and towards the use of such programming languages as Maya's MEL Script and 3d Studio Max's MAX Script, and various other time-based and code-based applications adopted from adjacent design, computation, mathematics and engineering disciplines.

Concluding in 2005, the DRL's three-year design research agenda, 'Responsive Environments', researched the relation of information to the distribution of matter in architectural design proposals as a means of designing real-time adaptive and responsive architectures endowed with increasingly life-like properties through the assembly of active components. Its current three-year agenda, 'Parametric Urbanism', focuses on the design of the 21st-century city, where the prediction of a future of ever-present global connectivity of control systems and networks has finally come to fruition. Large cities have comparable properties to other complex time-varying systems, including living organisms, environmental processes and artificial network organisations. Given our strategy to model, design and install complexity on the scale of urbanism, the DRL has begun working with Gehry Technologies' Digital Project software with the aim of achieving mathematically driven associative models through which to manage variation, adjustment and feedback within a modelling environment.

Other DRL projects are focusing on the ways in which algorithms can be applied parametrically in the formation of design systems in relation to contingent criteria by allowing for feedback, adjustment and the optimisation of specific

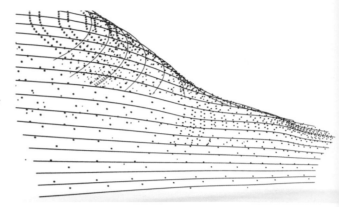

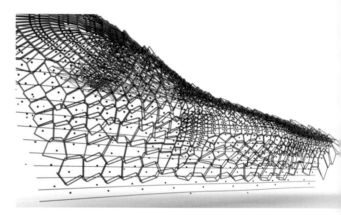

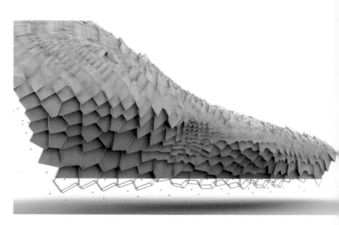

**G_Nome team, Net_Lab, Tom Verebes studio, DRL, 2004–06**
The design research work of the G-Nome team exemplifies how algorithms can be applied parametrically in the formation of design systems in relation specific contingent criteria. The Net_Lab series of computational procedures applies a 3-D Voronoi diagramming algorithm as a sequence of scripts generating iterative cellular spaces and material interfaces. Recursive computational design procedures allow for feedback, adjustment and optimisation of specific organisational conditions of a project brief.

organisational conditions in a recursive design process. For example, in the G_Nome project, the students applied the Voronoi diagramming tool as a three-dimensional design technique to explore the capacity to output continuous yet discrete cellular spatialities. A series of design systems was generated specifically to achieve parametric design variation according to a set of criteria related to each system. And in the YME project, the students applied Wolfram Research's Mathematica software to generate architectural spaces that nested two different densities of triply-periodic minimal level surfaces, formed via equations that are adjustable and controllable at the level of mathematical functions. These and other collaborative design research projects currently under way at the DRL apply such mathematical design tools to

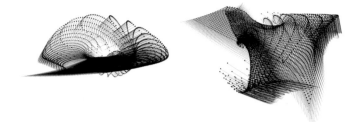

**P_FAX team, Soft Cities, Tom Verebes studio, DRL, 2005–07**
Generative vector force diagrams scripted in MAX Script, the scripting interface within 3d Studio MAX. These techniques are instruments to model environmental and contextual dynamic systems, including infrastructural flows, hydrological conditions of a wetland site and intensities of existing and proposed urban activation, as well as material systems generated from the optimisation of structural force.

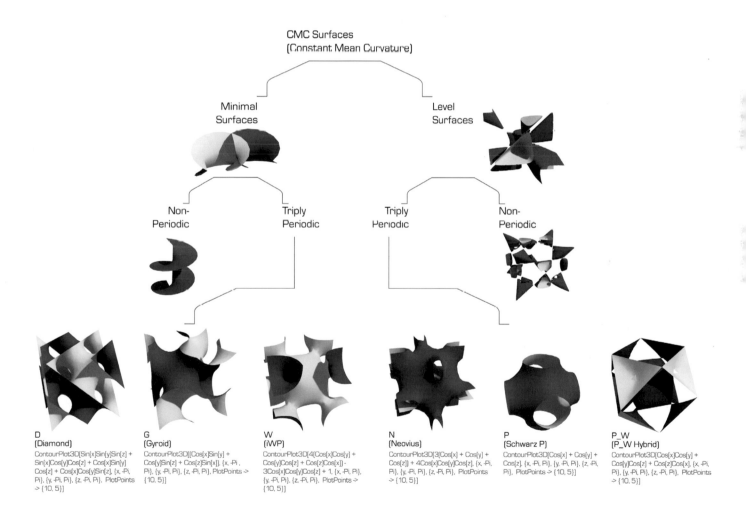

CMC Surfaces
(Constant Mean Curvature)

Minimal Surfaces

Level Surfaces

Non-Periodic

Triply Periodic

Triply Periodic

Non-Periodic

D
(Diamond)
ContourPlot3D[Sin[x]Sin[y]Sin[z] + Sin[x]Cos[y]Cos[z] + Cos[x]Sin[y]Cos[z] + Cos[x]Cos[y]Sin[z], {x, -Pi, Pi}, {y, -Pi, Pi}, {z, -Pi, Pi}, PlotPoints -> {10, 5}]

G
(Gyroid)
ContourPlot3D[[Cos[x]Sin[y] + Cos[y]Sin[z] + Cos[z]Sin[x]], {x, -Pi , Pi}, {y, -Pi, Pi}, {z, -Pi, Pi}, PlotPoints -> {10, 5}]

W
(iWP)
ContourPlot3D[4{Cos[x]Cos[y] + Cos[y]Cos[z] + Cos[z]Cos[x]] - 3Cos[x]Cos[y]Cos[z] + 1, {x, -Pi, Pi}, {y, -Pi, Pi}, {z, -Pi, Pi}, PlotPoints -> {10, 5}]

N
(Neovius)
ContourPlot3D[3{Cos[x] + Cos[y] + Cos[z]] + 4Cos[x]Cos[y]Cos[z], {x, -Pi, Pi}, {y, -Pi, Pi}, {z, -Pi, Pi}, PlotPoints -> {10, 5}]

P
(Schwarz P)
ContourPlot3D[Cos[x] + Cos[y] + Cos[z], {x, -Pi, Pi}, {y, -Pi, Pi}, {z, -Pi, Pi}, PlotPoints -> {10, 5}]

P_W
(P_W Hybrid)
ContourPlot3D[Cos[x]Cos[y] + Cos[y]Cos[z] + Cos[z]Cos[x], {x, -Pi, Pi}, {y, -Pi, Pi}, {z, -Pi, Pi}, PlotPoints -> {10, 5}]

**YME team, Hybrid Species project, Brett Steele studio, DRL, 2004–06**
Relational matrix of constant mean curvature (CMC) surfaces generated with Wolfram Research's Mathematica software to inform a catalogue of spatial component species. These seemingly mathematical types can be adjusted via a formula-driven design methodology of applying mathematics to the production of differentiated spatial organisations. In a recursive set of parametrically controlled operations, these techniques formed the basis of a thesis project that challenged compositional design strategies and the Maison Dom-ino model of slab and column tectonics.

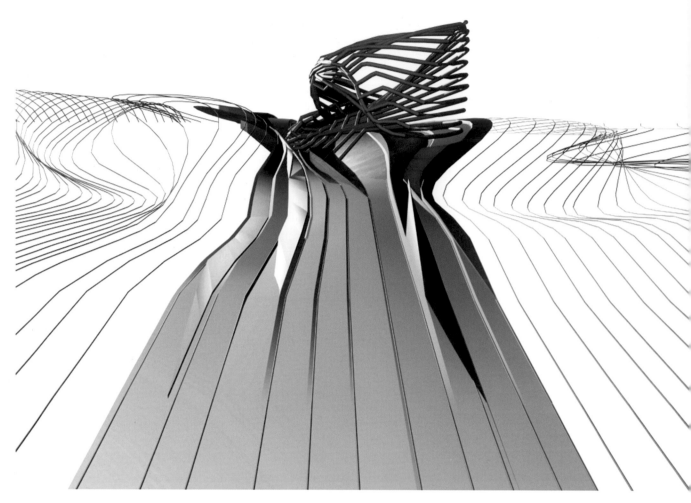

ocean D, Rabin Square Peace Forum, Tel Aviv, Israel, 2001
View of ocean D's proposal for an urban square in Tel Aviv. This was the first project in which ocean D instrumentalised MAX Script, in the formation of a modulated series of 18 scripted looped objects, each growing and changing serially. The flat field of the square is interrupted by the objects, where the position of each object causes a mathematical and spatial event. The parameters for the formation of the series of objects are the quantity of metrically equivalent line segments and the number of loops and their variable rotation and translation.

generate variable design components, with their eventual application tested at the scale of urban growth in terms of temporal growth and conditions of 'soft', or adjustable, control parameters.

In addition, in a recent project for an urban square in Tel Aviv, ocean D employed similar design techniques and software applications in the development of a modulated series of 18 scripted object configurations. The objects grow and change in incremental gradients as a serial event-field, both within each object as well as across the range of 18 objects. The homogenous parallel field is interrupted by the incorporation of each object, where the position of the object causes a mathematical and spatial event or singularity. The objects are all made of metrically equivalent straight-line segments, generating the appearance of curvilinearity. Using 3d Studio Max's MAX Script, the parameters generated by Felix Robbins include a constant of two weld connections per strand, and the rotation, translation, length and size of the

**The spatial objective is to challenge the persistent digital paradigm of architecture as surface and to promote a new material paradigm of volumetric aggregations of components informed by material sciences wherein scales of matter are understood to be composed of particulate organisation.**

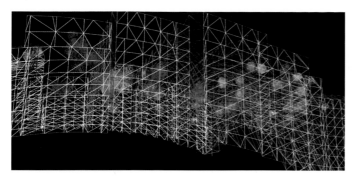

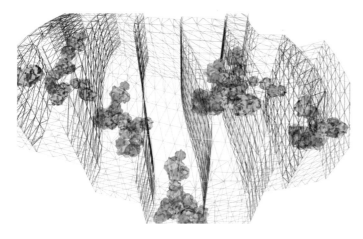

**ocean D, GenLITE, 2005–06**
Scripted design output testing the relation of a bounding container to the cellular growth and orientation in the formation of volumetric topologies. These techniques allow for sequential testing, evaluation and feedback, which aids the specification of a broad range of aggregated spatial arrangements of lighting cells.

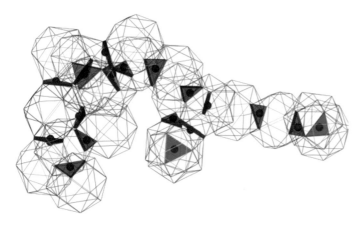

**ocean D, GenLITE, 2005–06**
Simple rules create a seemingly random and organic pattern of growth and orientation of polyhedra cells. The coplanar faces allow complex, multiaxial connections, surpassing Euclidian three-axis approaches to spatial coordinate systems.

components of each object, producing a highly differentiated set of continuously evolving spatial constructs. The modulation between each position and the preceding/subsequent position causes a topographical flow of convex and concave podia, evolving from the surface of the square. The result is an irrigated topography that interacts and responds to the geometric iterations of the objects embedded within the topography, operating as a mechanism of local reorientation between each object.

At the scale of product design, ocean D is currently developing an interactive domestic lighting system formed as an aggregate cloud-like organisation by small, lightweight, cellular illumination components that employ colour and luminosity as dynamic architectural media. By scripting the connection topologies, orientation and growth of these components, simple rules are embedded within the overall system and help to organise the extension and aggregation of three different sizes of small, volumetric polyhedra elements, giving order to highly specific patterns of growth and formation. The spatial objective is to challenge the persistent digital paradigm of architecture as surface and to promote a new material paradigm of volumetric aggregations of components informed by material sciences wherein scales of matter are understood to be composed of particulate organisation.

Through smart, performance-driven materials with embedded LED lighting elements, the user of such a system can 'play' with the aggregate organisation and, as the accumulation of light grows linearly, affect the colouring conditions, which are modulated through scripts. To this extent, the lighting system operates as a game-like interface whereby the users interact with the system to generate their own parametrically controlled aggregate organisation. The intended materials for the cells are primarily synthetic polymers, plastics or polycarbonates, optimising their lightweight strength and cost implications while maintaining the objective to use translucent, light-emissive materials to optimise the diffused lighting effects on the actual surface of the material.

Whether pursued in the form of academic design research within the present curriculum at the DRL, or within the professional design offices of ocean D, the new parametric design procedures outlined above focus on how spatial organisation can be informed by measurable and variable performance criteria. The tools described here point to increasingly malleable forms of spatial and material intelligence with increased capacities to adapt to contingencies of use and interaction. This potential reconfigures our design objectives away from conventions of permanence and towards producing environments that correspond to a world increasingly understood as complex and in a perpetual state of flux. Δ

# Designing Commonspaces: Riffing with Michael Hardt on the Multitude and Collective Intelligence

**Michael Hardt** has made an indispensable contribution to current understanding of the impact of globalisation on social, economic and political practice, especially in his two books *Empire* and *Multitude: War and Democracy in the Age of Empire*. In order to engage Hardt with many of the projects and ideas raised in this issue, guest-editors Christopher Hight and Chris Perry invited him to participate in a blog. The blog format enabled the resulting exchange between **Christopher Hight** and Hardt to be an open platform relating concepts like 'empire' and 'multitude' to contemporary design practice, and even raised challenges implicit in Hardt's own work. It also provided a productive alternative to the expropriation of a theorist's writings to legitimatise a particular design approach or methodology.

The blog tracked along three 'riffs' that emerged from an initial conference call between the editors and Michael Hardt. The general orientation of these three streams are: 1) the different topologies of space – geometrical, social and political – portended by both global capital and the multitude; 2) how design intelligence has become the paradigm of production; 3) the relationship of the first two to what used to be called 'the City', or a general notion of a 'metropolitan' condition.

## RIFF 1: BIOPOLITICAL TOPOLOGIES OF SPACE

### THE SIMULTANEOUS SEPARATION AND COLLAPSING OF THE PUBLIC AND PRIVATE SPHERES

The dialectic between public and private is constitutive of the sorts of political space we have been familiar with since the 19th century. In *Multitude*, Hardt and Antonio Negri note that today the distinctions between public and private have been fundamentally transformed, with that which was once thought private becoming the target of techniques of control and biopower, while that which was once considered public has been removed into 'private' control. For them, the multitude offers an alternative model of democratic social space, one that evades the new forms of control that operate despotically on the dichotomies of public and private.

*I would say there are two seemingly contradictory tendencies. On the one hand, there are many ways that, especially in the field of architecture, public and private are becoming ever more rigidly segregated. I am thinking specifically of the work by Rafi Segal and Eyal Weizman on the various walls of Israeli architecture, but one could also point to the generalised, international phenomena of the boundaries around private space becoming more rigid and impermeable – gated communities, for example – and public social*

*spaces becoming private – from common squares to shopping malls. So in some ways this involves a more radical separation of private from public and in others it means the destruction of public space altogether and a general privatisation.*

*On the other hand, however, there are other ways in which the borders have collapsed so that public and private are becoming indistinguishable. I remember being struck, for example, by a passage in a book by Lauren Berlant (The Queen of America Goes to Washington City) in which she argues that the feminist slogan 'the personal is political' has now returned distorted as a weapon against women in some of the public discussions in the US on abortion. No part of the woman's body is protected by privacy; rather it is totally open to social control. More generally, this is how the concept of biopower functions in many theoretical discourses today: to designate forms of power that reach down to the depths of the social field to engage and control all aspects of life. From this perspective there is no private space that is sheltered from public power, and hence no boundary between the public and the private.*

*So the first challenge for addressing the problem of the public and private – especially in the context of architectural design – is to think of these two apparently contradictory tendencies together: the increasingly rigid divisions between the two versus the collapse of all such boundaries; or, rather, the destruction of public space versus the elimination of the private realm. It is probably not as contradictory as I am posing it here, but it is a puzzle. After investigating this we might be in a better position to consider how the multitude might act differently and create forms of social space that evade these new forms of control.*

### THE FIELD OF ARCHITECTURE TRANSFORMED

Likewise, power no longer requires architecture as a figuring of institutional control in the way discipline did, epitomised in Foucault's famous example of the Panopticon. A pressing issue therefore becomes whether the architectural discipline responds by fortifying the boundaries of 'architecture' as a discipline or reconfigures its space of knowledge into different practices of 'design', of which the normative objects of architectural practice become only a part.

*I am intrigued by the relation you pose between architecture and design. This does seem to relate to the notion of a passage from a disciplinary society to a society of control, at least how I understand it.*

One aspect that was important to me in how Foucault and Deleuze conceive this passage is that disciplinarity does not evaporate or even lessen, but rather broadens the site of its application and becomes generalised. In disciplinary society, in other words, each disciplinary logic had a determinate site in a specific institution: there was a carceral discipline proper to the prison, an educational discipline proper to the school, a military discipline in the barracks, and so forth. Society was like an archipelago of these disciplinary institutions and each of us might move from one to another in the course of a life. In this current passage to the society of control, then, these disciplinary logics remain but they are no longer confined to specific institutions, so we may get out of school but never escape educational discipline, get out of prison but still be ruled by carceral discipline. In the society of control the disciplines mix and modulate.

Now it seems that you see a parallel process in the transformation of the field of architecture. It is not that architectural discipline, which oversees the design of constructed social space, has declined. Rather, it is tending to overflow the walls of the institution of architecture and invest with the logics of design various kinds of social activity. That is interesting to me.

POST-FORDISM AND THE REORGANISATION OF PRACTICE

A related issue is the organisation of practice as a mode of production. As Kevin Kennon points out in this issue, the dominant corporate model divides its labour, and thus knowledge, pool in way that has stifled specificity and innovation in favour of a singular identity. Today, many architects are attempting to develop more mobile business models, the network or distributed practice being foremost, that can opportunise post-Fordist modes of production and flexible knowledge exchange to shift architecture from a 'service profession' focused upon problem solving to a research-based practice focused upon innovation. This has drastic implications for the nature of what it means to be professionally qualified.

*I agree completely, at least with regard to labour and economic practices in general, that the passage from Fordist to post-Fordist regimes provides opportunities for innovation that we can seize on. One must keep in mind, of course, that the processes of making labour more 'flexible' and 'mobile' – the trademarks of the passage to post-Fordism – bring with them enormous suffering for workers. The pain for workers of the loss of long-term contracts and in general making employment more precarious is obvious and important. But it is crucial, too, not to romanticise the old Fordist factory arrangements and recognise in these current transformations the new*

*possibilities for the power of labour, through network arrangements, new forms of communication and cooperation, and other means. The workers might eventually be able to transform flexibility and mobility into their own weapons. The key for my work, in any case, is to confront the difficulties and forms of exploitation created by these transformations and yet, at the same time, recognise how they also provide enormous opportunities.*

RIFF 2: DESIGN AS THE MODUS OPERANDI OF KNOWLEDGE PRODUCTION

In this issue Philippe Morel argues that the only production left for human agency is the production of concepts. Another way of saying this might be that every form of production becomes a problem of design, whether one is thinking of mainstream genetic engineering, the conveyance of information and interfaces, or more fanciful examples. This raises the relationship of design to dominant forms of power and how one can practise in a way that is projectively productive rather than 'critical' or simply complicit.

# I think that the ubiquity of design, which you point out, is linked to a general transformation of economic production occurring today that places more emphasis on what might be called its immaterial products.

*I think that the ubiquity of design, which you point out, is linked to a general transformation of economic production occurring today that places more emphasis on what might be called its immaterial products. I do not just mean that the design of material commodities like automobiles and kitchen appliances is becoming a more important factor in the total value of those commodities, although this may be true. What I really mean is that the production of immaterial goods such as knowledge, images, code, communication circuits and even affective relationships is playing a more important role in the economy. Toni Negri and I claim, in fact, that industrial production no longer holds the hegemonic role it maintained for well over the last hundred years and that the tendency is for its place to be taken over by the production of such immaterial goods.*

*That claim requires an extensive argument, but for our purposes here consider the most dynamic debates in the field of property law – about copyrights, patents, the ownership of knowledges, genetic codes, music, images and so forth. All of these focus on immaterial goods. Looking backwards in the production process from this standpoint, then, we can see how the growing centrality of immaterial property today indicates the similar centrality of immaterial production.*

*Well, if you can accept this claim or hypothesis about the hegemonic position of immaterial production the ubiquity of design immediately becomes clear because design is really in many respects just a general name for the types of production we are talking about. Design often designates the production of the ideas or concepts or knowledges that inhere in a product. So from this perspective I would agree with Philippe Morel, even if I would say it in different terms. It is not so much that there is no other production left to accomplish, but rather that the economic position of design (or immaterial production) is becoming so hegemonic that there can be no production without it, at least in part. And that other forms of production tend increasingly to adopt the qualities of design.*

## If design is becoming central to the functioning of power – or, at least to economic production, as I have been saying – design practitioners such as architects are inevitably inside and in some sense complicit.

*One thing this means for design occupations such as architecture, it seems to me, is that there is no imagining oneself free from, or outside, the mechanisms of social power, no pure standpoint of critique. If design is becoming central to the functioning of power – or, at least to economic production, as I have been saying – design practitioners such as architects are inevitably inside and in some sense complicit. This is nothing new, of course, since critical architects have always had to struggle with their engagements with economic and political power structures. But if we are right about the tendency of the increasingly central role of design, that struggle will become ever more intense. And being inside or even complicit in this way does not seem to me a debilitating problem. On the contrary, it marks a position of great potential. But it does indicate a certain kind of critique and struggle that can be waged from within.*

RIFF 3: THE METROPOLIS OF THE MULTITUDE

Michael Hardt and Antonio Negri have suggested that perhaps the metropolis plays a similar role for the multitude as the factory did for the working class. Yet for many architects and urbanists, the metropolis as an object of knowledge is in crisis. For example, Jane Jacobs argued that the metropolis fuelled the de-territorialisations of modernity by producing a congested space where interactions between differentiated groups produced positive feedback loops, leading to further transformation, innovation and greater diversity. This

happened, she argued, at the micro scale of the street. One of the urban effects of information technology and so-called globalisation (or perhaps we could just say 'empire'), is a vertiginous jump from the individual and domestic to the macro/global system, bypassing the traditional public typologies of urbanism, such as the street. This is linked to the reconfiguring of public and private spaces discussed earlier. Given that, the question of where the multitude could reside perhaps requires alternative concepts of what constitutes the built environment.

*Let's step back to a philosophical level for a minute. What defines the metropolis for me is the production of, and access to, the common – common wealth in all its forms, including common knowledges, languages, habits. That is closely related to saying that the metropolis i defined by communication. When you think about it that way, then, it clear that the old divisions between town and country, urban and rural no longer hold. Rural life is no longer isolated and incommunicative. Instead, metropolitan life, along with the common and the communication that characterise it, is extending today across all the globe. (This issue of a transformation of the urban/rural divide is a larg topic, though, and needs to be worked out more fully and in more detai*

*In any case, what is essential here is the common (and its communication) because that's where the multitude resides. The common is a difficult concept, one that I don't think Toni and I have fully worked out yet. One can start from the early modern conception of the commons as open land, which was subsequently privatised by acts of enclosure. These commons were land available for use by the community. This is a good starting point, but the analogy is limited because the common I am referring to today is generally not somethin that is natural and pregiven, like the land, but rather something tha is constantly created through social interactions. This is clear, for example, in the case of common knowledges and common languages.*

*It is also important to highlight the fact that the common can be both beneficial and detrimental. The common in this regard is close t what economists call externalities. A park near one's property, or eve a neighbour's yard that is beautifully gardened, might be a positive externality and raise the value of one's property. Similarly, air pollution or traffic in a city might constitute a negative externality, lowering all property value in the area. With this notion of externalities economists are trying to grasp the value of the common, especially in a metropolitan context where the common predominate over all other factors.*

*So when I say that the multitude resides in the common that does not yet define a space. The common is a virtual location that is constantly being actualised*

In that light, it is significant that World Trade Organization (WTO) protests and the like often occur in the streets, but the do not take these as *a prori* typologies of public space, but as contested fields that need to be created through the event itself and which open on to larger, nonmaterial, networks. *I suppose modern political action has always focused on the streets, but you are certainly right that there is an added emphasis on that today. Take, for example, 'Reclaim the Streets' (RTS) – a wonderfully*

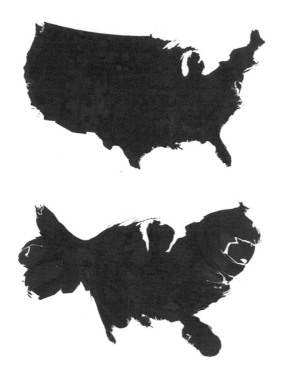

**Map and Cartogram of 2004 US presidential election by Michael Gastner, Cosma Shalizi and Mark Newman of the University of Michigan**
These images reveal the heterogeneity and complex topographies of political space, urbanisation and geography at the dawn of the 21st century. The first image of the 2004 presidential election presents a typical contour of the US, but rather than relying on opposition between red and blue political affiliation it uses gradients of purple based on percentage of votes. The second map is a 'cartogram' produced with a small software application that distorts territory to accurately map not geographic area but population density. The authors of the software suggest it gives a more accurate image of election results. In addition, it reveals how, as Hardt suggests, normative geographic typologies such as urban and suburban or rural need to be supplanted by more sophisticated spatial understandings of the networks and commons produced via communication.

*innovative organisation born in Britain that has now spread to North America and Australia. RTS generally acts by creating street parties and turning political action into carnival. You might say that such actions serve to turn back to the tendency of the privatisation of public spaces, opening them up once again to common access. Critical Mass is another group that comes to mind. They organise large groups of bicyclists to ride together on a street and thus effectively take it back from the automobiles.*

*These two activist groups are good examples because they show how the common must be created – or occupied – for the multitude to exist. But, as is always the case with such examples, these are just limited efforts involving relatively small numbers of people. They can serve as inspiration or suggest possibilities, but such ideas have to be integrated into social life in a much broader way to make real and significant the appropriation of the common.*

A rather different example might be the way the Right has been able to mobilise the newly communicative rural common, as evidenced in the last two elections in the US, by coupling it with the design of social affiliations that are

replacing the organs of liberal civil society. Post-Fordist religion, or televisual megachurches, for example, produce a common space that, not unlike the examples you mentioned above, unlink community from proximity and instead produce propinquity via information and communication technology. These are also constructed common spaces, ones that transverse nationality, class and race, but not in a necessarily liberatory way.

*There is nothing necessarily liberatory about the common. It should be thought of instead as a field of struggle, where the different political alternatives are worked out.*

Perhaps, then, the metropolis of the multitude lies not in reviving historical forms of urbanism as dense cities but in mobilising, through design, the scales of intimacy into networks for collective production, using the enfolding of the intimate and the global common-places for democratic and productive ends, using as models P2P network's challenges to intellectual property, WTO protests organised via text messaging, or even your references in *Multitude* to Bakhtin's carnivalesque. Perhaps there is a potential in much of the work in this issue to create intelligent environments and responsive electronic interfaces: to create an extended but intensive cybernetic urbanism as a site for the multitude.

*Yes, I certainly see this as an important and positive project for new architectures. And what interests me most, of course, is the design of democratic social relationships that architects participate in but extend beyond the limits of the architectural profession; that become a collective, social designing of space. Perhaps architects can be a model for others in this regard; and also, at the same time, architects can benefit from following the innovations of others, learning new ways to design social space and relationships from social movements and other creative social actors.*

Attempting to locate the relationship of the multitude and metropolis is difficult because it would not be defined by any existing discipline. There is a need for a 'collective intelligence' that enfolds and opens the boundaries of knowledge about space and politics and design. We need to design this commons of knowledge exchange.

*This certainly does involve a kind of collective intelligence, and it also focuses on the nature of the relationships that constitute that intelligence, insisting on democratic relationships defined by freedom and equality. It is hard to ask the question, as you say, and imagine such a multitude, but it is also true that we can recognise many social forces and desires pointing in that direction. This notion of the multitude is to me something that is at once strange and familiar, like something that you have dreamt about so many times that it seems already a reality.*

# Responsive Systems|Appliance Architectures

**Branden Hookway** and **Chris Perry** introduce the Responsive Systems Group (RSG), a newly formed design research collective at Cornell University's School of Architecture, Art, and Planning. Highly interdisciplinary in nature, the work here addresses questions of collective intelligence at a number of scales. In terms of practice, collaborative, group-based work is emphasised, with both the students as well as the instructors working in teams of three (Perry and Hookway are co-directors of the Responsive Systems Group along with Ezra Ardolino). The second scale addresses the technologies and methodologies of design itself, exploring problems of 'responsivity' in the context of artificial intelligence and the emerging fields of robotic and sensory interaction design. Finally, and by extension, the issue of scale itself becomes a site of inquiry as the RSG's work focuses less on 'architecture' and more on 'design', implicitly if not explicitly loosening general notions of disciplinarity as a means of revealing new sites for mixture and innovation.

RSG, Meteorologics, 2006
Responsive sonic-scrim (airport installation). A component of the Meteorologics project by Kenneth Lan, William Tan and Ting Ting Zhang (sonic-scrim system designed by Ting Ting Zhang), Responsive Systems|Appliance Architectures advanced research design studio, Cornell University AAP.

The Responsive Systems Group (RSG) defines itself through design methodologies and research interests. Its primary products are 'scenarios'. In the Appliance Architectures studio presented here, these are grouped as 'analytic' and 'design' scenarios, with research and design taking place concurrently and synthesised in a final project. Research interests focus on responsive systems, in which are found a useful distinction from the concept of interactivity. If 'interactive' suggests a unidirectional relationship, with a user performing tasks in an environment only flexible within constraints, 'responsive' suggests mutual reaction and exchange, with adjustments occurring continually on both sides of the use equation. This is seen both as a metaphor for working with digital technology, and as a model for social relations. As such, the RSG's interests extend beyond the digital: the computer is viewed less as a design tool to be mastered and more as a stage in the evolution of the sociotechnics of information processing.

This includes a wide range of developments – analogue and digital, organisational and technological, cultural and scientific, military and commercial, virtual and material. The traces of this lineage, both in precedent and in speculative projections into the future, actively implicate and determine the ways in which computers are used in the present. Instead of limiting architecture's engagement with the computer to the latest available design software – essentially limiting the role of architects to the uncritical production of form – the RSG chooses instead to see the computer as an opportunity for architecture to find common ground with other disciplines similarly concerned with problems of design and organisation.

Along with providing a venue to work with new techniques of digital visualisation, fabrication, organisation and design, the RSG's aim is to contextualise this exploration within architectural discourse while drawing new lines of connection to relevant outside disciplines (such as the history of technology, media theory and organisational theory). The group sees this as a way of both extending the conceptual range of architecture and finding new potential sites of design intervention.

The RSG is inherently configured as a collaborative venture. In the Responsive Systems|Appliance Architectures studio, both the critics and the students are working in groups of three, with team formation and negotiation considered explicitly as a studio problem. This refers to team-based approaches generally excluded from the architecture studio, such as the professional office, academic research laboratory and corporate think tank. In the formation of a collective intelligence within the studio, the group finds resonance with the studio research programme: the exploration of design responsiveness (including appliance design, interaction design, robotics, software and computer programming) as a means of producing flexible and adaptable environments, capable of adjusting to the variable and shifting needs, interests and programmatic desires of designers and users alike.

## Appliance Architectures

The Responsive Systems|Appliance Architectures research project locates architecture in the realm of circuitry, in assemblages of collectors, servomechanisms and transistors that absorb, process and redistribute matter, force and information. Here, the environments of the interventions are considered to be essentially active, comprised of moving parts, temporal components, the proliferation of electronic and digital equipment and interfaces, and the ebb and flow of information in real time. Investigations are not limited to the distribution of bodies (material, pedestrian, vehicular, and so on) within the form and geometry of a static architecture, but rather seek out behaviours of feedback and response, where intervention transforms environments and is likewise transformed in a continuous relationship.

The project focuses on the design of systems: collections of discrete parts that when correctly arranged form a complex or organic unity. Such systems may range from those formally developed in cybernetics, operations research and systems theory, to the more informal systems that might be referred to when 'beating' or 'gaming the system'. With any systems, design must take place simultaneously at the level of the object or node, and at the level of the wiring, connection or protocol. Thus, the studio takes the appliance, a discrete object wired for connection in a larger system, as its fundamental design unit.[1] The spatial and organisational qualities generated by assemblies of these objects and/or infrastructures are referred to as 'appliance architectures'.

This conception of space, as it emerges from the systematised deployment of equipment in networks, differs essentially from the conception of architectural space as delimited by enclosure or envelope. While the latter conception of space has most often been exemplified since the Modernists in notions of total design and *Gesamtkunstwerk*, produced through clear top-down authorial control and received by users as an all-encompassing experience, the former conception is far harder to describe or pin down as a controlled experience. While the system deployed in space may be every bit as totalising as any architecture, or even more so, and despite the fact that systems are primarily means of control, we are perhaps still unused to the idea that control may be augmented, not just diminished, through the blurring, flattening and dispersal of control hierarchies. In architecture we currently lack a vocabulary to describe the spatial effects of systems deployed in space, either in aesthetic or programmatic terms. The Appliance Architectures studio finds in this disciplinary blind spot a rich zone of operation.

## Systems Theory

'Systems' have again come into vogue in contemporary architectural discourse, and nearly to the point of over-saturation. This is not by coincidence. As the tools available to architecture become more sophisticated, architects have almost by necessity become more aware of systematisation in the contemporary world: from globalisation to urbanism,

## Responsive Systems|Appliance Architectures Analytic Scenarios

The images in this sequence are a sampling of references that serve to provide a larger cultural and technological framework for the general ambitions of the studio and, more specifically, the analytic research that was conducted by each of the three student teams. Taken from a wide range of fictional as well as nonfictional sources, the images suggest design processes, user groups, material logics and potential sites of intervention. From this general technocultural context, the studio began with the following problem: using a selection of readings and films drawn from postwar science fiction and futurology as a launching point, identify a sci-fi appliance or technology. Speculate upon one or more of the real-world sources the author may have extrapolated from in conceptualising this technology. Through text, images and diagrams, document the sci-fi appliance along with its real-world counterparts. Keep in mind the technological and cultural lineages leading up to the moment the particular appliance encapsulates, along with the potential energies it directs to the future. Possible areas of documentation include: What does it do? How is it made? Are other technologies necessary for it to function? Does it operate alone or in a network? Who are its users? Does its use require training? What kind of interface does it have? And, does the use of this appliance or technology have organisational implications?

AI takes command: Dave interfaces with HAL in Stanley Kubrick's *2001: A Space Odyssey* (1968).

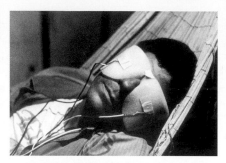

Time travel via VR rig: from Chris Marker's *La Jetée* (1962).

The Mars Rover's sophisticated sensing apparatus allows it to make tactical decisions at local scales.

From late-19th century typewriters and adding machines to mid-20th-century information management and telecommunications technologies to present-day home offices, equipment has continually driven the spatial and organisational configuration of the office.

The Chicago offices of JFN Associates, using Herman Miller's Action Office systems furniture (1964). The scale and configurability of component-based interior systems offers precedents and opportunities for responsive design.

The AbioCor Replacement Heart integrates biosensors, a flexible plastic simulating the reflexivity of human flesh and hydraulic pumps to model the complex rhythms of blood circulation.

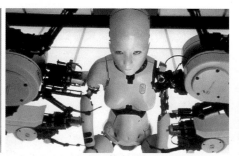

Left: A second-generation 'face robot' designed and developed at the Hara Kobayashi Laboratory/Science University of Tokyo expands the expressivity available to machine interfaces. Centre: Honda's Asimo – yet another attempt at machinic intelligence through sleight-of-hand anthropomorphism? Or a well-calibrated marketing move combining real advances in robotic ambulation with voice and visual pattern recognition? Right: 'All is Full of Love': Chris Cunningham's music video for the Björk song incorporates robotic systems originally developed for Stanley Kubrick's unfinished film project *A.I.*

The dreams of an intelligent and unfathomable ocean drive the scientists studying it to insanity and beyond. Andrei Tarkovsky's *Solaris* (1972) from the novel by Stanislaw Lem (1961).

from market forces to media culture, and from scientific speculation to the development of new materials and information technologies. In part, this confirms a basic insight of media theory: the tools we use shape our conceptualisation of the world. And if our tools and intuitions suggest that we can address such complex problems, the persistent question remains how.

Architecture has seen such times before. In the postwar era, architecture was informed by several waves of systems thinking – cybernetics in the 1950s and 1960s, pattern language and design methods in the 1960s and 1970s – producing a diverse collection of practices in response (Team X, Archigram, Gyorgy Kepes, Reyner Banham and many others). These were prefigured, in turn, by certain Modernist preoccupations (for example, the Futurists and the Constructivists, the Bauhaus and CIAM, Usonian planning and product streamlining, El Lissitzsky and Moholy-Nagy). We keep in mind these past responses of architectural discourse to technological change and complexity, from reaching out to other disciplines to enforcing disciplinary boundaries, and from formal innovations to changing notions of design practice and criticism.

We keep in mind as well the dangers of unrestrained technological enthusiasm. And yet, we feel that it is particularly urgent now that architects address disciplines outside their own, and particularly those concerned with relevant technologies and organisational behaviours. As a generalist discipline concerned with environments and spatial organisation, whose duty it often is to work with other specialist disciplines, architecture today looks forward to many new opportunities if it can successfully embrace an expanded field of operation. This likewise sets architecture in a privileged position from which to reflect on contemporary society, in that any claim to be critical needs to be deeply informed of that which it seeks to criticise.

## Hacks or Consultants?

Philip Johnson once dismissed an early space-planning firm as 'hacks'. When viewed against the ambitions of architecture in the heroic mode, it is no wonder the space-planners appeared banal: specialised, tied to the everyday business practices, beholden to client concerns, caught up in figures and calculations and, worst of all, uncommitted to a discourse whose aim was to justify the free expression of the architect's will to form.

Appliances – any object or assembly of objects with embedded intelligence, from kitchen appliances to systems furniture to iPods – often appear inaccessible to the generalist: they draw on multiple specialisations and often require specialist training to fully understand. Their invention can rarely be credited to a single authorial voice. More often than not, the producers are teams of experts or consultants, each addressing different aspects of the design problem.

For the discipline of architecture, the spatial effect of appliances is difficult to assess. Yet the influence of equipment in determining spatial qualities is increasingly difficult to deny. And so behind architecture's dismissal of the consultant might lie a certain suspicion: yes, the architect loses something in terms of control in becoming a consultant. But is there something to be gained? Or, even worse, is something lost to architecture when it ignores the space-making potential of appliances, or 'Great Gizmos' as Reyner Banham had it? And might it require a certain disciplinary humility, a willingness to engage other disciplines? Or even to adapt the kind of synthetic three-dimensional thinking that architects are so good at to a wider range of problems?

There is a resonance between the problem of appliance architectures and the role of computers in design. Much of the formal exploration celebrated in contemporary architecture would have been inconceivable without the computer, and it is an open question who is leading whom, the designer or the machine (yet another detraction from claims of authorial and critical sovereignty). In addition, the virtuality and temporality of computer environments stand in contrast to the materiality and sited-ness and being-there of architecture. Following William Gibson's definition of cyberspace, 'there's no there there'; the real action occurs virtually, it seems, in a nowhere between routers and terminals. On the one hand, this freedom from the material realm may be liberating; on the other it brings with it its own dangers, as extensions of vision always entail the production of blind spots.

## Site and Method

The methodology of the RSG is centred more on an interdisciplinary conception of design than architecture per se, taking advantage of the greater flexibility of the former term to incorporate disciplinary expertise outside the immediate vicinity of architecture (such as interaction design, robotics, software design, product and interior design). To this extent, the group understands architecture to be less about building than about building systems. Typical scales of focus might thus include reflexive and adaptable infrastructures for interior or small-scale environments. At the scale of the interior, this could be office, lobby and gallery landscaping systems, including the secondary scales of furniture, ceiling and partitioning systems, as well as lighting, sound and temperature infrastructures. At the scale of the exterior, it might include building skins, roofing landscapes and sidewalk furniture systems. At either scale, the group avoids conceiving of buildings as static or monumental, or of architects as master builders or form-makers. Instead it is interested in design systems that work a bit more like a software interface: a flexible and adaptable infrastructure through which users define their own individual and collective needs, potentials, and desires, with design configured as a machine or appliance for ongoing and unfolding userships and applications.

## Scenarios

Walter Benjamin prefaces his seminal essay 'The work of art in the age of mechanical reproduction'[2] with a revision of Marxian terms of substructure and superstructure: where Marx held that the economy was the substructure upon which

## Responsive Systems|Appliance Architectures
## Design Scenarios

The images in this sequence provide a sampling of design work from each phase of the studio's research and were produced by each of the three student teams: Kenneth Lan, William Tan and Ting Ting Zhang; Brian Carli, Morgan Ng and Katie Vitale; and Michael Curry, Roza Matreeva and Nicole McGuire. The design component of the studio involved the generation of digital abstract appliances. These responsive machines were built from the ground up using simple kinematic units (active skeletal components capable of basic motion behaviour) combined into larger assemblies. Working in AliasWavefront Maya, inverse kinematics were used along with expressions and scripts to model the potential behaviours of these machines. In the design, development, testing and refinement of the machines, suggestions for how to proceed were drawn from the ongoing analytic research and the evolution of the machines themselves. As such, the studio explored the generative or inventive potential of working with active systems; while the machines were configured by a designer, the numerous points of adjustment and dynamic variables, along with the influence of the software environment itself, ensured an element of unpredictability. To this extent, the process of design became one of discovery within an environment of continual testing and refinement, looking inwards at the abstract behaviour of the machines and outwards at the potential uses such machines could have in the world. The relationship of the designer to the object or environment of design was inherently responsive; each is bound up in a continual feedback loop of information, influence and exchange.

The networked deployment of appliances in an airport responding to programmatic demands including security, way-finding and communications.

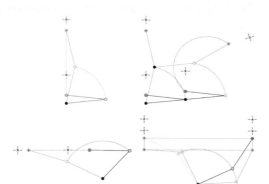

A single component tracing a scanning path with its information flow diagram.

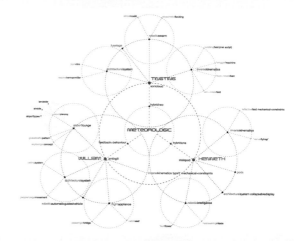

Diagram of the collaborative process within one of the research teams.

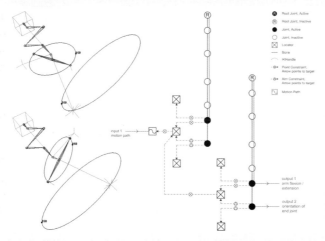

The range of motion in a single component.

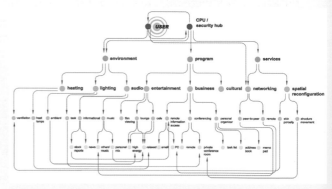

Diagram of user/system responsivity mapping various forms of dynamic interface and engagement between the design environment and its user/s.

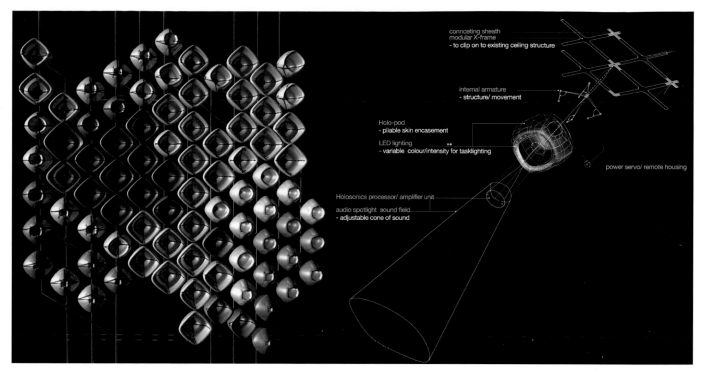

Rendering of a responsive ceiling system, looking from below, and an exploded axonometric of the unit incorporating directional sound and lighting as well as general scanning and tracking capabilities.

the superstructure of culture rested, Benjamin responds that the 'dialectic [of class struggle] is no less noticeable in the superstructure than the economy' and proceeds to argue the inseparability of technology, economy, politics, media and culture in modernity.

Without an ideological framework to help tease out the strands of historic causation, we arrive upon the scenario. Scenarios today are a widely used technology, from economic outlooks to trend forecasting. The Cold War turned the scenario into a fine art, with game theory as its language of discourse. But the RSG's favourite form of scenario-building is science fiction. Even the appliances of science fiction are miniscenarios in themselves, where the author has extrapolated alternate future technologies from the existing. Other scenarios address the organisation of scientific endeavours, and even the potential dangers of misjudging and applying scenarios. The group therefore hopes to learn from science fiction's facility to project ideas into the future, and to trace connections between existing appliances from the postwar era to the present to counterpoints drawn from science-fiction milieus.

Its research thus follows two primary and parallel trajectories: analytical scenarios (oriented towards technology and human–machine relations including speculative/fictional and historical/technical research), and inventive scenarios (oriented towards design innovation through the development of responsive machines using computational design software and robotics technology). However, each of these investigations can be enriched only when developed simultaneously with the other. This is not to say that the RSG

does not appreciate the value of pure design invention unfettered by critical concerns, and likewise that of research unfettered by design considerations, but in separating the two hopes to maximise the invention and production of ideas, tools and strategies for their eventual synthesis – not a synthesis of opposites, as in a Hegelian clash of thesis/antithesis, but rather a coming together, enmeshing and mutual enhancement of two systems to create a richer, more complex set of relationships.

Scenarios often have a way of turning out drastically wrong. Yet, in the territory of scenario-based research, even an interesting failure can be a success. Science-fiction author Stanislaw Lem knew this well: in *Solaris*, the dreams of an intelligent and unfathomable ocean drive the scientists who mean to study it to the brink of insanity, while in *The Invincible*, the would-be conquerors of a newly discovered planet are roundly thwarted by a species of mechanised fly. In short, the best-laid plans often go awry. ⌀

**Notes**
1. '…[I]t is in the very readymadeness and superficiality of these objects that we may discover what is radical about them: each bears within itself an abstract mechanism for producing political and social transformations at even the minutest scales of existence.' In our conception of appliances, we are indebted to Brian Boigon and Sanford Kwinter's 1990 studio brief developed at the University of Toronto and subsequently published as 'Manual for 5 Appliances in the Alphabetical City: A Pedagogical Text', in *Assemblage* 15, MIT, 1991.
2. Walter Benjamin, 'The work of art in the age of mechanical reproduction', in Hannah Arendt (ed), *Illuminations*, Schocken (New York), 1969, p 217.

Parallel Processing
Design/Practice

in the late 1990s servo emerged as a young design collaborative embracing new forms of distributed practice as enabled by the advent of telecommunications technologies. In this section, **David Erdman, Marcelyn Gow, Ulrika Karlsson** and **Chris Perry** write about how these organisational principles are at work not only in the context of their practice, but in the design work itself, which stretches across a variety of design disciplines to incorporate areas of expertise particular to information and interaction design, as well as a number of manufacturing and fabrication technologies. Many of servo's projects have focused on small-scale interior infrastructures, typically in the form of gallery installations, furniture systems and exhibition designs. This particular scale has allowed the group to focus on the development of full-scale prototypes, exploring a wide range of potential innovations at the point of integration between various technological and material systems.

## Responsive Design Networks

*Today you have interaction with hardware. You also have the opposite, that is, hardware changes according to the human being and the human being is interacting with the hardware – you have design, you have clothes, and we know that in the future expo of the 21st Century, it will be people.*[1]

Anticipating the conflation of the biological and technological that drives contemporary ideas of architectural operating systems, Bell Laboratories engineer Billy Klüver made this comment in the context of the Osaka '70 World Expo. The 'living responsive environment' that Klüver and the Experiments in Art and Technology (EAT) organisation developed in the Pepsi Pavilion for Expo '70 attempted to perform, in an exhibition context, the man–machine dialogue that proliferated in the semivisible electronic channels and interchanges through which the bits and bytes of the information society coursed.

Significant in this early description of interactivity is the suggestion of the partial 'erosion' of materiality as a site of exchange and the dichotomy posed between the physical attributes of a space and its operating procedures, between static materiality and more immaterial, dynamic attributes of

a space or, in Marshall McLuhan's formulation, between 'art form' and 'environment'.[2] The terms 'hardware' and 'software' are useful to describe this dichotomy as they have been instrumental in shaping both a history of computation and a cultural discourse in the 1960s, and have a renewed relevance for the current architectural discussion.[3]

The spatialising of the informational paradigm has a bit of a circuitous history, one which is manifested through a number of seminal architectural and urban projects from the 1960s, but which also emerges simultaneously in the context of several artistic practices, for example in the work of EAT, that can be understood as parallel processes. Considering computation as a nexus of interacting communication channels and a site of data management, processing, storage and retrieval – rather than simply as hardware – is crucial to an understanding of how this technology was reflected in the architecture and art of the 1960s as well as its impact on contemporary practice. A look at projects like the Pepsi Pavilion reveals a more multivalent implementation of this nexus than that described through the hard dichotomy of image or performance, and one that resonates with servo's approach to an 'architecture in-formation'.

Klüver's observation that 'hardware changes according to the human being' suggests a degree of feedback. The interaction in Osaka between hardware and the human being took the form of 'live programming' that was to involve visitors to the pavilion in developing their local environment at the expo. EAT attempted to create this responsive environment through augmenting the pavilion's physical structure with a series of dynamic layers of media, or software, which included a programmable low-hanging stratus cloud surrounding the structure, an interactive floor-loop sound system whereby visitors could mine the interior of the space for local audio output, a programmable multi-channel speaker grid, and a series of motorised 'floats' whose trajectories across the pavilion plaza could be influenced through contact.[4] A very important aspect of the EAT pavilion is the fact it used the space of the exhibition itself as a site not to show off technology or to show representations of experimental work, but to experiment on work in real time (literally 'live programming') and to engage an audience into actively shaping their surroundings. In essence the pavilion acted as a kind of large-scale operating system, or proto-computational environment, into which the expo visitors were invited to co-author and inform the exhibition itself. It performed as an ambient machine, in which hardware is subsumed by the atmospheric effects of software, and materiality de-instantiates itself into responsive networks.

These kinds of responsive networks act as parallel processes in the work of servo. As contemporary practitioners, servo inevitably operates in the context of the information age, and this shift from a mechanical paradigm to a data

---

**servo, Lattice Archipelogics, 2002**
Detail view: elevation drawing of Lattice Archipelogics cell cloud.

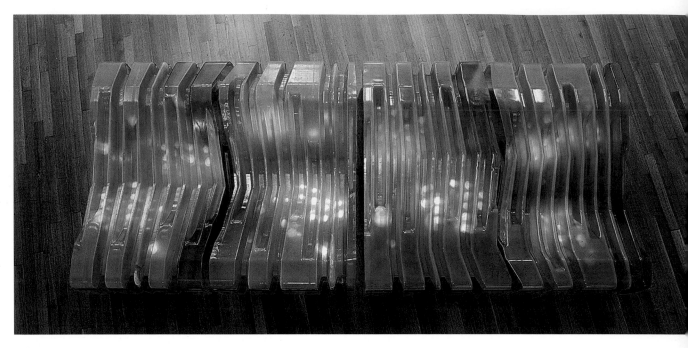

**servo, Thermocline, 2002**
Thermocline installed at the 'Mood River' exhibition at the Wexner Center, Ohio State University.

paradigm resonates in its work on several levels. The extent to which the exchange of data instantiates itself in the material properties or organisational qualities of a space, and the extent to which this exchange is sometimes more immaterial in nature, becomes a primary impetus; in early exhibitions issues of the storage and relay of information within a network were reflected both in the form and material organisation of the architecture, as well as in the more immaterial fallout, which results in the production of secondary effects.

The Thermocline project, a furniture system that could be occupied in the exhibition space and acted as a channelling device between sound and light patterns, merged two primary strains of connectivity – the material and the immaterial. On the one hand it incorporated material techniques for forming plastic to structurally support bodies, and simultaneously housed small-scale hardware networks of LED lighting and speakers in an interior landscape of contours.

Thermocline was originally designed for the 'Mood River' exhibition at the Wexner Center, Ohio State University, and servo later collaborated with the Emonic Collective from MIT's Media Lab to upgrade the piece for the 'Non-Standard Architectures' exhibition at the Pompidou Centre. This upgrade involved programming the system to pick up ambient sounds in the gallery from visitors and importing them into a custom mixing software where they were layered with other sounds and used as inputs to inform the lighting patterns of the LEDs, and emitted through the speaker network. The surface acted as an interface between these embedded interior systems and the exterior systems of the gallery and its occupants. Different zones of luminosity and

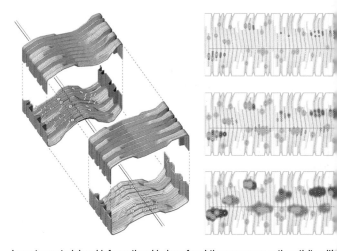

In part a material and informational index of real-time programmatic activity with the space of the gallery, Thermocline incorporates a network of LED fixtures and microsonic speakers to generate responsive lighting and sound patterns.

sound intensity were generated as it gathered sound from th surrounding space through microphones and as different quantities of people moved on and around it. The surface, in sense, became infused with information.

In Lattice Archipelogics, a collaboration between servo an the Smart Studio of the Interactive Institute in Stockholm, th informational nexus was pushed to a more immersive scale i the gallery. A dynamically responsive field was produced within an archipelago of plastic cells. The cells became luminous through the integration of LEDs and were interwoven with a matrix of proximity sensors. Lattice Archipelogics operated as a porous illumination device wher

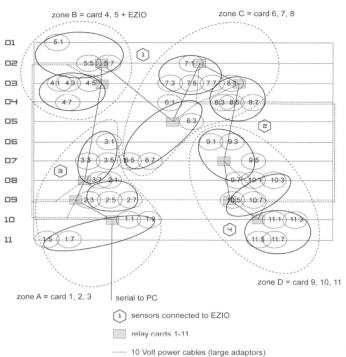

zone B = card 4, 5 + EZIO    zone C = card 6, 7, 8

01   5:1
02      5:5  5:7      7:1
03   4:1  4:3  4:5    7:3  7:5  7:7  8:1
04      4:7         6:1    8:3  8:5  8:7
05                6:3
06         3:1      9:1  9:3
07   3:3  3:5  6:5  6:7      9:5
08   3:7  2:1      9:7  10:1  10:3
09   2:3  2:5  2:7      10:5  10:7
10         1:1  1:3      11:1  11:3
11   1:5  1:7      11:5  11:7

zone A = card 1, 2, 3    serial to PC

zone D = card 9, 10, 11

1   sensors connected to EZIO

▨   relay cards 1-11

┈┈  10 Volt power cables (large adaptors)

**servo, Lattice Archipelogics, 2002**
In the Lattice Archipelogics project, a network of motion-sensing technology, custom software and LED fixtures
provides an infrastructure for the generation of variable lighting patterns in response to programmatic activity.

the light levels produced at any given moment were dependent upon the number and sequence of people moving inside the archipelago. Various densities of physical haze were moved through the space by people walking through the cluster of cells. This archipelago of physical matter and light, and its potential for dynamic modulation, dealt with a series of phase shifts. Here, the notion of materiality shifts between solidity and fluidity was considered in terms of fabrication techniques by using stereolithography and vacuum casting, and in terms of computation and programming as the algorithm-generated fluid light paths of virtual agents migrating towards the sensors and activating individual cells as they moved. When left in its inert state, Lattice Archipelogics sampled from the catalogue of stored movement patterns to perform them iteratively. A materialised drawing at the scale of the sinuous lattice elements and their assembly in space was coupled with a sequence of performative, three-dimensional luminous drawings sketched by visitors through their bodily manipulation of the digital interface.

More recent projects continued to develop the idea of creating software for interaction in a public space which is ultimately infused in materiality in order to generate secondary fallout or effects. The Genealogy of Speed was a display infrastructure designed by servo in collaboration with the graphic design firm SKDP in 2004 for 30 of Nike's most technologically innovative athletic shoes. The primary approach to display was to bring all the content away from the walls, to disperse and spatialise the genealogy of shoes in a way that was transformative. The design effectively accelerated the architecture and slowed down the visitor. The installation was broken into three different speeds, or modes of experience: fast/ceiling, slow/clusters, idle/furniture system. Comprising modular components, plastic strands combined to form a virtual surface/ceiling that operated as a substrate from which to suspend the shoes, levitating them in the space. A series of plastic tubes docked into these strands, each containing a single shoe with its individual diagnostics sandblasted on the exterior.

The interactive aspect of the project occurred through the manually reconfigurable display vitrines. A pool of eight genealogical groupings was sorted throughout the course of an event into three clusters, each comprising five tube-like vitrines that through a laser-cut detail were remountable. The ceiling 'dripped' into the tubes in a stalactite-like formation, tracing the fibre-optic lighting system down to the bottom of a tube where a shoe was located and spotlit. Each tube was arranged around others to form clusters where relationships were established between individual shoes. The clusters re-organised existing pedestrian circulation, slowing visitors down as they manoeuvred around them to examine the focus of the show − Nike's innovative athletic shoes.

In servo's design for 'Dark Places', an exhibition curated by Joshua Decter for the Santa Monica Museum of Art in 2006, the idea was to develop a space that would be tied to the media of display, respond to it and mutate because of it. The

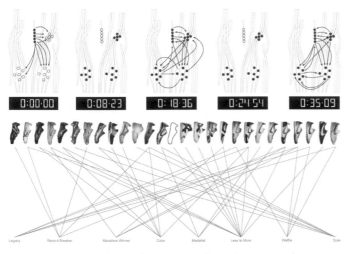

**servo, The Genealogy of Speed, Nike, 2004**
The Genealogy of Speed exhibition system allows for display material to be redistributed according to variable curatorial speeds and themes by providing a series of removable shoe canisters.

The Genealogy of Speed exhibition environment allows for varying conditions of display, integrating passive systems (ambient lighting conditions produced through horizontally distributed fibre-optic technologies) with active systems (display clusters comprising reconfigurable vertical vitrines).

exhibition needed to accommodate the work of 76 artists in 325-square-metre (3500-square-foot) space, and the content was inherently active and temporal, a series of video projections and digitised photographs all dealing with the film noir genre. The two primary aspects of the project were the use of light in the exhibition and developing a spatial organisation for the art work that was not linear, but temporal, with the capacity to produce affiliated relationships between pieces.

A family of components was developed around projection, touchscreens, sound, fibre-optics, constraints of packing, shipping and assembly. The project was conceived of as an active growth in the space, inhabiting and mutating it over the duration of the exhibition. As a result there were components that behaved more like emitters, or terminals, within a network. This traced the flow of information and data through the system, from input to output, the primary intention being the configuration of different pulses of art in the gallery, each with a different cadence or tempo which then allowed for cross-referencing and simultaneous autonomy among the pieces.

The interactive component was limited to touchscreens, and the mode of output was exclusively projection. Since all the art work in the exhibition was projected, its media (light) was captured and expressed by the network of architectural components that made up the exhibition. This enabled a focus on the way light would shape the strands, in particular using the front projectors where the pitch and angle of projection had to be calculated to eliminate interference, basically inflating the section of the piece to allow light to be thrown on to walls at these four locations. With the rear projection areas, the presence of light was registered as a splitting open of the surfaces in these locations to capture the projected 'image scrape' and hold the projection screen, in essence making the luminous matter three-dimensional. Visitors could browse an online catalogue of the contents of each individual strand at the touchscreen. Every time the screen was touched, the individual strand's fibre-optics appeared to breathe as light pulsed from the touchscreen area to the projector emitting the content. In this way an ambient, luminous environment was produced through the exploration of data in the space.

## Responsive Practice Networks

*We are seeing the combination of network communications and social networks. Whenever a new communications technology lowers the threshold for groups to act collectively, new kinds of institutions emerge.*[5]

The Internet has fostered and accelerated communication in exceptionally sophisticated ways, but usually towards simple notions of efficiency (the Internet allows for companies to expand without jeopardising their solidarity). For example, corporate practice utilises new communication networks of

## servo, 'Dark Places', Santa Monica Museum of Art, California, 2006

The 'Dark Places' exhibition environment provides the gallery user with both active as well as passive forms of engagement. Responsive fibre-optic lighting continually adjusts the ambient conditions of the gallery as users interface passively with both rear- and forward-projected imagery and actively with a series of touchscreen monitors providing direct access to the exhibition database.

General view of the 'Dark Places' exhibition space.

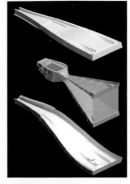
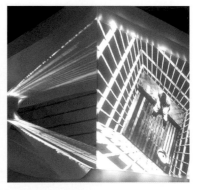

The rear projection system integrates various degrees of material information, from the plasticity of its vacuum-formed acrylic shell to the liquidity of data rendered in the form of projected imagery across the surfaces of the shell.

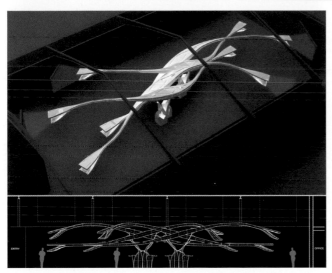

Axonometric and elevation views of the exhibition infrastructure.

Ground components, each of which hold CPUs carrying the digital content of the exhibition in addition to touchscreen monitors for user interaction.

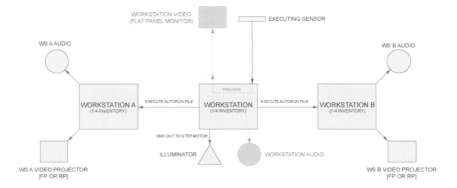

Diagram of the display infrastructure, integrating audio, visual and interactive technologies in the formation of a responsive exhibition environment.

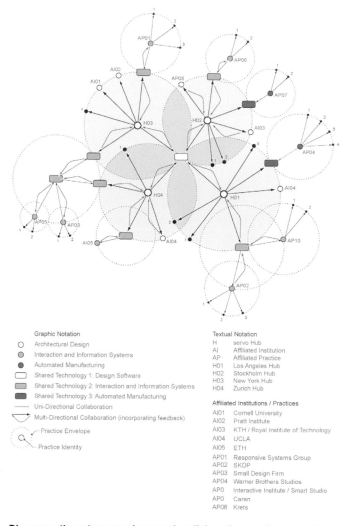

**Graphic Notation**

○   Architectural Design
◔   Interaction and Information Systems
●   Automated Manufacturing
▭   Shared Technology 1: Design Software
▭   Shared Technology 2: Interaction and Information Systems
▭   Shared Technology 3: Automated Manufacturing
──   Uni-Directional Collaboration
▽   Multi-Directional Collaboration (incorporating feedback)

  Practice Envelope

  Practice Identity

**Textual Notation**

| | |
|---|---|
| H | servo Hub |
| AI | Affiliated Institution |
| AP | Affiliated Practice |
| H01 | Los Angeles Hub |
| H02 | Stockholm Hub |
| H03 | New York Hub |
| H04 | Zurich Hub |

**Affiliated Institutions / Practices**

| | |
|---|---|
| AI01 | Cornell University |
| AI02 | Pratt Institute |
| AI03 | KTH / Royal Institute of Technology |
| AI04 | UCLA |
| AI05 | ETH |
| AP01 | Responsive Systems Group |
| AP02 | SKDP |
| AP03 | Small Design Firm |
| AP04 | Warner Brothers Studios |
| AP0 | Interactive Institute / Smart Studio |
| AP0 | Caran |
| AP08 | Krets |

**Diagrammatic system mapping servo's collaborative practice network**
This diagram was designed by Aaron White with the intention of registering the various organisational qualities and effects of servo's design practice. According to White, 'the diagrammatic system employs networks that are both provisional and heterogeneous in nature, made up of temporal affiliations between both human and nonhuman actors. The "nonhuman" actors could be understood as various forms of technology (for instance, design software, automated manufacturing processes and interactive technologies). Comprising a larger technomachinic membrane, the nonhuman element should not be considered passive, but rather as something that provides various forms of material resistance to its human counterparts, actively altering the information that flows through it in unpredictable yet potentially inventive and productive ways. Within this context of provisional and heterogeneous networks, there are three primary configurations. "Random networks" are typically characterised by the fact that most nodes have approximately the same number of links, exhibiting what is known as the "small world property", which means that the path length from one node to any other node tends to be relatively short. "Scale-free networks" are characterised by the fact that some nodes (called "hubs") are much more connected than the average node within the graph. These networks are ultrasmall and exhibit no inherent modularity. Finally, "hierarchical networks" are characterised by sparsely connected nodes that are part of highly clustered areas, with communication between clusters maintained by only a few hubs. In the case of the servo diagram, it is primarily through technology (various forms of design and production software, manufacturing processes and information systems) that a variety of otherwise discrete practices become integrated with one another. Ultimately, then, the diagram operates as a momentary actualisation of specific instances, at a specific point in time, and within a larger field of potential connections, meaning the diagram can best be understood only as a statistically probable set of relations fundamentally provisional in nature, constantly disassembling and reassembling itself over time.'

repetition and expansion to further its productive capacity, but often at the expense of innovation. The multitudinous employment of communication networks, however, is at once more organisationally horizontal and reflexive. Its focus is less on communication as an efficient tool, and more on communicability as proliferation, an intensive exchange and feedback of information that leads to the innovation of ideas (or of entirely new institutions, as Howard Rheingold suggests in the quote above). This potential for feedback extends beyond the scale of the individual user to one involving entire disciplinary fields. As Manuel Castells described: 'What characterizes the current technological revolution is not the centrality [in importance] of knowledge and information, but the application of such knowledge and information to knowledge generation and information processing/ communication devices, in a cumulative feedback loop between innovation and the uses of innovation.'[6] It is this feedback, or reflexivity, which differentiates information technology from other technologies: 'The novelty of the new information infrastructure is the fact that it is embedded within and completely immanent to the new production processes.'[7]

In terms of our contemporary cultural condition we see these effects of relexive invention in a number of relatively recent social phenomena, particularly in user-generated political organisations such as moveon.org, or file-sharing communities such as BitTorrent and flickr. What these organisations have in common is the degree to which they challenge conventional models of social practice, employing the Internet and its decentralising effects to reconfigure the very nature of cultural invention and production. Through reflexive communication, these distributed networks are sites not only for the exchange of information, but for the invention of new information.

As a collective practice, servo has in part learned from these kinds of open-source, peer-to-peer models of distributed exchange and production, extending these logics to a reconfiguration of the conventional design office format by recasting it as an international, intergeographic, design-based, file-sharing community. Taking the form of a network of geographically discrete and yet informationally integrated 'hubs', servo's four principal partners operate out of four different cities, bridging the design cultures of Europe and the US. Utilising open-source methods of communication and exchange to allow each local hub to inflect the others (as well as the collective whole), design work is initiated and developed at neither exclusively global scales (online and as a single, unified entity) nor local ones (in a particular city/office and thus as an individual or separate entity), but somewhere between these two conditions. To this extent, the practice is able to draw upon and incorporate aspects particular to the design cultures of the various cities in which it is located, allowing the work to be more interregional and international in nature (as opposed to being fixed to European, American or even West Coast versus East Coast influences and, as a result, identities).

In addition to this internal network of four primary partners, servo's practice has incorporated a second tier of collaboration with a number of secondary external agents and institutions. In part a reflection of the increasing interdisciplinarity of the design work (as described at the beginning of this essay, in terms of the incorporation of particular areas of disciplinary expertise such as information and interaction design), this second tier expands the professional envelope of the practice to include a number of areas of design specialisation outside the immediacy of architecture. As mentioned earlier, this has included collaborations with institutions like MIT's Media Lab and the Interactive Institute's Smart Studio, both leading research

## If informational media, from interactive sensory systems to telecommunications, have radically reconfigured our relationship with technology, it is due to their lack of specificity. Digital technology is not fixed to particular uses as determined by a given discipline and its skill sets, but is rather a universal abstract machine.

groups in the areas of computation and interaction design. In addition, servo has worked with graphic design firms such as SKDP, motion typography offices such as Small Design Firm, fine artists like Karen Kimmel and Perry Hall, and other interdisciplinary design practices such as biothing. servo's practice organisation thus expands beyond the immediacy of the primary partnership to include a larger interdisciplinary network of agents and participants. It is therefore not simply a means to transfer existing information between the four partners, but a mode for the invention and production of new information, not only between the partners but between a number of external design practices and, by extension, their respective disciplines, actualising in the form of a design practice what has previously been referred to as 'communicability' in a social organisation.

### Summary/Synthesis

If informational media, from interactive sensory systems to telecommunications, have radically reconfigured our

relationship with technology, it is due to their lack of specificity. Digital technology is not fixed to particular uses as determined by a given discipline and its skill sets, but is rather a universal abstract machine.[8] Rather than being assigned to one function, limiting itself and, by extension, its user, the computer's flexible infrastructure allows for the possibility of its user/s to perpetually redefine its productive capacities. Thus, one sees an increasingly blurred condition between user and technology, between man and machine. What is of particular importance with this shift is the degree to which modes of production, distribution and consumption are no longer passively related. In the Fordist era of industrialisation, manufacturing processes were more or less isolated from user or market processes. Information about user demand had a difficult time reaching and, ultimately, re-informing manufacturing processes. Toyotism[9] represented an early advance in bridging this gap within the limits of a still-industrial era, but it was not until the emergence of the computer that an active relationship between technologies of production and cycles of use began to affect one another in substantial ways and reconfigure the very architecture of the technology. ∆

### Notes

1. Billy Klüver, 'Transcript of an Interview for the *Ueno Reporter*', Osaka, 27 June 1969, Experiments in Art and Technology. Records, 1966–1993, Getty Research Institute, Research Library, Accession 940003, Box 43, Folder 35.
2. Marshall McLuhan, 'The invisible environment: the future of an erosion', *Perspecta 11: The Yale Journal of Architecture*, Yale University (New Haven, CT), 1967, p 165. Edited version of a lecture entitled 'Technology and Environment' given at the Vision 65 conference 'New Challenges for Human Communication' at Southern Illinois University in October 1965.
3. The integration of electronic and digital media into a popular cultural context was addressed by a number of exhibitions, like Jack Burnham's 'Software. Information Technology: Its New Meaning for Art', Jasia Reichardt's 'Cybernetic Serendipity' at the ICA in London in 1968, and Kynaston McShine's 'Information' at MoMA in 1970, and had obvious ramifications on the status of the object in artistic practice that played out somewhat differently in Pop Art, Conceptual Art and Art and Technology.
4. For a complete description of the project, see Billy Klüver, J Martin and B Rose (eds), *Pavilion: Experiments in Art and Technology*, EP Dutton (New York), 1972.
5. Howard Rheingold (author of *Smart Mobs: The Next Social Revolution*) from an interview for 'How The Protesters Mobilized' by Jennifer Lee, *New York Times*, 23 February 2003.
6. Manuel Castells, *The Rise of the Network Society*, Blackwell Publishers (Oxford), 1996, p 32.
7. Ibid, p 298.
8. Frank Webster, *Theories of the Information Society*, Routledge (London), 1995, p 291.
9. Toyotism represents an important shift in mass-production processes whereby feedback from consumers was incorporated with increasing speed so as to more actively inform the ongoing design and development of the technology as it was being produced (as opposed to consumer feedback arriving after the completion of the production cycle when it is too late to affect the process).

# After BitTorrent: Darknets to Native Data

What are the implications of the inherent reflexivity of the Internet for the design professions? **Anthony Burke** argues that radically innovative and distributed forms of information exchange such as BitTorrent suggest a general shift away from the traditional conception of the architect as master builder to one more in line with the collaborative remixing and patching tactics of the hacker. BitTorrent is a communications protocol that allows massive information exchange across infinite users with minimum resources. Through its sheer force of collectively pooled imagination, it provides a potent example of the sorts of platforms of information exchange that foster the new forms of communal organisation that Michael Hardt and Antonio Negri term the 'Multitude', and which productively challenge conventional models of cultural invention and production. In this context, Burke raises questions about the implications of this broader shift for the design professions' business organisation, as well as their more general methodologies.

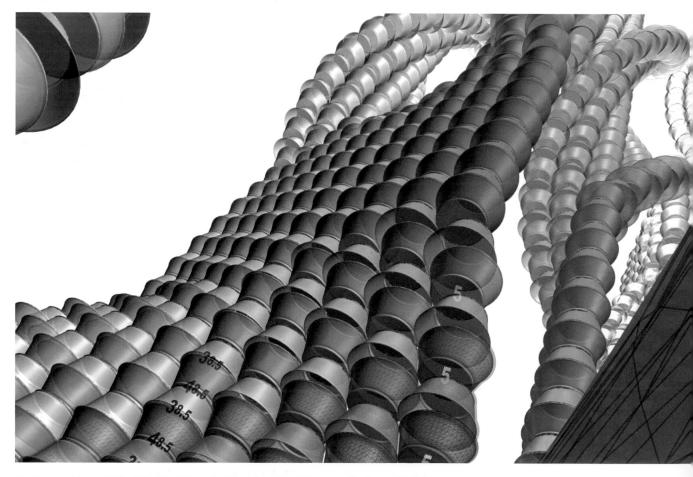

**Student work from 101 Arch Studio, Stripmall v2.0, University of California, Berkeley, September 2005**
Developmental studies of collective component intelligence based on simple local relationships. Students: Byron Chang, Christine Chang and Joseph Chieng.

*Nothing is easier than to admit in words the truth of the universal struggle for life, or more difficult – at least I have found it so – than constantly to bear this conclusion in mind.*

Charles Darwin, *On Natural Selection*[1]

Architecture is undergoing a radical transformation in the face of developing organisational imperatives resulting from an intense period of theoretical, technical and social co-evolution of the logics of networks and complexity. As a result, the status of design more generally is being deeply interrogated and requalified. Witnessing the progression from object to operation to organisation fuelled by complexity theory and advances in information technologies over the last decade, the potentials of metastructural architectures of organisation are now being explored by designers, as much as the potentials of a new architect. While it is true that we are undergoing a kind of network fever,[2] postcomplexity network logics offer a highly integrated philosophy of relational orders in an ecology of instrumental contextual registers that exceed the cultural/aesthetic interpretations of network thinking from the 1960s and 1970s by articulating a clear mathematical logic as well as material practice within its schema.

While architecture owes much to the precedents of the Metabolists, Archigram and New Babylon, today's network structures exceed the imperatives of architecture's visual/social regimes, instead looking past the singular object to the operational and structural continuums of dynamic organisations of massively distributed agents and resources, and the evolution of contextually responsive information ecologies.

At stake for architecture is the requalification of design as an act of negotiation, simultaneously more intrinsic and more extrinsic to the traditional notion of practice. That is to say, in many disciplines, as well as architecture, the relational logics that organise flows, that parse information, that allow interaction, be they biological, chemical, material or spatial, have moved from a model of external, or predefined, form as applied to matter, to an intrinsic model where form is the expression of the interaction and characteristics of the material intelligence that constitutes it.[3] Form, then, is not imbued or fixed; rather it must be encouraged and drawn forth through the expression of contextual, internal and material forces, and it is the negotiation between these factors that determines ultimate expression. Both extrinsic in that this thinking places the role of the designer in a meta-relationship to the object, instead working as a strategist and negotiator, organising networks of relationships to 'breed' a fitter species, and intrinsic in that the expressions of that negotiation are dependent on properties of material (molecular) organisation.[4] Hence the enthusiasm after complexity in the study of network logics over a broad range of disciplines as an activation of potentials embedded precisely within those organising relationships.

This material philosophy[5] now has the mathematical laws of small-world networks and power laws to corroborate and explain many natural and social phenomena. Duncan Watts

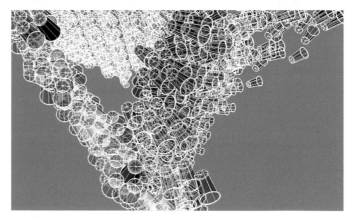

**Student work from 101 Arch Studio, Stripmall v2.0, University of California, Berkeley, September 2005**
Developmental studies of collective component intelligence based on simple local relationships. Students: Christian Olavesen, Alina Grobe and Andrew Dominitz.

**Anthony Burke and Eric Paulos, 180x120 installation, San Franciso MoMA Member Sessions Event, 24 October 2005**
Using 180 RFID tags to track and plot location over time, guests to this installation collectively construct a register of the event and the installation itself through building a history of movement throughout the space over 120 minutes. The projected histogram builds over time, revealing crowd intelligence, patterns of crowd distribution, zones of intensity and preferred locations as well as interaction with the screen itself. This installation was created by Anthony Burke and Eric Paulos with the assistance of Tom Jenkins and Karen Marcelo for an SFMoMA member sessions event held on 24 October 2005.

A tessellated paper screen embeds the anticipated histogram within the depth of the geometry of each tile unit. The overlay of projected real-time information updated every 60 seconds reveals the gap between forecast and reality.

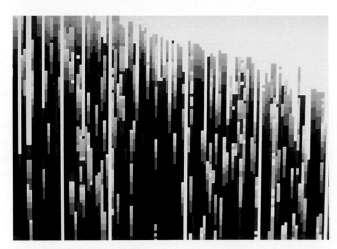

Screenshot of histogram build.

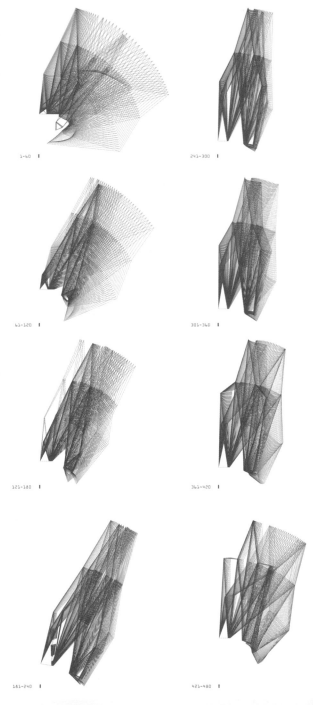

Laser-cut templates for the creation of each unique tile.

and Steven Strogatz summarise the potentials of small-world networks, stating in their ground-breaking paper 'Collective dynamics of "small-world" networks' for *Nature* magazine in 1998 that: 'Models of dynamic systems with small-world coupling display enhanced signal propagation speed, computational power, and synchronizability.'[6] That is to say, understanding how to recognise and utilise the dynamics and organisational structure of networks of coupled dynamic systems leads to vastly improved communications, intelligence and coordination within any system – social, technical or chemical. These relationships organise around both hierarchically clear (exogenic) and emergent (endogenic) structural logics that necessarily coexist in the development of complex systems and are most highly optimised in a state 'somewhere between these two extremes'.[7]

As the threshold of autonomous computational agents surfaces as an active constituent of both our design space and our environment, we are compelled to recognise the combined intelligence of the material environment and the virtual environment (or software agents) and to bring them into an information-rich design space. Negotiating the balance of design partners along these lines opens the potential of this active communal space for design, and capitalises on a collective systemic intelligence that embeds multiplicity (both/and) within the reformulation of the structural relationships of network performance, invoking entirely novel trajectories for material expression and spatial organisation in the process.

The shift in status of information itself also signals an imminent regime change for design, and it is both the currency and superfluity of information that enables these networked developments. According to Hans Christian von Baeyer,[8] all material systems can be understood as a function of their informational content, and reduced to the basic atom of information, the bit, with the qubit[9] extending this logic into the quantum universe. The structural logic that organises fluid informational molecules from qubits to feature-length movies and gives them meaning underpins a reconsideration of design practice, product and place in light of new orders of performance involving human, environmental and informational (artificial intelligence) collaborators. The challenge for architecture, then, is more social than technical. As the frame of reference around design is projected into an engaged and productive space of negotiation, an architecture mired in the cult of the object is unable to utilise the advantages of collective organisation and interconnection, preferring tidy distinctions and clear boundaries over protocols of exchange within deep networks.

### The Distributed Underground

Studies of the creation of information show not only a profoundly massive amount of data being produced every year, but that more than 550 times more data resides in the 'deepnets' and 'darknets' well below the radar of browsers and search engines than is visible in the surface net.[10]

A darknet is a private virtual network benignly equated to friend-to-friend networks or, in more provocative terms, the domain of the illicit file-sharing communities and home to the digital resistance. The term was coined in 2003 by Microsoft researchers who state that: 'The darknet is not a separate physical network but an application and protocol layer riding on existing networks.'[11] Darknets are networks limited to a select group of users through encryption and structural security measures paradoxically built around logics of extreme distribution and flexibility. Darknets, Deepnet and Dark Internet are terms that have arisen to articulate the balkanisation of information space into differing structural regimes responding to environmental parameters such as privacy, anonymity, community and security.[12] As the attorneys of the Hollywood studios and the recording industries continue to pursue legal action against the likes of BitTorrent[13] through targeting file indexes and traffic hubs, they continue to unwittingly push the pace of development for content distribution systems and cement attitudes of information freedom in the file-sharing public, sending the development of distributed structures and their supporting technologies on a trajectory aimed deeper and deeper underground. Rather than the democracy of information of the Internet, in Web 2.0[14] the vast majority of data will be dark.

In this light, many theorists believe the copyright wars we are in the midst of are the death throes of mass media as we have known it. The underlying architectures of networks no longer favour large companies with the infrastructure and equipment required to both create content and distribute it. More importantly, the operational understanding of distributed systems has become socially entrenched, so that to a whole generation of users, accessing distributed content is a fundamental right and simultaneously as pedestrian as email. File-sharing networks have grown to accommodate a generation of users where, as Clay Shirky describes, 'everyone is a media outlet ... There are no more consumers because in a world where an email address constitutes a media channel, we are all producers now.'[15]

While users now expect all content to be mutable, fundamentally a worldview of collective organisation and fully distributed content spread over contextually scalable networks rivals, if not replaces, the culture of the commercial monolith, constituting the conditions for a postconsumer mentality.[16] The development of distributed file-sharing structures over the last five years not only charts a sophistication of the advanced structural logic of network theory as it becomes instrumentalised, but mirrors a societal transfer of organisational logics from the stabile to the mobile. While we were downloading MP3s we were also trading paradigms.

### Activating Organizational Structures

*... centralized schemes work poorly for illegal object distribution because large, central servers are large single points of failure.*[17]

BitTorent creator Bram Cohen, as well as Freenet principals Ian Clark and Oskar Sandberg, quote from network theorists such as Barabasi (*Linked*)[18] as well as Watts and Strogatz ('*small-world' networks*), discussing the structural logics of small-world networks, power laws and superhubs that underpin the current metastructural preoccupations in design. The creation and success of these file-sharing peer-to-peer networks constitute some of the first implementations of advanced network theory springing from complexity studies at the Santa Fe Institute in the early 1990s to be instrumentalised in popular culture and simultaneously make Hollywood and the recording industry insanely anxious.

*Any new technology, any extension or amplification of human faculties when given material embodiment, tends to create a new environment.*

Marshall McLuhan[19]

The implications of network logics have already begun to reorganise the sciences and humanities, and architecture is no exception. If we look at architecture as a practice of spatial, material and, even, intellectual organisation then it is clear that the effects are potentially profound. But these patterns of organisation that we are now aware of in everything from beehives to movie stars (the popular game 'Six Degrees of Kevin Bacon', for instance) also challenge the current normative modes of architecture and raise questions and unique opportunities for this emerging generation of designers. The impact on the forms of practice, the nature of design and the nature of the spaces we design are open for exploration and reinvention as the current ties to representation, form and practice are unable to negotiate the complexity with which we work. So it is that we see new forms of practice emerging, sitting at the edge of traditional disciplines and existing between research and practice, as well as between disciplines. And, as the theory and implementation of postcomplexity organisational constructs mature, the implications are rapidly extending beyond the digital environments of information and communication systems to combinations of physical systems of sensors and ubiquitous computational and real-world agents.

In the late 1990s the US military responded to these conditions by announcing its broad-based Network-Centric Warfare (NCW) initiative intended to integrate all aspects of military operations and resources into a collectively intelligent force. Recognising the ineffectuality of large traditional military forces, the military has been pumping money into tactics and strategies that focus on information superiority. Through the networking of all information within the vast military complex, both active situational information as well as static (inventory, specifications and so on) data, the military hopes to regain the advantage in the field that it lost to small, nimble, semi-autonomous groups of loosely affiliated guerrilla cells spread across an unbounded and decentralised battlespace.

Through initiatives such as the Global Information Grid (GIG)[20] and a host of experiments in all aspects of C4ISR[21]

## The Self-Healing Minefield (SHM)

Among a sea of initiatives to operationalise network strategies within the US military, the 'self-healing minefield' (SHM) is one example of a generation of autonomous strategic and tactical systems under development. The project, sponsored by Advanced Technology Office (ATO) of the Defense Advanced Research Projects Agency (DARPA), began in June 2000 and was fully tested at Fort Leonard Wood, Missouri, in April 2003.

*The SHM is comprised of a system of Antitank Landmines (ATLs), each of which has mobility, RF communications, ranging, and distributed computation subsystems. Upon deployment, the ATLs autonomously assemble a totally ad hoc wireless network via their frequency hopping spread spectrum (FHSS) radios. This peer-to-peer network, which is logically flat and does not rely on any predefined routing, rapidly detects and adjusts when an ATL leaves or enters the network.*[22]

Activating the operational logics of networks, the SHM has the capacity to assess its own status and operate in one of three operational modes, 'gracefully' degrading over time and use. The aim of the SHM is to literally heal itself once munitions have been expended and nodes drop from the network by autonomously redistributing the field of mines to seal any breech. Literally, each individual mine is a 2-kilogram (4.4-pound), rocket-propelled node in a flat ad hoc network that recognises the location of all the other mines in the field through a continual monitoring over a frequency-hopping spread spectrum radio with the capacity to jump as far as 12 metres (39 feet) in any direction to ensure field integrity.

The activation of the field into a meshwork of mines that are able to organise and work in concert with each other is a small example of the potential of the Network-Centric Warfare once larger groups of multiple systems are linked. The intelligence of the system comes from the quality of the information gained from networking each node in a local informational context, or 'habitat', that allows 'high-quality situational awareness information and understanding'.

The Self-Healing Minefield, fully tested in 2003, both exemplifies the collective intelligence of a synchronous network of agents, and is one of the first active environmental applications of the theories of network logics within the US military's Network-Centric Warfare initiative.

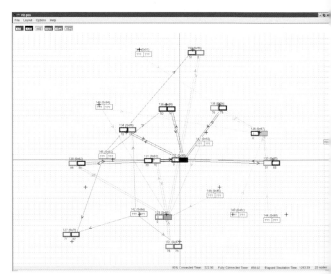

Screen capture demonstrating network connectivity and relative geolocation. Ground truth positions are shown by the crosses.

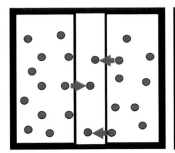 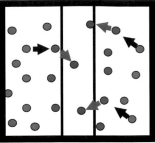 

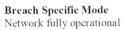

**Breach Specific Mode**
Network fully operational

**Nearest Neighbor Mode**
Network partially operational

**Random Mode**
Network inoperable

The multimodal healing algorithm allows for graceful performance degradation.

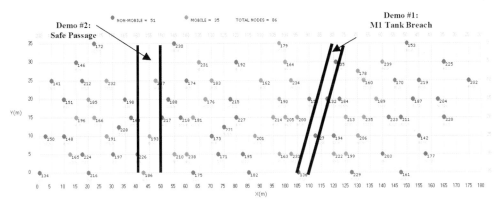

Node in flight

Node launch

Self-healing minefield mobile node test-hopping out of a ditch.

Location of the first two demonstrations relative to the viewing stand.

that bring network theory into network practice, the military is already testing a slew of distributed weapons, surveillance and overlaying information gathering, processing and analysis networks that are as physically active as they are informationally.

*In the Network-Centric Warfare (NCW) paradigm, battlespace agents autonomously perform selected tasks delegated by actors/shooters and decision-makers including controlling sensors. Network-Centric electronic warfare (NCEW) is the form of electronic combat used in NCW. Focus is placed on a network of interconnected, adapting systems that are capable of making choices about how to survive and achieve their design goals in a dynamic environment. ... The grids carry a flood of data and information among the entities that can be used to increase the tempo of operations. This flood will overwhelm human actors and decision-makers.*[23]

Embedded organisational intelligence takes over the day-to-day information gathering and processing while human interactions with these intelligent systems exist at the strategic level and humans become tuned to a higher-order structural and operational intelligence schema. As data breeds, or automatically assembles and constitutes new data, interaction with human actors is not only marginalised at the level of the field, but actually problematic. We are out of the immediate decision loop because our capacity to make large amounts of time for critical low-level decisions from vast arrays of interconnected factors is inadequate. As sensor devices and AI engines propagate in the fertile conditions of their own information ecology, human participation in networks of communication and decision-making has at an immediate level become categorically undesirable. Our networks are thinking for us.

## Native

*Another study in Nature, looking at the global network's growth dynamics of the Web, confirms the idea that the World Wide Web follows natural laws and can be studied as 'an ecology of knowledge'.*[24]

The power laws, small-world behaviours and superhubs of network theory, while applied to information and communication systems, were initially revealed not in information science, but through mathematics, biology and sociology. Structures of networks are based on mathematical laws, but biological and social systems exemplify these structures and formally describe the complex processes that capitalise on the evolutionary properties of a networked and collaborative intelligence.

As self-generating data frees itself from our control it could be said to go native, developing more complex informational ecologies and necessarily changing our interaction with it. Technically we become unencumbered by the need to create the raw material that our sensors now do for us, and as negotiator/designers we are motivated to organise and edit as

a creative act. Like botanists, as information ecologies flower we will trim (delete) unproductive or overly productive branches of data and splice and graft (copy/paste/hyperlink) streams of information to cultivate new hybrid species (threads). As data goes native, we can speculate on the possibilities of cultivating large crops of information types for mass consumption (for example, popular music) as well as lavish and manicured parcels of highly articulate but private or limited gardens of code (such as private banking). Finally, we can consider the extremes of truly wild data, venturing into those forests for recreation or prospecting.[25]

The act of design strategically broadens and we are not only working in a context of data, but with data as a partner. The ability to operate in this medium will depend on the intelligence of the tools we can create and the partnerships with our software intelligences that can be cultivated. Developing and maturing relationships with a larger computational intelligence in this context is highly likely, and it is entirely possible that given the growth of AI, practices will develop their digital personas as an enduring set of design processes and preferences that represent a collective of like-minded designers. This highly 'practice-specific' software, trained over an extended period, ultimately embodies an evolved ethos of design amounting to a collective and directed design intelligence. Again, this is to some degree already in place with dumb software, where a design office will develop way of working with it that suits them, collecting information that is continually used or referred to, creating their own hacks and patches and essentially activating collective intelligence in a fairly benign way. Similarly, the nature of traditional disciplinary discrete practice is challenged, as what could be thought of as intellectual property of one discipline or another (say, architecture or engineering) is transformed into a common project space and with it the space of a design ethos rather than a disciplinary speciality.

*The surface properties of a living being were controlled by the inside, what is visible by what is hidden. Form, attributes and behavior all became expressions of organization.*[26]

Similarly forecast is the change in the nature of our relationship to the processes and tools we develop and use and consequently, the expression of those tools and processes in the generation of form. The negotiation between architect and software (intelligent or routine) both disempowers the architect from the sole genius role and empowers him or her through the integration of information and a continually evolving range of intelligent computationally derived generative techniques. The architect as director essentially stages the project, guiding final formal outcomes as a product of intrinsic processes engendered from the collective power of the informational environment that surrounds the design space. Form from within is shaped, tested and reshaped, built on a series of related informational (molecular) constraints and the possibilities of their material and organisational expression.

As the environments we design are themselves becoming intelligent, they require something more like an ongoing relationship to negotiate or manage their evolution over a much-extended period. Integrating aware surfaces, and computational power, designers will come to approach project spaces the same way they approach software, installing updates, tweaks and working out bugs periodically while adjusting to new environmental parameters, entailing ongoing monitoring and analysis. Ultimately, 'patching' and 'hacking' environmental systems will become a new strain within the purview of the evolved discipline and its new architects.

Architecture in this context can be seen not as the production of built products, but the development of ideas and methods that result in vectors of research marked by built moments. In this sense, practice itself becomes a locus of design where formal inconclusions or delay are not a temporary moment before reaching some ideal architecture or final form, but rather an ideal state in and of itself. It is the goal: to remain open, responsive and fluid, to negotiate and renegotiate as new contextual pressures become apparent; to imagine practice as a project within which projects may be built but are never complete, but are always in a state of evolution.

*Information wants to be free.*[27]

As a generation of users executing a mastery over media we expect to engage with a two-way interactivity completely unlike unidirectional traditional media and architecture, where assembly and organisation create meaning, forecasting the transformation of the figure of the architect necessarily along the lines of the negotiator. Design becomes the ability to activate patterns and relationships and to construct intelligent tools. The architect becomes a builder of spatial contracts, organising computational agents towards specific performative goals achieved through designing the relational matrix of the design space. The role of the architect is to arrange these agents into a hierarchy of prominence, to foster a community of intelligent agents to work towards sympathetic goals through mediation of the protocols determining the flows of highly networked information. The transfer of the architect's role requires trading in the romance of form as an end point for the courage to embrace a distributed and expansively operational disciplinary trajectory of collaborative intelligence within a network-centric framework. ∆

**Notes**
1. Charles Darwin, *On Natural Selection*, Penguin Books (New York), 2004, p 1; extract taken from *On the Origin of Species*, first published in 1859.
2. Mark Wigley, 'Network Fever', in *Grey Room 4*, MIT Press (Cambridge, MA), 2001.
3. Manuel DeLanda has written extensively on this philosophical framework: see Manuel DeLanda, *A Thousand Years of Non-Linear History*, Zone Books (New York), 1997. See also Ludwig Von Bertalanffy, *General Systems Theory: Foundations, Development, Applications*, George Braziller (New York), 1969, as a precursor to an integrated organisational schema overlaying many disciplines, most notably with regard to the effects on morphology within mathematics and biology.
4. Ibid.
5. This materialist philosophy has been articulated through a philosophical trajectory that includes Spinoza, Deleuze and DeLanda among others.
6. Duncan J Watts and Steven H Strogatz, 'Collective dynamics of "small-world" networks', *Nature*, Vol 393, 4 June 1998, p 440.
7. Ibid.
8. See Hans Christian Von Baeyer, *Information: The New Language of Science*, Harvard University Press (Cambridge, MA), 2003.
9. A qubit is a quantum unit of information – 'it is a concept not a thing. Where a bit can have the value of zero *or* one, a qubit is defined as a quantum superposition of zero *and* one.' From Christian Von Bayer, op cit, pp 183–4.
10. Peter Lyman and Hal Varian, 'How much information 2003?', SIMS, University of California, Berkeley, c 2004. http://sims.berkeley.edu:8000/research/projects/how-much-info-2003/.
11. Peter Biddle, Paul England, Marcus Peinado and Bryan Willman, 'The Darknet and the Future of Content Distribution', Microsoft Corporation, http://msl1.mit.edu/ESD10/docs/darknet5.pdf.
12. Briefly, the deepnet holds file locations on the public World Wide Web that are inaccessible to conventional search engines, and the dark Internet is a network of computers inaccessible to the World Wide Web. According to one study the amount of information contained in the deepnet is 550 times greater than the surface net, in the words of the Microsoft researchers who coined the phrase.
13. BitTorrent is a peer-to-peer file transfer protocol created by Bram Cohen in 2001. For more on BitTorrent see www.bittorrent.com.
14. The next-generation Internet, reported widely as Web 2.0, will feature context-sensitive information capabilities and predictive information through linking many different sources of information based on user histories and profiles.
15. 'RIP Consumer, 1900–1999'; http://www.shirky.com/writings/consumer.html.
16. Ibid.
17. Biddle, England, Peinado and Willman, op cit.
18. Albert-László Barabási, *Linked: The New Science of Networks*, Perseus Publishing (Cambridge, MA), 2002.
19. Marshall McLuhan, 'The relation of Environment to Anti-Environment', in Eric McLuhan and W Terrence Gordon (eds), *Marshall McLuhan, the Unbound project (04)*, Ginko Press (Corte Madera, CA), 2005, p 6.
20. See 2002 Milcom Proceedings, 'Global Information Grid – Enabling Transformation Through 21st-Century Communications', copyright 2002, IEEE (IEEE Copyrights manager, NJ) 2002.
21. C4ISR: command, control, communications, computers, intelligence, surveillance and reconnaissance.
22. Glenn Rolader, John Rogers and Jad Batteh, 'Self-healing minefields', in Raja Surech (ed), *Battlespace Digitization and Network-Centric Systems IV*, Proceedings of SPIE, Vol 5441, SPIE (Bellingham, WA), 2004.
23. John C Sciortino Jr, James F Smith III, Behzad Kamgar-Parsi and CDR Randall Franciose, 'Implementation of battlespace agents for network-centric electronic warfare', in Raja Suresh (ed), *Battlespace Digitization and Network-Centric Warfare*, Proceedings of SPIE Vol 4396, 2001.
24. Alan Boyle, 'Measuring the Web's "diameter"', http://www.msnbc.com/news/309085.asp?cp1=1.
25. 'The ecology of ideas' is elegantly discussed as a social/cultural phenomenon by Pierre Lévy in 'Towards a language of collective intelligence', in Christine Schopf and Gerfried Stocker (eds), *Code: The Language of Our Time*, Hatje Cantz (Ostfildern, Germany), 2003.
26. François Jacob, *The Logic of Life: A History of Heredity*, Vintage Books (New York), 1973.
27. From R Polk Wagner, 'Information wants to be free: Intellectual Property and the mythologies of control', *Columbia Law Review*, Vol 103: 995, p 999. (http://www.law.upenn.edu/polk/wagner.control.pdf). Though it has clearly taken on a life of its own, most people attribute the origins of the phrase to Stewart Brand: see Stewart Brand, *The Media Lab: Inventing the Future at MIT*, Penguin, reprint edition, 1988.

# Working with Wiki, by Design

**Andrew Burrow** and **Jane Burry** explain the use of online platforms, such as wiki, employed
by the Spatial Information Architecture Laboratory (SIAL) at RMIT University in Melbourne. As
they demonstrate, these platforms enable projects whose participants span the globe, in turn
situating SIAL within an internationally distributed design research network incorporating
diverse forms of expertise. This includes the academic research under way at SIAL, much of
which is done collaboratively with various other design and research entities, as well as the
international work of SIAL's director Mark Burry, who has been developing innovative design
and fabrication methods for the completion of Gaudí's complex proposal for the Sagrada
Família church. SIAL's wiki platform collapses geographic and temporal distance to allow
geographically dispersed agents to collaborate in unprecedented ways, integrating widely
diverse sets of knowledge into the design process.

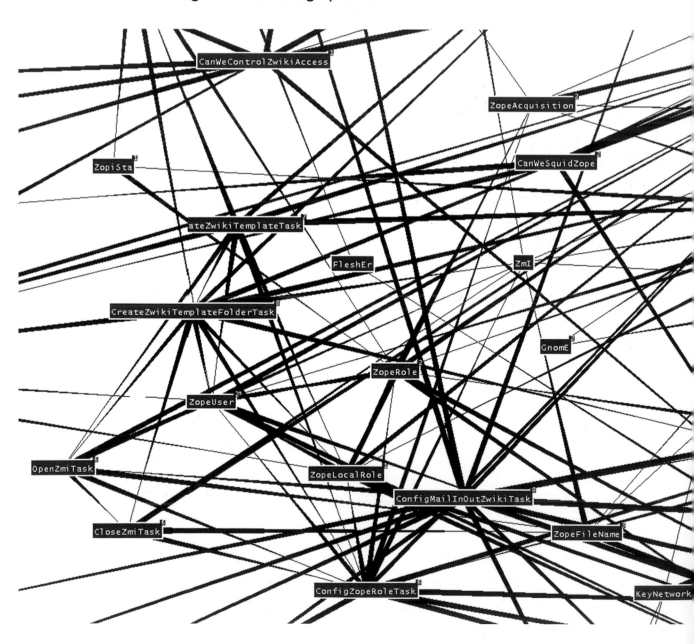

The existence of the World Wide Web has, from a current vantage point, an extraordinarily short history. The web came into existence at CERN only in the early 1990s. But its conceptual history stretches back much further than the technology necessary to realise it.[1] One of the pressing problems it has been seen to address, 'information overload', was so named only in 1970[2] but, as a very apparent widespread condition in all institutions in society, it too had been driving the development of the hypertext systems we now embrace from earlier times. Long-distance cooperative and collaborative work involving multiple contributing correspondents in multilateral communication also has a much longer history than the web.[3] Historically, we can see the evidence in linear activities and where there is a request for information and an instruction or piece of information is sent in response; and also in the wonderful collections of letters from the past in which creative souls test and share ideas with their contemporaries.

Architects and designers in academia leapt at the opportunity to experiment in collaborating through electronic link-ups before the establishment of the web. In 1988 computer-supported cooperative work was a new but already wide-ranging technical and sociological research field. From that time on university-based designers started to establish 'virtual design studios.'[4] In the late 1980s and early 1990s electronic mail was hailed as the greatest of networking tools, not as yet a channel of signal-drowning noise. In the late 1990s electronic mail was at last becoming mainstream outside academic environments.

Hence it was email that acted as the site for feverish creative exchange on a number of projects at the time, among them a project that drew together a group of individuals from many organisations in architecture, mathematics, programming, structural engineering, electronic engineering, ballistics, pneumatics and more, distributed almost evenly around the globe. This was dECOi's Aegis hyposurface project, a risk-taking experiment not only in inventive and artistic terms but in its exploration of a wholly new type of creative practice underpinned by computer-supported communication. Aegis is the competition-winning kinetic interactive wall designed as an art installation for the entrance to the Hippodrome theatre in Birmingham, then in design.[5] The design phases from original competition entry to full-size working prototype spanned the period from late 1998 to 2001. The diverse and dispersed nature of the team was as novel as its objectives. It came together from a range of academic institutions, architecture and engineering practices, and manufacturing-based design. The roles were new and negotiated, and fitted no familiar artistic, architectural,

industrial design or engineering pattern for design or realisation. Electronic mail was the default medium of communication and, in the absence of a more formal system of knowledge capture and management, the main common resource for the project.

Informal observation of the communication throughout this project – the challenges of working and creating in a team where many of the contributors never met face to face, had to negotiate their roles with different disciplinary foci, had quite different levels of familiarity with different media of communication from computer code to animation and even ascribed different meanings to the same term – led afterwards to an Australian Research Council grant application by universities to investigate tools to support design collaboration.

Clearly, a shared democratic web-based communication environment should be able to improve life, leading to a world where project information accumulates and is searchable, but also perhaps to a world that is a partially 'proactive' environment that brings together related topics and documents, unobtrusively contextualising and raising participants' awareness of what has gone before. Wiki presents itself as 'the simplest online database that could possibly work' (as defined by Ward Cunningham, the original creator). Already, as we write, a world without Wikipedia[6] seems unimaginable. It is perhaps the closest thing in existence to HG Wells' vision of an encyclopaedic, cross-referenced 'shared brain'. Memex is now real. Coincidentally, and perhaps fortuitously for us, Wikipedia came into existence in January 2001, the month the research proposal for investigating tools to support communication in design collaboration was submitted.

This research was carried out in the Spatial Information Architecture Laboratory (SIAL), a centre set up at RMIT University in 2001 to research innovation in the practice of design that brings together many disciplines and explores the appropriation of new technologies and techniques across discipline lines to put them to new use. It is led by Mark Burry, whose application of parametric design using aeronautical software to the modelling of Gaudí's Sagrada Família church has been an exemplar of the potential in this way of working. It has a broad research base, ranging from space as information (design of virtual spaces for interaction, communication and presentation of complex system information) to information as space (exploring new ways of modelling and communicating design information for construction and fabrication, and experimental affective technique). With a particular emphasis on the nexus between research, practice and education (rather than simply any two of these) the communication network supporting any of the

**Andrew Burrow, Wiki map: detail of the network**
Each node is labelled with the name of the page it represents; each edge represents a link between two pages, directed from the text of a page to a referenced page. The proximity of pages is measured in links; if you pass through many pages in tracing the links from one page to another they are distant and might be expected to have only distantly related content.

projects can become very involved, and there are many synergies between different research projects. There is a sizable and growing postgraduate community.

Wiki is a series of linked pages that is generally open to all who wish to contribute and edit. While writing one page it is simple to create links to new, related pages. It is a lattice rather than tree structure, which means it supports the most lateral of links. Through the page names and links the hypertext has a tacit structure. It builds, and provides access to, a project history and simultaneously generates a largely self-organising social or community-of-interest map. Particular areas or clusters within the wiki are known as gardens and editing of the page structure or edification of the content and presentation is referred to, charmingly, as wiki gardening.

Since 2002 we have experimented with the use of wiki to support this growing community and provide an online

communication and networking environment for all activities from multidisciplinary undergraduate studios and electives to collaborative research projects with practices and government organisations, and working together on projects such as the Sagrada Família church where the team is distributed internationally. For two in every six to eight weeks, Mark is based on site at the church in Barcelona while other members of SIAL continue to work on the project in Australia. The wiki is a vital forum for sharing meetings, making decisions as events occur on site and discussing responses or models being prepared in Melbourne. The pages can easily be organised around particular projects within the building, and particular site visits, issues and collaborators. A single page might be a collection of images and comments (including hand sketches) to elucidate a particular issue.

A garden is developed within the wiki for each undergraduate studio or elective and individual students cultivate their own cluster of pages, recording and presenting their work week by week. This has been a particularly simple and valuable way to bring students together in multidisciplinary groups. It is a collective environment for studio reviews where students can both upload images as html and attach related files. The graphical interface throughout each garden or cluster of pages may be customised to reflect the particular flavour and preoccupations of that studio. The students' work is closely linked to their studio page but they can navigate out more widely and continuously review work in other courses. One page in a student's own collection of linked pages within an undergraduate design studio is shown on the left. Postgraduate students use wiki and often need the potential for restricted access rights while also using open gardens for sharing and discussion. SIAL researchers have had a series of design collaborations with architects, engineers, artists and other organisations such as city councils – for instance, the City Sounds projects I and II, which are interactive-game type environments for sampling, commenting on and ultimately finding information to help ameliorate noise issues within the city; or research with Arup into automation of the complex documentation of the London Australian War Memorial (http://www.sial.rmit.edu.au/Projects/City_Sounds.php, http://www.sial.rmit.edu.au/Projects/Australian_War_Memorial.php). For the last year, this commitment to the triangle of research, practice and teaching has been strengthened through the embedded-practice postgraduate programme. A cohort of postgraduate students is now based within innovative architecture and engineering practices in Australia researching new modes of practice from within a particular practice context. Here they undertake projects and have close supervision by, and interaction with, members of the practice. They return to the university weekly for academic supervision and group seminars, and at least twice a year for symposia involving the practice supervisors and collaborators, students and academics. This subnetwork, which links SIAL, the practices and their collaborators and the wider university

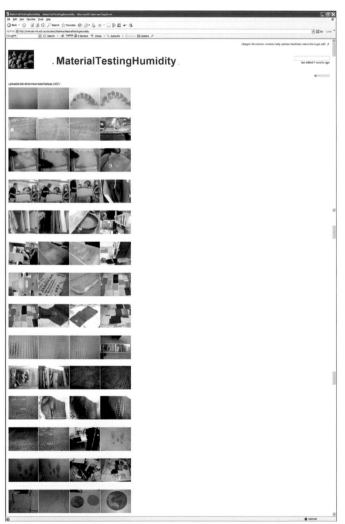

**RMIT upper pool architecture and industrial design studio, AIR, 2005**
This is a page from an undergraduate group's own 'garden' within the AIR studio 'garden', within a large open wiki called TheHive. This page has been used to compile thumbnail images recording a series of experiments exposing a range of materials to different humidity conditions as part of the design of a humidity-experience centre.

community, is another example of how wiki provides a shared online environment accessible from both within and without the immediate organisation.

The basis of the specific research into wiki within SIAL is to find the most appropriate ways of enhancing its characteristic openness while providing some differentiation between the levels of access and types of page within the wiki. There is a need for selective exposure while new ideas are nurtured and sometimes inevitable confidentiality for third parties. Documents can change their roles over their lives. The network diagrams (right) illustrate a proposed mercantile model of offering or progressively publishing pages to a wider, more inclusive group which can operate very simply within the existing syntax for creating links. The poetry here is in maintaining the brush-stroke simplicity of constructing a strong usable set of documents without interrupting the flow of communication, allowing the network to remain 'self-organising'. This means making the interface even simpler to use and more graphic in revealing its structure.

Within SIAL we have found that the simplicity, openness and hyperlink structure give hypertext the robustness to be the communication and recording medium of choice, one that is warmly embraced and personalised, and provides the complex and defining network of links throughout the organisation. Of course, for day-to-day communication it does not displace phone, text, instant messaging or email although it can be linked to log these.

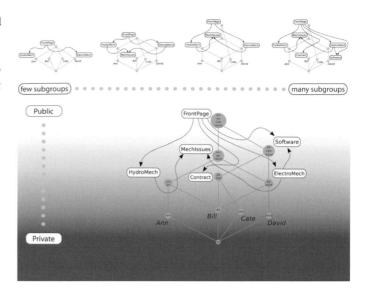

**Andrew Burrow, Diagram of the lattice-structured wiki**
The development of subgroups within a project is illustrated by a sequence of diagrams. Over time, pages are added to a wiki, represented by the curved nodes and edges. In this example four participants working on four aspects of a collaborative design project – fluid mechanics, electronics, software and contract details – access the pages and form subgroups represented by the circular nodes in the underlying lattice.

Acknowledging that there is little in communication that is analogous to the transfer of information between machines, we need nevertheless to capture and revisit much that transpires in our transactions, and often this is a collective need. This is achieved with little proscription through the invention of hyperlinks in the wiki, which seems to support communication between people without threatening all that is performative in the act. Hyperlinked, the *art* of communication and the *art* of design still appear to have the potential to remain closely intertwined. ⚙

**Notes**
1. In 1937, HG Wells expressed the view that global indexing and access to information were lagging behind other technology-supported activities and he provided a vision of a shared brain-like resource in the future. Vannevar Bush wrote about Memex in 1945 and Doug Englebart protyped oNLineSytem (NLS) in the 1960s.
2. The term was coined in Alvin Toffler, *Future Shock*, Random House (New York), 1970.
3. The compilation of the *Oxford English Dictionary* in the 19th century is a prime and well-known example. It was to some extent a line management process with a one-directional flow of contributions from community volunteers who provided word meanings, and how the words were used in literature, to a central office where they could be catalogued and cross-referenced. For a concise history: http://en.wikipedia.org/wiki/OED.
4. See Nancy Cheng's presentation on the history of a virtual design studio from 1992 to 2000:
http://darkwing.uoregon.edu/~design/nywc/vds99/HTML/v01.html.
5. Mark Goulthorpe, 'Aegis Hyposurface: Autoplastic to Alloplastic' in *AD Hypersurface Architecture II*, Vol 69, 9–10 (Academy Editions), 1999, pp 60–5.
6. For the history of Wikipedia: http://en.wikipedia.org/wiki/Wikipedia.

Text © 2006 John Wiley & Sons Ltd. Images: p 96 © Andrew Burrow; p 98 © Jane Burry; p 99(b) © Mark Burry and Foo Chin Sung, SIAL; p 99(t) © Andrew Burrow and Dominik Holzer, SIAL

This schematic diagram of the Spatial Information Architecture Laboratory (SIAL) organisation shows the principal streams, activities and partnerships as overlapping pinwheels. All these areas and their many individual participants share the wiki as a network for communication and accumulated project knowledge. There are project-specific and subcommunity-specific clusters within it, but the links also span these clusters.

# Computational Intelligence: The Grid as a Post-Human Network

Research and design collaborative **EZCT Architecture & Design Research** has adopted grid computing to produce a series of furniture systems and other small-scale prototypes using genetic algorithms in combination with automated fabrication technologies. Here, cofounder **Philippe Morel** relates this design practice to the broader technical and social implications of various grid-computing projects, such as the online organisation Folding@Home, which utilises grid computing and distributed communities for the production and exchange of postindustrial knowledge. He argues that these 'knowledge farms' which create an 'ambient factory', are perhaps the ultimate form of social-economic production, transforming not only the evolution of design but of the communities that produce and eventually consume its products.

*Indeed, today, it has sadly become very fashionable to reject, in an obscurantist way, many more things in the subconscious than is necessary: it is much nicer to adore the 'primitives' and to note, happily, a 'bankruptcy of the rationalist mind' ... than to realize, once and for all, without equivocation, that the age of physics, far from becoming extinct, is just beginning!*

Arno Schmidt, *Calculus I.*[1]

*The scientific man is the ulterior development of the artistic man.*
Friedrich Nietzsche, *Human, All Too Human*[2]

### 'Distributed' Paradigm

During the past five years, most of my (post-) 'critical-political time' has been spent dealing with a new idea of collective intelligence that replaces the one implicitly defined, a century ago, by Gabriel Tarde[3] or, explicitly, 10 years ago, by Pierre Lévy.[4] This intelligence first evolved from communication networks ranging from the newspaper to the telephone, the fax to the Internet. Today, it finds its fullest expression in grid computing, the distributed computing paradigm *par excellence*. Grid computing is a protocol for linking discrete but geographically dispersed machines into a distributed parallel processing network. Grid computation has given rise to a distributed computational intelligence that renders the classical concept of singular and autonomous intelligence obsolete.

As important as the technology itself are the consequences of this phenomenon, namely the rise of a new kind of people – geographically isolated scientific farmers who exchange their postpolitical concepts in symposia[5] – and the rise of a posturban environment that I call the 'Ambient Factory'. What are the constituents of this factory? An early example, SETI@home, participated in deciphering extraterrestrial radio signals for signs of extraterrestrial intelligence. And this experiment has recently been transformed into a new model of industrial production with projects such as Folding@Home, Evolutionary@Home, XPulsar@Home, Fightaids@Home,

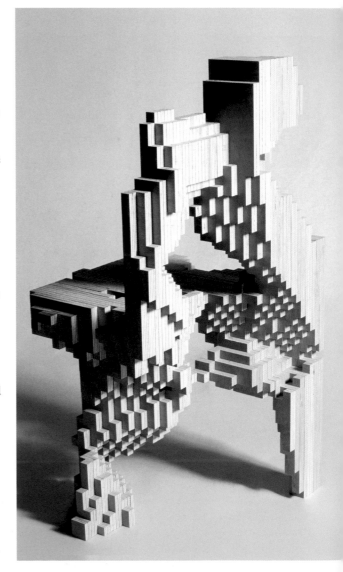

Chair 'Model T1-M', after 860 generations (86,000 structural evaluations).

Genome@Home, Models@Home and HIWTNI (Home is where the network is).[6] All these examples of grid computing use the downtime of geographically dispersed PCs (at the moment often running as screensavers, but there is no doubt that computation power per se will become a global market – take, for example, the polluting rights market and the recently created Powernext Carbon)[7] to process the immense amounts of data involved in investigating a scientific research problem. Through a home PC, which becomes a piece of e-laboratory equipment, any user therefore participates in a community of scientists and nonscientists in producing knowledge. This effectively creates a carpet constructed of autonomous but interconnected 'farms': computer farms, energy farms and so on. The term 'farm' may seem anachronistic, but it is appropriate because it connotes the sorts of new living practices these networks produce.

The questions such projects raise for (a-)spatial and (a-)social organisations of production for the present are as significant as Ludwig Hilberseimer's recognition of the electrical power grid in 1955 as 'the real force toward [urban] decentralization', since 'even the smallest settlement can be supplied with water, electricity, heat and light'.[8] Today, grid-computing networks not only allow the multitudes to communicate and to give an existence to the 'world brain', they allow computers to communicate in autonomous ways as a pure infrastructure that is at once global, abstract and standardised. This infrastructure allows a new kind of distributed computational and linguistic production, revealing what previously was called human production[9] as what it truly was all along: reproduction. Indeed, because of the growing complexity of all production (for example, in biotechnology, material science, pharmaceutics and computer sciences), all that is left for human labour is conceptual work. Everything else, in any field, is done by computers or numerically controlled machines.

### 'Quantitative' Shift

Why use ideas of industrial production, post-human networks or disappearing cities in reference to bionetworks and the multitude? Contemporary production seems to be driven by scientific rather than social forces. If so, understanding science means understanding real characteristics of our civilisation driven by 'quantitative concepts' such as numbers, statistics, approximation tools and methods, and mathematical precision. Quantity sounds abstract if, in the field of architecture, we consider Hilberseimer's diagram *H Bomb on Chicago*, dated 1946, but it also appears as a very practical concept if we listen to Max Planck's comment on the same nuclear power problem (1947): 'An appropriate calculation has shown that the quantity of energy liberated in this way in a cubic meter of uranium oxide pulverized in a hundredth of a second would be enough to raise a load of a billion metric tons to a height of some 18,000 meters. Such a quantity of energy could replace the combined production of all the world's most powerful plants for a good many years.'[10]

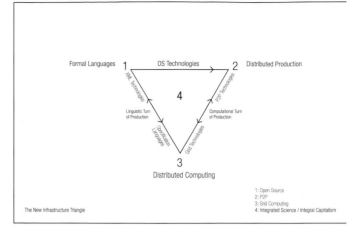

The New Infrastructure Triangle

1: Open Source
2: P2P
3: Grid Computing
4: Integrated Science / Integral Capitalism

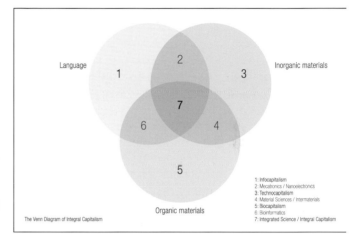

The Venn Diagram of Integral Capitalism

1: Infocapitalism
2: Mecatronics / Nanoelectronics
3: Technocapitalism
4: Material Sciences / Intermaterials
5: Biocapitalism
6: Bioinformatics
7: Integrated Science / Integral Capitalism

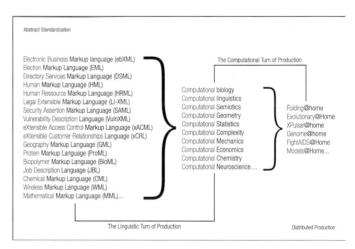

**Philippe Morel/EZCT Architecture & Design Research, Integral capitalism diagrams, from 'The Integral Capitalism', Philippe Morel Masters thesis, 2001–02**
The diagrams are part of a global analysis of contemporary science-based capitalism – through the linguistic/computational turn of contemporary production – developed by Philippe Morel over the past four and a half years. This study insists on the merging of three inseparable forms of capitalisms (infocapitalism, technocapitalism and biocapitalism) into an integrative economy: the Integral Capitalism. The study has to be considered as a post-Koolhaas (as well as postSassen) analysis of globalisation.

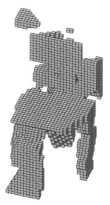

**EZCT Architecture & Design Research with Hatem Hamda and Marc Schoenauer, Studies on optimisation: computational chair design using genetic algorithms, 2004**
The 'Bolivar' model is evaluated for a multiple load strategy (it is always stable, whatever way the seat is positioned). This model (prototype and drawings) is part of the Centre Pompidou Architecture Collection.

Here, quantity is a concrete problem, as concrete as Robert Musil's definition of the traditional newspaper – 'filled with a measureless opacity' that 'goes far beyond the intellectual capacity of a Leibniz'[11] – a definition often envisioned for our contemporary information overload. In this respect, thinking about collective intelligence means thinking about the way it works and the way problems are solved. Quantitative questions in fact pose their problems and their solutions simultaneously. Algorithms solve searching problems, peer-to-peer storage problems, open-source collaborative practices' problems[12] and open technologies standardisation and communication problems. An answer to a technological problem is always a technological answer. Then, what is grid computing if not an appropriation, for industrial purpose,[13] of a new kind of productive paradigm? Is not SETI@home, which processes each year the equivalent of 400,000 years of computing time by a single processor, the new paradigm for industrial production, for 'collaborative computational practice' in any field, including architecture? It seems that corporations have already answered positively to this with their employment of the SETI@home model,[14] and I believe that grid computing is the next step for collective intelligence – an infrastructure-based computational intelligence.

## Tools and Concepts

The integration of concepts like distributed partial machine intelligence within the design process is an integral component of EZCT Architecture & Design Research's work. However, the practice not only refers to ideas of technology and science in their analyses of technology, but makes use of them. Architects should not metaphorically depict technology but use it, in a flat model, beyond any representation. Finally, because EZCT is part of the multitudes whose work concerns the 'ultimate production of human imagination' – that is, concepts – the practice also builds proofs for these concepts a design projects constructed through computers and programming languages.

For example, the practice has recently moved towards a grid model of design conceptualisation and production, extending its long-standing use of Mathematica, software normally oriented towards scientific communities, as a design tool, by using its grid-computing variant. GridMathematica leads to more efficient collaborative practice while alleviating the constraints of a single computer's calculation power. Its use has allowed EZCT to reinforce its long-term collaboration with physicist Bruno Autin (author of the Geometrica software package, formerly of CERN) and mathematician Maryvonne Teissier (Paris VII University). Of course, GridMathematica is not the only way to achieve distributed computing. During the summer of 2004, EZCT led a project wherein a series of chairs were computed using genetic algorithms for optimisation using a cluster of 12 computers from the École Polytechnique in Paris. They were controlled by Hatem Hamda, from a geographically distinct lab (INRIA), using a Linux platform and open-source libraries and software including Evolving Objects (an evolutionary computation library) and xd3d (a scientific visualisation tool). In this process, first a human collaborative practice was evidently implied in the previous development of the open-source libraries, software and so on, and second a computational and 'post-human' collaborative practice became the paradigm since a very limited number of people were able to appropriate a vast amount of computational resources.

Thus we should not underestimate the fact that collaborative practice does not necessarily mean a human collaborative practice, and take into account newly emerging concepts; for example, that of productive autonomy. **Δ**

**EZCT Architecture & Design Research with Hatem Hamda and Marc Schoenauer, Studies on optimisation: computational chair design using genetic algorithms, 2004**
Data analysis, 'Bolivar' model, Mathematica drawings. Because the data was structured for mutations and evaluation via finite element methods, it needed to be rearranged for fabrication. Mathematica was therefore used for writing different algorithms in order to ease pricing, cutting and assembling. The drawings are part of the Centre Pompidou Architecture Collection.

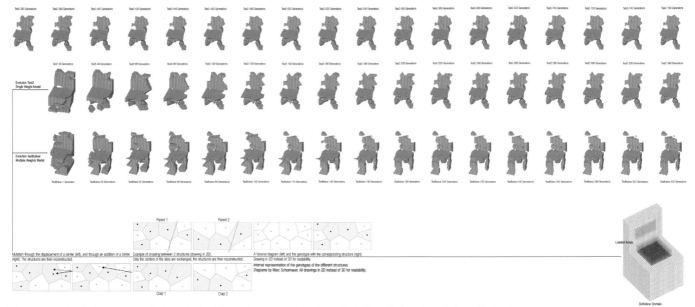

The process sheet shows seven chairs optimised through a mono-objective optimisation strategy, two chairs optimised through a multi-objectives strategy, and the optimisation process for Model 'Test2'. The sheet shows the crossing-over internal representation based on Voronoi diagrams. This high-level representation strategy, developed by Marc Schoenauer, allows for a better correspondence between the genotype representation and the phenotype of the real chairs.

Preliminary structural studies for a lounging chair (unrealised).

## Notes

1. Arno Schmidt, 'Calculus I' (Berechnungen I), in *Texte und Zeichen*, No 1, 15 January 1955, reprinted in Rosen & Porree, Stahlberg (Karlsruhe), 1959.
2. Friedrich Nietzsche, *Human, All Too Human: A Book for Free Spirits (Menschliches, Allzumenschliches. Ein Buch für freie Geister)*, trans Marion Faber and Stephen Lehmann, Penguin Classics (London), 1994.
3. Gabriel Tarde, *Les lois de l'imitation: étude sociologique*, F Alcan (Paris), 1890.
4. Pierre Lévy, *Collective Intelligence: Mankind's Emerging World in Cyberspace*, Perseus Books Group (New York), 1997.
5. Those who are not scientists, who are, by implication, in marketing or business, exchange their ideas in trade shows or technology conferences, places where, following Nietzsche's sublime prediction, our whole civilisation affords 'buying or selling as a luxury of our sensibility'. Friedrich Nietzsche, *The Gay Science (La Gaya Scienza)*, 1882.
6. I used this HIWTNI abbreviation, developed by the McKinsey quarterly, in my work 'Living in the Ice Age' (2001–02), which is an explicit theorisation of what I only evoke in the present article.
7. Due to the Kyoto Protocol, companies and countries now trade polluting rights on this dedicated marketplace (Powernext Carbon).
8. Ludwig Hilberseimer, *The Nature of Cities*, Paul Theobald (Chicago, IL), 1955. The Ambient Factory concept actualises not only Hilberseimer's but also Mies' parallel comment: 'There are no cities, in fact, any more. It goes on like a forest. That is the reason why we cannot have the old cities anymore; that is gone forever, planned cities and so on. We should think about the means that we have to live in a jungle, and maybe we do well with that.' Ludwig Mies van der Rohe, Interview with J Peter, in Phyllis Lambert (ed), *Mies in America*, CCA, Whitney Museum & Harry N Abrams (New York), 2001.

9. The classical one theorised by Adam Smith then Karl Marx.
10. Max Planck, 'The Meaning and Limits of Science', 1947. Lecture given at the Harnack-Haus, Berlin-Dahlem.
11. Robert Musil, *The Man Without Qualities (Der Mann ohne Eigenschaften)*, first edition Rowohlt Verlag, Hamburg, 1930.
12. Open source is an answer from contemporary capitalism to itself: 'I've worked for IBM in Linux for more than six years, and it has become big business for us, it's a fundamental part of IBM's business. We're not into Linux and open source because it's cool. It's nice that it's cool, but it's good business. We're making billions.' Daniel Frye, 'From Open Source Software to Open Technology: How a Phenomenon is Turning Into an Exciting New Industry', InnoTech Conference, Portland, Oregon, 9 March 2005.
13. Keep in mind that everything is industrial – it is pharmaceutics, high-energy physics experiments, education, and so on – and that some distinctions between laboratories on one side and transnational corporations on the other do not really hold any more.
14. Arcelor or AstraZeneca: 'Large-scale clusters allow us to manage and share computing resources across the entire Discovery Function, accelerating drug discovery, design and time-to-market, and realize our investment in hardware. Platform LSF has more than proved itself so far and is now the preferred solution for managing compute farms in AstraZeneca.' Sandra McLaughlin, AstraZeneca's senior systems administrator for physical and structural sciences, in 'Platform to accelerate drug discovery, design at AstraZeneca, *HPCwire*, 3 January 2002.

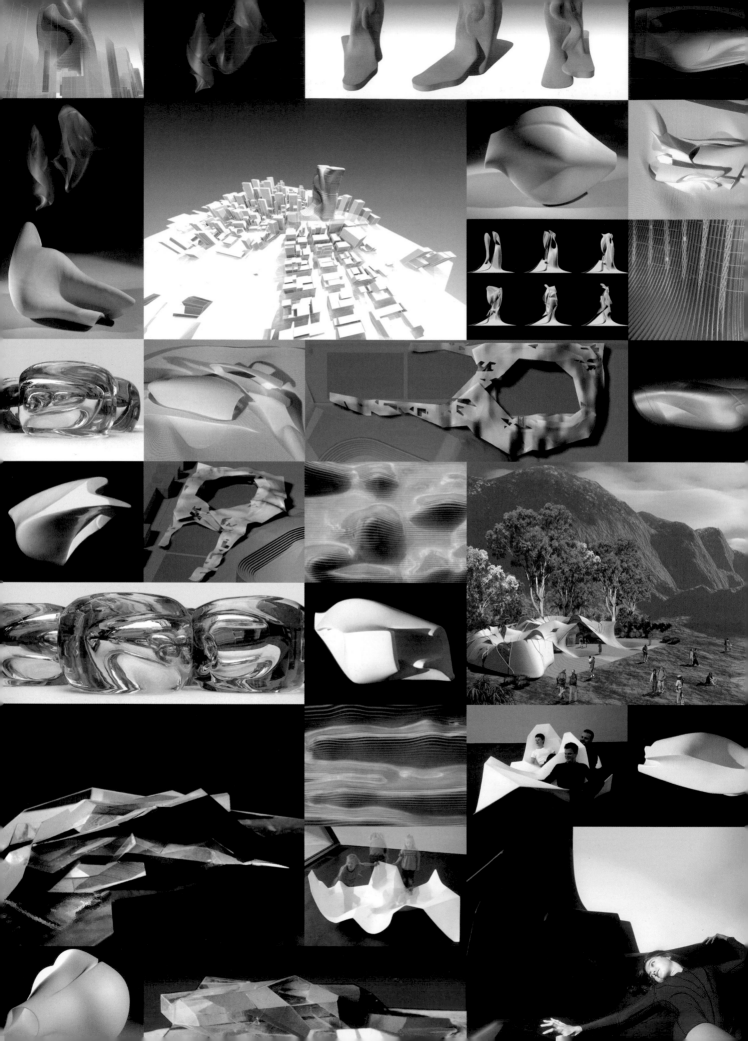

# Evolving Synergy: OCEAN Currents, Current OCEANs and Why Networks Must Displace Themselves

Founded in the early 1990s, OCEAN was one of the first collaborative geographically distributed practices to realise the potential of telecommunication and digital design technologies. Here **Michael Hensel** recounts the various mutations and fluid transformations of the experimental groupings that came to form OCEAN net. Accordingly, Hensel's account is more akin to a band biography than a staid sociology of a professional office. Moreover, he explores how the molecular model of distributed authorship presents difficulties, either by confounding external expectations of a singular identity or signature behind the various design processes, or internally as a stable whole of identities attempting to re-emerge and fix its collaborative mixings into a rigid hierarchy. As OCEAN's biography attests, true collaboration is inherently flat, distributed and transformative, situating architecture as more than just a service profession and transforming it into an intensive practice of living. Collective intelligence in these terms is embedded in the distributed evolutionary processes of the practice as a design project in itself.

The OCEAN displaces itself alongside with its shoreline.
*Orphan Drift*

OCEAN surfaced and claimed its ground as the first collaborative design network of its kind in 1994, the same year Kevin Kelly's iconic book *Out of Control* was launched.[1] Pattern recognition will show us not only that both network and book start with the letter O, significant though this may be, but also, in time, that the title of the book actually and suitably describes OCEAN's distinctive and happily crazy brand of network collaboration. OCEAN's ongoing transformation started with the group becoming a geographically dispersed network of collaborators, with backgrounds in architecture, urban design, and industrial, interior, furniture, glass and ceramics design as well as agricultural sciences. This network has for most of its existence since 1994 undergone permanent changes and remained as an organisation largely elusive even to its members, while becoming renowned for its design output. In other words: while OCEAN's work has become widely known, it has itself remained a mirage that cannot quite be discerned even with eyes squinted like a snake. It is this article's monumental task to map OCEAN's currents, current OCEAN's and their place in architectural hysteria. Here is the result.

## Prologue: 1992 ANYONE around?

The beginning of time: 1992. Vast, blank, pointing, incongruent and intensively coherent folded and striated black stuff (see Greg Lynn, *AD Folding in Architecture*, 1993) made up the ingredients of a postgraduate primordial soup cooked up by Jeffrey Kipnis at the AA.[2] From this emerged a few startled postgraduate organisms. Among those were Chul Kong, Nopadol Limwatanakul, Johan Bettum and I, all shaped from utter filth through Kipnesque Deformation. Thus we entered a world of architecture full of new wonders but rather void of ANY fitting architectural niches. And so, in utter trepidation, I slipped back into the fold of the AA to teach with Jeffrey Kipnis and Bahram Shirdel.

## 1994 Life in the OCEANs (David Attenborough ho!)

In contrast to this Chul Kong reached escape velocity and changed from the AA's primordial to the Korean Space Soup, where he wrote a series of articles on emerging practices for *Space* magazine. He extended an invitation to me to publish

Projects include: Extraterrain by OCEAN Helsinki (1996); Canberra Finnish Embassy (1996) and Töölö Open Arena by OCEAN Helsinki and OCEAN Oslo (1997); Synthetic Landscape Phase 03 by OCEAN Oslo and OCEAN Cologne (1998); a_Drift Time Capsules by OCEAN NORTH, finalist entry in the *New York Times* competition (1998); Ambient Amplifiers by OCEAN NORTH (2000), received FEIDAD Design Merit Award in 2000; Formations Small Objects by OCEAN NORTH (2002); Frozen Voids by Ernesto Neto and OCEAN NORTH (2003); The World Centre for Human Concerns by OCEAN NORTH (2001–04), exhibited at the Venice Architectural Biennale 2002; Mountain Hut by ocean D (2004), exhibited at the Venice Architectural Biennale 2004

**Beholder, drifting by your eye is work
by OCEAN net, OCEAN Oslo, OCEAN Helsinki, OCEAN UV,
OCEAN NORTH, OCEAN UK, OCEAN US and OCEAN D,
and all the other OCEANs that may yet be
or what in them might lurk.**

some work. Since I didn't have any work I teamed up with Tom Verebes, Bostjan Vuga, Ulrich Königs, second-generation Kipnesque organisms, who also didn't have any, to form a group which we put together under the name OCEAN. And so this became the dedicated expression of the will to extend the group into a network of collaborating designers. Instantly, due to a well-studied reflex, OCEAN undertook a series of design competitions, until the end of 1994, when Bostjan Vuga and Ulrich Königs decided to move back home. Up to this point the work of OCEAN had taken place in London. How would our group continue to exist upon geographic dispersal? But then we might well become a geographically distributed design collective consisting of local groups if we could manage to communicate productively across long distances.

We quickly focused all our creative attention on renaming: OCEAN became OCEAN net with local nodes in different places. In consequence we listened to a lot of drum-'n'-bass and also decided that the European continent was the first to be settled upon. Bostjan Vuga and Juri Sadar founded Sadar in Vuga Arhitekti in Ljubljana. Tom and I stayed in London. In 1995 we invited Johan Bettum to join and he settled in Oslo and started a group there. With the new key members Birger Sevaldson, Bonsak Schieldrop and Kim Bauman Larsen they got some work done indeed. The latter three brought a brand-new digital sensibility and tool-set to the network and through Birger Sevaldson's contacts it became possible to collaborate with Steiner Killi, who, in turn, made it possible to tap into Rapid Prototyping technologies: the dawn of the oceanoidal dust-monkey! The outcome was the Synthetic Landscape Phase 01-03 (1995–8) and the Synthetic Landscape Pavilion (1997–8). Tom and I continued to claim further landmass for OCEAN. In result of a workshop at the University of Art in Design in Helsinki, Kivi Sotamaa and Markus Holmstén were invited to join and formed a group in Helsinki. This group was subsequently joined by Toni Kauppila, Lasse Wager and Tuuli Sotamaa.

In the short time between mid-1995 and the beginning of 1996 the OCEAN net had expanded into four local groups with a rapidly growing portfolio, which we could show in an exhibition at the AA in 1996. Bostjan and Juri had won the competition for the Slovenian Chamber of Commerce, and the OCEAN net entry for the Nordic Countries Embassies had received an honourable mention. OCEAN Oslo and Helsinki collaborated on competition entries for the Finnish Embassy in Canberra (1996), the Töölö Open Arena (1997) and the first phase of the Jyväskylä Music and Art Centre (1997). A lot of work did not survive studio parties held on Friday nights in Curtain Road and Merritullin Katu, and what remained was

later thoroughly chewed by Kivi's dog, culminating into what became the world's largest model cemetery.

Birger Sevaldson, Professor of Industrial Design, Markus Holmstén, a spatial and furniture designer, and Tuuli Sotamaa a glass and ceramics designer by training, introduced a strong industrial-design approach and sensibility. OCEAN Oslo's introduction of a cutting-edge composite material approach and computer-aided design and manufacturing expanded the network's scope of skills and work.

### 1997 OCEAN's divide

Soon we started exhibiting in different places and to grow ou profile, to the effect that upon the event of our second exhibitio at the Hennie Onstad Art Center in Oslo in 1997 our egos had become so large that we didn't fit into one space any more.

The point of conflict was marked by the question whether to assume a vertical structure or remain a horizontal organisation. And so the nodes that had become offices remained offices and the nodes that remained nodes continued to remain nodes, but now separate from one another.

Bostjan Vuga and Juri Sadar continued their very successful office and Tom Verebes continued OCEAN UK, with Laura

**During the golden summer of the year 2000 Jeff Turko came up with an idea to form a larger network concerned with cultural production, named the do-group, that would take on some of the promising aspects of the network characteristics of the early OCEAN net, while being at the same time much more multidisciplinary.**

Gimenez, Alex Thompson, Felix Robbins and Yan Gao joining the collaboration. By 1998, Tom Verebes and Robert Elfer had joined with Wade Stevens to undertake their first collaborative project together, working between Boston and New York. Rob and Wade formed OCEAN US and were later joined by Kevin Cespedes and Erik Hanson. Ocean D was formed in 2001 as the consolidation of OCEAN UK and OCEAN US into a new network of practices in London, New York and Boston.

We then thought: well hey! In result of this realisation OCEAN Oslo, Helsinki and Cologne joined forces.

We quickly focused all our creative attention on renaming: OCEAN Oslo, Helsinki and Cologne became OCEAN NORTH with local studios in different places. OCEAN NORTH might well become a geographically distributed design collective consisting of local studios if we'd all learn how to travel by air and use email. And so this time became incredibly fruitful, for our network, various northern European airlines and duty-free shops, due to the intensive travelling of members who collaborated on the projects of that time: the Chamberworks installation (1997), a_Drift Time Capsules (1998); the third phase of the Synthetic Landscape Research and the scheme for the Sandefjord Museum (1999). This was a time of great intensity. It was possible, for example, to run several weeks of workshops in parallel at the University of Art and Design in Helsinki and the Technical University in Vaasa involving four groups of students from three countries, with OCEAN NORTH members travelling back and forth, while running a design charette on the Sandefjord Hotel and other projects in the Helsinki studio, organising and coordinating a series of public lectures, and late-night sauna, whisky and cigar sessions at Hvittrask, the studio of Eliel Saarinen, Lindgren and Giselius out in the sticks in Finland. Ask Ben. Rockband style: burning it fast. Thinking back I am still exhausted. Some others burned out too and left henceforth the net out of their work: Johan Bettum and Kim Bauman Larsen left the group in Oslo and Markus Holmstén, Toni Kaupplia and Lasse Wager left the group in Helsinki. And then there were only four: Kivi and Tuuli Sotamaa in Helsinki, Birger Sevaldson in Oslo and myself, by choice now mainly located in Helsinki. And here the story ends.

No it doesn't. Stay here!

**2000 Fresh Waters**
During the golden summer of the year 2000 Jeff Turko came up with an idea to form a larger network concerned with cultural production, named the do-group, that would take on some of the promising aspects of the network characteristics of the early OCEAN net, while being at the same time much more multidisciplinary. A mission statement and a five-year programme was drafted together with Christopher Hight, and members were invited including servo. All members of OCEAN NORTH joined and formed, together with Jeff Turko and Christopher Hight, the motor of the do-group for the next two years. The first year of the do-group in 2000 brought 30 members from Europe, North and South America and the Near, Middle and Far East together in London for two workshop sessions entitled 'Space of Information'. In 2001 a smaller group gathered in Helsinki for a session, entitled 'Space of Extremes', that led to the publication under the same name. However, since work makes work the do-group imploded without trace but with a ghastly sound in 2002. Anticipating this collapse OCEAN NORTH organised the d-Fusion seminar and exhibition, in Aalto's Finlandia Hall and around the archipelago of Helsinki in the midst of summer 2001, which turned into a continuous white-night

**The *modus operandi* of network collaboration emerged during the mid-1990 when OCEAN was formed. Many architects and designers followed in the footsteps of OCEAN; however, they soon disintegrated or settled back into common corporate or franchise operations.**

Projects include: Lasipalatsi Media Square by OCEAN UK (1996); Habitare Furniture Exhibition by OCEAN Helsinki (Helsinki, 1997); Jyväskylä Music and Art Centre Phase 01 by OCEAN Helsinki and OCEAN Oslo (1997); Chamberworks installation by OCEAN NORTH (Oslo, 1998); Intensities installation by OCEAN NORTH (Helsinki, 2000); Landsc(r)aper Urban Ring Bridge by OCEAN NORTH (2000); Agora sound-active installation by Natasha Barrett and OCEAN NORTH (Oslo, 2001–03), received the Edward Prize in 2004; Jyväskylä Music and Art Centre Phase 02 and 03 by OCEAN NORTH (2004–06), exhibited at the Venice Architectural Biennale 2004

party with many of the do-group members and new cultural activists joining in: seminars, cultural events, exhibitions, lectures, boat trips, island hopping, sauna and BBQ sessions, and some minor drinking excesses with renowned activists from the Baltic region. That was the fun part and then it was back to work with network hangovers better than the best cantilever! Ever!

And work it was: the Landsc[r]aper Urban Ring Bridge produced for the 'Living Bridges' exhibition (2000), the exhibition design for ARS 01 at Kiasma (2001), the Agora sound-active installations (2001). With Achim Menges joining OCEAN NORTH fresh vigour ensued and more work got done: the World Centre for Human Concerns for the Max Protetch exhibition 'A New World Trade Centre' (2001) and the Venice Architectural Biennale 2002, Formations at the Trussardi Foundation in Milan (2002), and the reworking of the Jyväskylä Music and Art Centre for the Venice Architectural Biennale 2004. The bridge and the World Centre projects were done in collaboration with Jeff Turko's Nekton. After burning bright and fast, finally, in early 2006, Tuuli and Kivi Sotamaa left the group in order to pursue their work more steadily as a design practice under the name of Sotamaa Design.

## 2006 Chasing the Distant Horizons
Well, my friend, the seven seas ain't for the fainthearted. And so, watch out Captain Ahab! We, the three remaining buccaneers, will hoist the Jolly Roger and take to the vast sea once more and no siren will ever again lure us ashore …

## Epilogue: 2006 MANYONE around?
The modus operandi of network collaboration emerged during the mid-1990s when OCEAN was formed. Many architects and designers followed in the footsteps of OCEAN; however, they soon disintegrated or settled back into common corporate or franchise operations. It is negotiating multiple egos with time- and project-specific group interests that requires a dynamic structure of task- or interest-based regrouping. This condition is always both precarious and normal, as one can see from the constant change of members joining and leaving. When the balance can no longer be struck the network either dissolves or changes into a hierarchy dominated by one or few individuals. Due to this difficulty, design culture remains dominated by iconic individuals or mighty corporate structures.

The fact that networks change all the time is not a bad thing, though. In fact, what gives the network its productive edge is the mutual learning, exchange of knowledge and skills, and the very particular design work, that results from changing interactions and collaboration. Network collaboration is therefore about co-evolving towards individual and collective self-development to facilitate novel design production.

Over the 12 years of the existence of the OCEAN network collaboration many transformations occurred due to group-external events, individual life changes and group-internal changes, or the experience of working together on a particular project. Regrouping and retooling became thus entwined and yielded new synergy in productivity and innovative potential.

However, the perceived need to create an image of the network for the outside is in fundamental conflict with the dynamic nature of collaborative networks. Once there is an increasing tendency of members to value the external image for the sake of membership recognition, and therefore as predominantly a means of launching individual careers, there also evolves an inclination to view internal change as detrimental to the external image. This oftentimes results in the view that the portfolio should reflect valued expectations and thus the range of projects and design experimentation begins to narrow down.

The latter reduces the need for retooling, other than for the purpose of problem solving, and, in turn, reduces the need for regrouping. These tendencies deliver the work back to normative practice: individuals begin to acquire fixed roles and duties. Hierarchies emerge and inequality disillusions members who find themselves lower in the hierarchy, as well as the emerging leaders who begin to wonder, strangely enough, about the fact that they have to shoulder more responsibilities.

While OCEAN NORTH is renowned for its design work, the structure of the group has remained a source of curiosity for outsiders, and also for the members of the group. Is OCEAN NORTH still a collaborative network? What is the minimum operational size of a network that is capable of synthesising individual differences into a functioning collective endeavour that can yield operative synergy and novel design output? Whatever the next manifestation of OCEAN NORTH may be, it will likely not be its final one if it is to remain a network. For that to be possible, differences need to be reincorporated and cultivated through inviting many new members into the network.

We did not focus quickly all our creative attention on renaming: OCEAN NORTH remained OCEAN NORTH. After all, life in the OCEAN might well be more productive and interesting if we learn how to let it become so. Perpetually! P … we have just been joined by Steinar Killi. Rock'n'roll baby! Δ

## Notes
1. Kevin Kelly, *Out of Control: The Rise of Neo-Biological Civilisation*, Fourth Estate (London), 1994. Kelly describes the characteristics of distributed networks, which seem to largely coincide with the characteristics of OCEAN throughout its numerous yet transitory manifestations.
2. Jeffrey Kipnis established a formal graduate design programme at the Architectural Association during the academic year 1992–3. During this year he and Don Bates taught the graduate design course combined with Diploma Unit 4. In the following year, 1993–4, the graduate design programme, now dubbed the Architectural Association Graduate Design Group (AAGDG), was taught by Jeffrey Kipnis and Bahram Shirdel assisted by the author. Jeffrey Kipnis and Bahram Shirdel continued to teach AAGDG together until 1995. From 1995 to 1996 the programme was taught by Bahram Shirdel and the author. From 1996 onwards the programme was directed by Brett Steele and Patrick Schumacher, now redubbed the Design Research Laboratory (DRL).

# Treatment 1: Notes from an Informal Discussion on Interinstitutional Design Research and Image Production

Since 2003, **Benjamin Bratton** and **Hernan Diaz-Alonso** have conducted a series of parallel theory seminars and design studios at SCI-Arc (Southern California Institute of Architecture). These collaborations have addressed questions of collectivity at varying scales: *personal* (between two individuals, each with separate professional practices), *institutional* (between two disciplinary positions, one analytical and the other creative) and *cultural* (between what is inside and outside the architectural imaginary). The work featured in the article represents another primary mandate of their interinstitutional project: the transdisciplinary implications of *design* as a general form of practice as opposed to the historical definitions of 'architecture' or the architect.

The following notes are the result of an informal discussion between Benjamin Bratton and Hernan Diaz-Alonso regarding their continuing interinstitutional design research project spanning a three-year period between 2003 and 2006. The research curriculum comprised so far a total of four sets of design studios and theory seminars, taught collaboratively over the course of four semesters at SCI-Arc (and replicated at Columbia University where Diaz-Alonso also teaches). The collaboration between the architect and the sociologist also extends to their respective professional practices, Xefirortarch and The Culture Industry.

### Innovation and Novelty: Design as Research

When we started to teach advanced vertical studios at SCI-Arc we decided to conduct the studio collaboratively, in part because we've always been interested in production and technique, and wanted to eliminate the conventional notion of how research is conducted in a typical design studio. This involved a general reconfiguration of design as research, aimed very much at privileging the projective act of innovation and novelty, as opposed to the more traditional, reflective form of research as retrospective criticism.

As an extension of this interest in open-ended innovation as a legitimate form of design research we were more specifically interested in the degree to which highly involuted geometrical forms could be interpreted programmatically, or in terms of having latent narrative potential. In other words, how might conventional architectural programmes be productively mutated (if not entirely mutilated) by the organisational influence of formal and geometrical effects? Advanced modelling software generates the potential for what we began to see as a productive migration away from conventional notions of programme (that which is typically thought of in planometric terms) and towards a

Hernan Diaz-Alonso/Xefirotarch, Design Series 4, 'SANGRE', San Francisco Museum of Modern Art, California, 2005–06
Detail of the display system.
Project architects: Jeremy Stoddart and Josh Taron
Design team: Ben Toam, Mirai Morita, Robert Mezquiti, Greg Derrico and Klaus Ransmayr

reconsideration of programme as something much less determinate. We began to think of programme as being less quantifiable in nature and more the product of specific qualities, in particular the notion of space and programme as an embodied experience.

In the context of these general research interests, the first set of seminars and studios taught collaboratively was on airports. We treated the arc of flight from one city to another as a temporally contiguous space and asked students to

**SCI-Arc design studio, Terminals, spring 2003**
Aerial perspective of the Long Beach airport variation 1.
Students: Kevin Sperry and Asako Hiraoka

design three airport locations and two cabin spaces along a single itinerary. Rather than tracing a space of flow as a formal surface organisation, we experimented with constructing a cinematic continuity of experience, a travelling POV shot, through the design of form and atmospherics. These investigations led to the second set of studios and seminars, which addressed the single-family home as a straightforward architectural typology. The seminar focused on issues particular to post-Oedipal family dynamics, a notion of the plural body of the biological family and the way in which architecture operates as a kind of prosthetic projection to exacerbate, accommodate and confound intimate social economies. We discovered that architectural design became a means by which to construct narratives about new kinds of

social bodies. In fact, the results of the design work became the production of a 'body' as much a 'building'. Whether the students were conscious of it or not, these 'houses' transformed into self-portraits. This suggested dispensing with the 'building' altogether, and having each student focus instead on the design of a body, or what we eventually came to consider a kind of 'animal'. This evolution towards the production of a body or animal led to the third set of studios and seminars, in which we continued to shift the research down in scale, focusing on the invention and production of bodily 'organs'. By the time we reached the fourth set of studios and seminars (in progress when this discussion took place), our focus was on the viscous formal capacities of 'blood

### Software Isomorphism: Design as Image

Many of these interests regarding forms of innovation and novelty raise questions of design technology and, more specifically, design software. There has been a striking de-differentiation of design disciplines in the last few years.

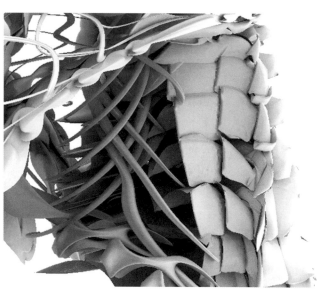

**SCI-Arc design studio, Fleshology, spring 2005**
Detail perspective of the final version of the tower/species replacing the Freedom Tower at the World Trade Center.
Students: Hunter Knight, Nick Pisca and Jason Mah

Graphic designers, architectural designers, shoe designers and car designers all once had forms of expertise particular to their specific sets of tools and their techniques of production with those tools, thus helping to distinguish each skill as a predominantly separate and distinct design practice. More recently, the tools that differentiated designers from such diverse fields have converged with the rapid proliferation of computer technology and, more specifically, 3-D digital modelling programs, the effect being the production of a kind of 'software isomorphism'. It is now common practice that most if not all designers work with similar if not the same software applications, regardless of the scale or function of the design products they are generating (a logo, a shoe, a building, etc). We see one predominant effect of this 'isomorphism' being the aggregation of diverse forms of design intelligence into an almost universal condition of image production.

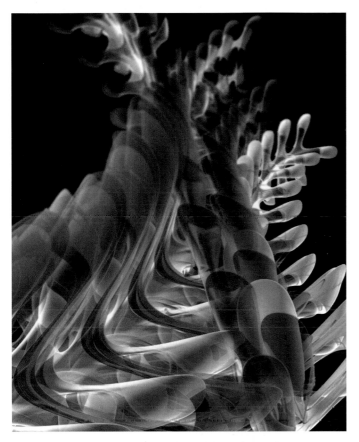

**Graduate School of Architecture Planning and Preservation (GSAPP), Columbia University design studio, Fleshology, spring 2005**
Detail of the genetic code of tower/species evolution.
Student: Robert Mezquiti

Design always concerns a translation between forms and formats of image. More than 'textuality' or even 'iconography', its very form is a secondary function of how it performs as an image. Perhaps some might see this as a triumph of superficiality over depth, but it's certainly also an intensification of the conjectural and fictive logics of design, of its ability to mobilise a social imagination and with it a series of potential futures. We see this as a real and complex demand that global network culture makes on producers of architectural content.

**Our Certain Los Angeles-ism: Design as Cultural Production**
Another implicit (if not explicit) interest particular to this research project is the embrace of Los Angeles (and perhaps more specifically 'Hollywood' – less a place than a condition)

as a cultural milieu. Even if superficial and banal, LA continues to have a very particular and profound influence on the shaping of contemporary aesthetic culture (particularly in terms of the entertainment industry and the general spectacle of celebrity). To this extent, our interest in the question of the image (as mentioned in the previous section, architecture or design-as-image-making) has its origins in a culture in which image is quite literally 'everything'. This condition, however, provides a different context for each. Hernan makes images in a city of image-making. Benjamin positions himself more as an 'intellectual', a 'permanently absurd identity in Los Angeles', a perspective that he uses nevertheless as the basis of critical and professional production.

In the collaboration across their professional practices 'Hollywood' becomes as well a model for the informal and opportunistic circulation of ideas and strategies across disciplines. Our exchanges, however, are never directly programmatic, nor ideological, but rather they mutate and migrate across the different purposes to which they are put.

**SCI-Arc design studio, Hemastology, autumn 2005**
Detail perspective of the final version of the bridge/species replacing the Brooklyn Bridge.
Students: Brian De Luna and Chikara Inamura

In this, the pedagogical collaboration within the context of the institution often functions as a forum for unexpected and unplannable innovation. What is learnt there is idiosyncratically applied to practical problems elsewhere. Hernan also characterises this back and forth in the musical terms of improvisational compositional techniques. 'It's like a four-year-long jam session,' he smiles.

# Contributors

**Chandler Ahrens** is a partner of Open Source Architecture (O-S-A) located in Los Angeles, where he received a masters degree from UCLA. His research and design methodology derives from an investigation into both tangible and virtual environments engaging various modes of spatiality, materiality, fabrication techniques and the implementation of computational technology to inform and evaluate the design process. He is co-curator of the forthcoming exhibition 'The Gen[H]ome Project'.

**Alisa Andrasek** is an experimental practitioner of architecture and computational processes. In 2001 she founded biothing, focusing on the generative potential of physical and digital computational systems for design. In 2005 she initiated CONTINUUM, an interdisciplinary research collective focusing on advanced computational geometry and software development. She teaches at Columbia University and Pratt Institute, and has lectured and exhibited worldwide. She was co-winner of the Metropolis Next Generation Design Competition in 2005, and received a FEIDAD Design Merit Award in 2004.

**Benjamin H Bratton** is a theorist and strategist. He teaches design and theory at SCI-Arc. At UCLA's Design/Media Arts department he co-directs the Brand Lab, teaching organisational brand analysis and development as a critical practice. His book on design and terrorism will be published by Semiotext(e) in 2007. His professional work is based in the semisecretive consultancy known as The Culture Industry. See www.bratton.info.

**Anthony Burke** is a designer based in San Francisco, director of offshorestudio.net and assistant professor at the University of California, Berkeley, where he explores the relationship between network culture and architecture and researches urban computing with the Intel Research Lab. A graduate of the Advanced Architecture Design Masters at Columbia University and the University of New South Wales, in October 2004 he co-convened the international symposium 'Distributed Form: Network Practice' and is co-editing its forthcoming publication.

**Andrew Burrow** is a research associate in the Spatial Information Architecture Lab (SIAL) at RMIT University. His research interests include ontology-based design collaboration, transdisciplinary design communication, and analysing representations for incremental update in order to bring direct manipulation interfaces to sophisticated information systems.

**Jane Burry** is an architect and researcher in the Spatial Information Architecture Laboratory (SIAL), RMIT University, where she is leading research and teaching in the area of mathematics and design. Further links and details of projects and publications can be found at www.sial.rmit.edu.au/People/jburry.php.

**Pia Ednie-Brown** is a senior lecturer in the architecture programme and the Spatial Information Architecture Laboratory (SIAL) at RMIT University. She teaches design and theory at undergraduate and postgraduate levels. Her performatively oriented research practice, Onomatopoeia, involves interactive installation projects, animation, sculpture, creative writing and theoretical analysis.

**Hernan Diaz-Alonso** is the principal and founder of Xefirotarch, an award-winning design firm in architecture, product and digital motion in Los Angeles. He teaches studio design and visual studies, and is the thesis coordinator at SCI-Arc, Los Angeles. He is a design studio professor at the GSAPP, Columbia University.

**David Erdman** is one of four founding members of the research design collaborative servo. He has been a full-time faculty member at UCLA's Department of Architecture for six years, teaching design and conducting technology seminars focusing on the development of new modelling, representational and production techniques. He has also taught at the KTH Stockholm, RPI and the Southern California Institute of Architecture, and is currently the Esherick Visiting Professor at Berkeley.

**Alexander R Galloway** is author of *Protocol: How Control Exists After Decentralization* (MIT Press, 2004) and is an assistant professor in the Department of Culture and Communication at New York University. He is the founder of the Radical Software Group, an award-winning collective devoted to experimental software design. He is also the author of *Gaming: Essays on Algorithmic Culture* (University of Minnesota Press, 2006).

**Marcelyn Gow** is a partner and founding member of servo. She has lectured internationally and teaches design, research and technology seminars at UCLA's Department of Architecture and Urban Design. She has also taught at the Royal Institute of Technology in Stockholm and the ETH in Zurich. She is currently a doctoral candidate at the ETH. Her forthcoming dissertation, explores the relationship between aesthetic research and technological innovation.

**Michael Hardt** is professor in the Literature Programme at Duke University. He is author of *Gilles Deleuze* (1993) and co-author of *Labor of Dionysus* (University of Minnesota Press, 1994), *Empire* (Harvard University Press, 2000) and *Multitude: War and Democracy in the Age of Empire* (Penguin Books, 2004).

**Michael U Hensel** is an architect, urban designer, researcher and writer. He is a partner in OCEAN NORTH and the Emergence and Design Group, and a board member of BIONIS. He has taught, lectured, exhibited and published globally. Publications include AD *Emergence* and AD *Techniques and Technologies in Morphogenetic Design*, both with Achim Menges and Michael Weinstock, and *Morpho-Ecologies: Differentiated Structures and Multi-performative Systems in Nature and Design* with Achim Menges.

**Christopher Hight** is a theorist and designer. Currently an assistant professor at the Rice University School of Architecture, he has practised in the US and in Europe. His research on formalism and post-humanism will be published by Routledge Press as soon as he can finish it.

**Branden Hookway** teaches at Cornell University and is a co-director of the Responsive Systems Group. He has worked as an architect, and graphic and industrial designer and writes on issues of technology, society and design. He is the author of *Pandemonium* (Princeton University Press, 2000), and is currently working on a dissertation at Princeton University.

**Ulrika Karlsson** is a partner and founding member of servo. She has lectured internationally and teaches design studios at the Royal Institute of Technology in Stockholm, where she is a doctoral candidate. Her dissertation explores the parallel development of Modern architecture and radio technology. She is a board member of AKAD and has been a guest teacher at UCLA's Department of Architecture and Urban Design.

**Ed Keller** is a designer, professor, writer and musician/multimedia artist. He founded aCHRONO in 1998, and co-founded a|Um Studio in 2003. He is a member of the faculty at Columbia University GSAPP and SCI-Arc, and a visiting professor at the University of Pennsylvania, Pratt Institute and Parsons School of Design. *Chronomorphology* (Columbia Books on Architecture, 2003) documents the work of 12 of his advanced design studios at the Columbia GSAPP.

**Kevin Kennon** founded Kevin Kennon Architect in 2003. He is a director of the Institute for Architecture and Urban Studies and founding principal of United Architects, selected as a finalist for the World Trade Center Design Competition. Previously a design partner for KPF Associates, he is the recipient of more than 30 major design awards and has been a visiting professor at Yale and Princeton, and an adjunct professor at Columbia.

**Carla Leitao** is an architect, designer and professor. She co-founded Umasideia (Lisbon) in 1999, and co-founded a|Um STUDIO in 2003. She currently teaches at Cornell University. She is a fellow in the artist-in-residence programme of Schloss Solitude and has received grants from the Gulbenkian Foundation and the Luso-American Foundation. She is editor of *32BNY* and has edited and co-edited several publications for Columbia Books on Architecture, including *City Fragments Beijing*.

**Philippe Morel** is cofounder of EZCT Architecture & Design Research, adjunct assistant professor at the École Nationale Supérieure d'Architecture Paris-Malaquais, and has written extensively about the consequences of technological phenomena on global disurbanism. He lectures around the world, including, at Harvard, MIT and Columbia, across Europe and, recently, Tokyo.

**Eran Neuman** is a partner of Open Source Architecture (O-S-A). He received his PhD from the Critical Studies in Architectural Culture Program at UCLA. His research focuses on the history and theory of technology and science in architecture. He has received numerous research grants, for example from the Lady Davis Post-Doctoral Fellowship, the Center for Advanced Holocaust Studies Fellowship and the German-Israeli Foundation Fellowship. He is co-curator and co-editor of the exhibition and book 'The Gen[H]ome Project'.

**Chris Perry** holds a Masters of Architecture degree fro Columbia University. In 1999 he co-founded the collaborative design practice servo, the work of which has been featured in numerous exhibitions and publications including the 2004 Venice Architecture Biennale and *10x10_2* published by Phaidon Press in 2005. Since 2000 he has taught design studios and theory seminars at the graduate schools of Columbia, Yale, Cornell, the University of Pennsylvania, RMIT in Melbourne and Pratt Institute. In 2006 he co-founded the Responsive Systems Group (RSG), a newly formed interdisciplinary cultural and technological design research organisation, the work of which will be featured in the 2006 Architecture Biennial Beijing.

**John Rothenberg** is a designer and programmer living in Cambridge, Massachusetts. For the past three years he has been working at Small Design Firm, building electronics and programming graphics for interactive installations. He is a co-founder of sosolimited, an audiovisual performance collective, and is currently a Masters student at the MIT School of Architecture and research affiliate of the Computing Culture Group at the MIT Media Lab.

**David L Salomon** received his PhD in architectural history and theory from UCLA's Department of Architecture. His current research focuses on the historical and contemporary interaction between Modern architecture and capitalism. He currently teaches architectural theory at Cornell University.

**David Small** completed his PhD at the MIT Media Laboratory in 1999, where his research focused on the display and manipulation of complex visual informatio His thesis examined how digital media, in particular three-dimensional and dynamic typography, will chang designers' approach to information. His work has been exhibited at the Museum of Modern Art, Documenta11, the Centre Pompidou and the Copper-Hewitt. He is the principal and founder of Small Design Firm.

**Aaron Sprecher** is a partner of Open Source Architecture (O-S-A) and an assistant professor at Syracuse University School of Architecture. His researc focuses on the potentialities of the fusion between information technologies, computational languages and automated systems. He is Fellow of the Syracuse Center of Excellence, and has lectured extensively at institutions throughout the US and Europe. He is co-curator and co-editor of the forthcoming exhibition ar book 'The Gen[H]ome Project'.

**Brett Steele** is a director of the Architectural Association School of Architecture, and a former director of the AADRL. His links, writings and course syllabuses can be found online at www.resarch.net.

**Eugene Thacker** is an assistant professor in the School of Literature, Communication, & Culture at Georgia Tech. He is the author of *Biomedia* (University of Minnesota Press, 2004) and *The Global Genome: Biotechnology, Politics, and Culture* (MIT Press, 2005) and i currently working on a new book called *Necrologies*. He also works with the Biotech Hobbyist collective, which aims to bring an intellectually open and ethically informed practice to the life sciences.

**Therese Tierney** is currently a doctoral scholar at the University of California, Berkeley. During 2005 she pursued design research at MIT on emergent systems. She is the author of *Abstract Space: Beneath the Media Surface* (forthcoming) and co-convened the interdisciplinary symposium and edited the book, *Distributed Form: Network Practice*. Her essays on architecture, digital technology and interactive art hav been published in *Leonardo* and *arcCA: Architecture California*. A practising architect in San Francisco and Dublin, she has taught at the University of California and California College of the Arts.

**Tom Verebes** is an architect and educator based in London. He co-founded OCEAN and has since directed OCEAN UK and been a partner in ocean D, with offices in London, Boston and New York, working across a range of design scales and typologies. He is co-director of the Architectural Association's Design Research Lab (DRL) where he has taught for a decade. Tom has presented, published and exhibited the work of ocean and the DRL internationally.

# C O N T E N T S

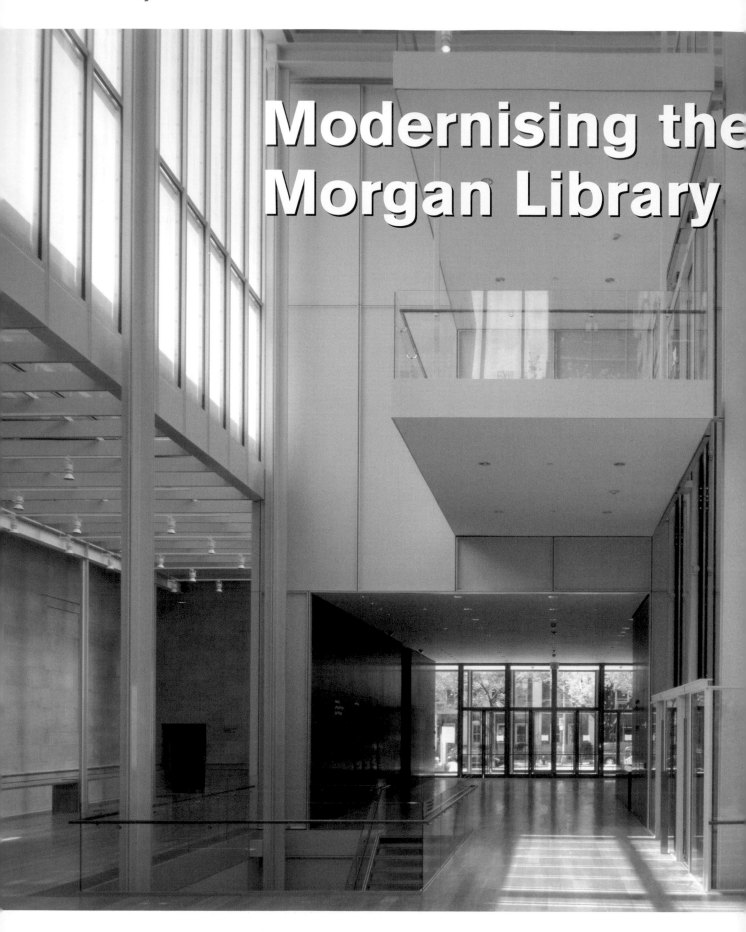

# Modernising the Morgan Library

Renzo Piano's recent addition to the Pierpont Morgan Library in New York is of interest in its own right because it radically alters the experience at one of the city's most appealing and unique institutions. But it is also worth considering, **Jayne Merkel** argues, because Piano is now working on more major museums than any architect in the world. At the Morgan, he subtly transformed a magnificent Renaissance Revival private library into a full-fledged modern museum with fine facilities for displaying parts of the collection and making its resources available to scholars. The old parts look as magnificent as ever, though they are now somewhat side-lined. The new parts are strong and elegant. The two are daringly juxtaposed, and the planning for 14,028 square metres (151,000 square feet) of facilities that more than doubles the size of the whole on part of a cramped Manhattan block is skilful.

Piano is unquestionably one of the world's great architects. His unusually competent and versatile firm, the Renzo Piano Building Workshop, is accomplished at designing a wide range of building types. But is it as uniquely qualified to design galleries as its current portfolio of commissions suggests?

It was, after all, a museum of sorts that first made Piano famous. Even though the Centre Nationale d'Art et de Culture George Pompidou, which he built in Paris with Richard Rogers between 1971 and 1977, was controversial from the start and the galleries it contained soon went out of style, the building revived a whole section of Paris and remains the epitome of a certain moment in time. It was not, however, the million-square-foot, million-dollar Pompidou that launched Piano's career as a museum architect. That was the tiny, exquisite, sophisticatedly modest Menil Collection Museum in Houston, Texas, of 1982–6. Yet it was not until Frank Gehry's wildly popular Guggenheim Museum in Bilbao opened in 1997 that Piano began to get one sought-after museum job after another, while Gehry, who had become the most famous architect in the world, did not receive a single one (though he was inundated with commissions of other kinds).

In the 1980s, when word of the 9290-square-metre (100,000-square-foot), $24 million Menil Collection's distinctive character and exquisite natural light began to spread, Piano's gallery commissions were, curiously, more modest and closer to home. First came the 700-square-metre (7,500-square-foot) Lingotto Exhibition Spaces in an abandoned Fiat factory in Turin of 1983–2003, then the 9290-square-metre (100,000-square-foot) Museum of Contemporary Art at the Cité Internationale trade fair centre in Lyons, begun in 1986 (and still ongoing), and the small but impressive Pompeii Visitor Centre Library in Naples of 1987. Of the earlier commissions, only the 6615-square-metre (71,200-square-foot), $37 million Beyeler Foundation Museum, near Basel, of 1992–7, was similar in programme (if not, perhaps, in success) to the Menil, since it houses a private collection and is rather small.

After Bilbao, however, the Renzo Piano Building Workshop was invited to

---

**Renzo Piano, Pierpont Morgan Library addition, New York, 2006**
The new entrance to the Morgan Library, around the corner from the historic buildings, on Madison Avenue, leads into a three-storey, light-filled courtyard with white-painted steel and glass pavilions, overhanging balconies and glazed elevators. The original architectural treasures, however, are not immediately visible as they are tucked away behind doorways to the left.

Piano's new Madison Avenue facade of the Morgan Library complex juxtaposes a rectangular white-painted steel box to the articulated stone facades of the older Morgan buildings on either side, offering a sharp contrast between old and new. The addition, however, is visible only as the visitor approaches. From just a block away, only the historic buildings can be seen.

expand one major American museum after another – and therefore revise the work of one celebrated architect after another. At the High Museum of Art in Atlanta, it was a building by Richard Meier of 1983. At the Chicago Art Institute it is an 1893 building by Shepley, Rutan & Coolidge with a series of additions by Howard Van Doren Shaw, Holabird Root & Burgee, Skidmore, Owings & Merrill, and Hammond, Beeby & Babka. At the Los Angeles County Museum it is a problematic building of 1964 by William Pereira with a Japanese Pavilion by Bruce Goff and additions by Hardy Holzman Pfeiffer from the 1980s. At Harvard, it will be Coolidge, Shepley, Bulfinch & Abbott's 1925 Renaissance Revival Fogg Art Museum, James

Stirling's postmodern 1984 Arthur M Sackler Museum of Asian Art, and Gwathmey-Siegel's 1991 Werner Otto Hall at the Busch-Reisinger Museum. And at the Whitney Museum in New York, if he succeeds where Michael Graves and Rem Koolhaas have failed to win community support, Piano will be adding on to the 1966 work of Marcel Breuer and a 1998 addition by Richard Gluckman. He is also renovating London Bridge Tower and designing a Museum of Contemporary Art in Sarajevo-Bosnia-Herzegovina, as well as the *New York Times* Building and a master plan for the expansion of the Columbia University campus in Manhattan.

At the Morgan, a starkly rectangular, white steel and glass pavilion, which opened on 29 April

this year, connects three historic buildings on the block to form what the library is now calling a 'campus'. The masterpiece is JP Morgan's magnificent private library, designed by McKim Mead & White in 1902 in a scholarly Renaissance Revival style. Eleven years after the famous banker death in 1913, his son Jack (J Pierpont Morgan, Jr) decided to open the library to the public, demolished his father's mansion, and engaged Benjamin W Morris to build a compatible structure with galleries and entrance facilities for visitors. It opened in 1928. In the 1980s, the library acquired an 1853 brownstone across the block that had once belonged to Jack and recalls the character of the neighbourhood where the Morgans lived there.

The 6968-square-metre (75,000-square-foot), $106 million Piano addition replaces an elegant, only 15-year-old veined white marble, limestone, steel and glass Garden Court designed by New York architect Bartholomew Voorsanger. This also connected the three historic buildings, and the $12 million structure, with a piano-curve roof, oxidised brass, bronze and seeded art glass, made the transition with so much grace and charm that the Morgan began to attract crowds as it never had before, and the court generated $600,000 a year in revenue from private hire. Inexplicably, when library officials decided that its popularity merited additional gallery and gathering space, Voorsanger was not invited to submit a proposal, but instead two celebrated New York firms, Tod Williams Billie Tsien and Associates and Steven Holl Architects, were asked along with Piano – who reportedly was only interested in the job if he was the sole applicant. Thus we will never know, as we did at the Museum of Modern Art, what the other contenders would have done had they been allowed to contend.

What Piano, working with Beyer Blinder Belle of New York, has done is intelligent, thoughtful and absolutely straightforward. Yet it is so beautifully detailed that it has real elegance. The central courtyard rises three storeys to contain an interior garden as well as, on the third floor, a bilevel study room with a surrounding balcony recalling those in the Morgan Library itself, a long low-light gallery for the display of manuscripts on the second storey, and a pristine cubic gallery space on the ground floor for other treasures. A pair of glass-walled elevators serve all

Piano's addition replaces an elegant Garden Court by Voorsanger Architects of New York. Although it was frankly modern, since it was made of veined white marble, limestone, oxidised brass, bronze and seeded art glass, and capped with a graceful piano-curve roof, it met the historic buildings on their own terms and created transitions subtly.

these spaces as well as a sensuous underground auditorium and functional education centre.

Unlike Voorsanger, who used materials as sumptuous as those in the original buildings, Piano chose frankly modern faceted steel panels and high-transparency, low-iron glass. The steel is coated in a (barely visible) rose-hued off-white paint that contrasts effectively enough with the fine natural materials of the original building in the courtyard, but appears somewhat harsh from the street. The 36th Street facade, however, is beautifully proportioned. Here, the steel panelling is set back, and since it contains much less surface area than the stone walls the composition as a whole is successful.

On Madison Avenue, where the main entrance is now located, the new pavilion is recessed enough to be invisible even a block away. But up close, the gigantic steel box overpowers its neighbours and looks too mechanical in its grand historic context. Much-too-heavy 2.7-metre (9-foot) tall bronze entrance doors fail to create a connection. Instead, they present an obstacle to all but the toned professional athlete. And because the entrance no longer leads directly into the addition to the historic library on 36th Street, the gem that should be the primary experience is now tucked away in a corner.

The spaces inside the historic buildings, however, continue to captivate. They have been beautifully preserved or, in the 19th-century house, redesigned with a lovely new dining room, café and store. Piano has succeeded in knitting the entire complex together graciously on an almost impossibly tight urban site. It is a considerable achievement. But it is not astounding enough to explain his unprecedented popularity as a museum architect. ⌂

The pièce de résistance of the institution is still J Pierpont Morgan's three-storey private library, designed by McKim, Mead & White in 1902 in an academically 'correct' version of the Italian Renaissance style. Stairways to the upper tiers are concealed behind movable bookcases. The setting may seem inconceivably luxurious today, but the collection it contains is even more extraordinary.

One of the most welcome features of the new addition is a fine auditorium, Gilder Lehman Hall, 280-seat underground space that will allow the library to hold performances in a beautiful, comfortable, acoustically controlled new hall with a sloping floor, cherry-wood walls and ceilings, and lush red upholstered seats. The auditorium will feature music drawn from the library's superb collection of music manuscripts, as well as literary readings and lectures inspired by the holdings.

# Cyber House Rules: James Law Cybertecture International

After training at the Bartlett in London and an influential period working in Itsuko Hasegawa's studio in Tokyo, James Law returned to launch his own practice, James Law Cybertecture International, in Hong Kong. Working globally and across media and disciplinary lines, Law has captured the imagination of his home country – he was recently awarded the Microsoft/Esquire 'Cool Guy Digital Lifestyle Award 2006' by the general public as the personality most symbolic of the new digital lifestyle of Hong Kong. **Anna Koor** puts Law's brand of 'cybertecture' under the spotlight and describes the mechanism of his uniquely responsive practice.

James Law Cybertecture International, ICC Tower Observation Deck, Hong Kong, 2006

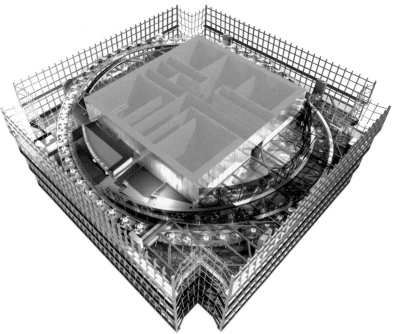

**James Law Cybertecture International, ICC Tower Observation Deck, Hong Kong, 2006**
Located on floors 100 and 101 of the Hong Kong International Commerce Centre, the public observation deck combines viewing and dining, not on separate levels but intertwined via gently sloping ramps and terraces. Law's desire for visual enhancement is played out in the double-height volume of the observation deck, promoting the sense of panorama and verticality. In plan, the deck logically radiates outwards from the building core in circular ramps and terraces that intersect each other. Each 'halo' of space is fitted with interactive info-tainment technology

Hong Kong Chinese architect James Law operates somewhere beyond and between the fringes of a typical practice, but where precisely is difficult to pinpoint. Although Hong Kong provides a ready and willing canvas for him to explore the yet-to-be-imagined, he also has visionary clients next door on mainland China, as well as in Denmark and Sri Lanka. Technology is undoubtedly the driving impetus of Law's work, which is why he adopted the term 'cybertecture' to describe his avenues of thought.

Cyber. To many the very utterance of the 'C' word induces an audible 'euwwh', closely followed by a stifled yawn. But this cybertect is no space cadet. His choice of title is well reasoned. 'I never thought of the "cyber" part of the term "cybertecture" as something related to the transient fashion of cyber design that prevailed during the 1990s,' insists Law. 'The word "cyber" actually does not relate to technology at all; it means "of another", so I use the word "cyber-tecture" as meaning "the fabric of another"; that is, something beyond conventional physicality ... something more than "archi-tecture".'

As far as Law is concerned, there is nothing more sinister about 'cyber' than the straightforward 'symbiotic balance between architecture, space and technology'. With that sorted, one still worries that the moniker, James Law Cybertecture International, could put off some clients from knocking at his door. However, for every potential doubter there are plenty who respond positively. A phone call to Law from 'the secretary to Director Wong' was prompted by googling the word 'cyber'. The mystery caller transpired to be phoning on behalf of the acclaimed film director Wong Kar Wai, whose films have achieved cult status worldwide. A few lengthy chats led to Law being invited to contribute his expertise as cybertechnology consultant for the epic *2046*.

The 'dream commission' torments the minds of most architects throughout their lengthy careers, but working with an eminent film director was an experience Law had not planned for, though in hindsight it made absolute sense. Law was asked to conceptualise a number of set designs for the movie; however, he discovered that the creative process of architecture, even at its furthest technological edge, bears little resemblance to film-making. Endless ideas were floated around, but nothing tangible ever seemed to materialise. It was not a case of being presented with a brief that could be challenged then executed. 'Our discussions were so broad yet so detailed, I really wasn't used to working in such a conversational mode, I'm used to making something concrete, creating something,' Law reasons. Nevertheless, he turned the situation around by documenting the discussions in the form of a Lonely-Planet-inspired travel book. It presented a method for Law to set down parameters and link information together in a project situation where there was little in the way of a fixed script or linear story. It has since been printed as one of a sequence of essays on Hong Kong urban experiences, in *HK Lab 2* by Map Book Publishers.

The methodology might differ, but read into Law's analysis of his *2046* experience and, at one level, it poignantly goes some way to explaining the cybertect's broader success. 'Wong Kar Wai has developed this visual language that's very good for story-telling ... the audiences have come to accept his films not as simple linear storylines, but as vignettes of experiences. Just like our own human memories, we don't think in a linear fashion – we make associations, they overlap and clash.' Delve into Law's portfolio and much of his work owes its richness to an ability to extract, codify and orchestrate, thereby re-creating life's complexity from the broadest of parameters.

Whilst he never consciously decided to part with conventional architecture, Law saw an opportunity to 'morph into a new realm which encompasses new possibilities, all of which are based on the fundamentals of architecture, but embellished by the vocabulary, tools and techniques available in the modern

**James Law's apartment, Kowloon Tong, 2004**
Sci-fi technology and hybrid furniture delineate the multifunctional live-and-work space where doors, panels, light, projection and sound are controlled from Law's wireless Cybertecture Home Automation System.

technological and information-driven world'. Having trained at the Bartlett under the tutelage of Peter Cook, the courage to innovate and explore was anything but subdued. The same experimental focus was undoubtedly reinforced within the studio of Itsuko Hasegawa – Law's initiation into 'real' practice – in Tokyo during Japan's economic boom of the 1990s.

Though he does not claim to have yet reached a level of recognition that enables him to plug into a global network, this international exposure so early in his career may have helped Law stray from the path of conventional architecture. It also helped when he resettled back in Hong Kong. 'Certainly one must think beyond borders and cannot confine one's identity to just one city – especially for me, who has lived and trained overseas,' he says. After a period working for larger, more corporate architecture practices doing relatively mainstream work that is bound by the many frustrating limitations placed on Hong Kong's process of making architecture, Law eventually created a new niche. 'Over a period of 10 years I came to realise that my own potential did not lie in developing myself into just another competent practitioner,' he maintains.

In this respect Law is perfectly poised to interface with China's unique economic situation. Its turbocharged building and infrastructure boom is hardly compatible with old-school architecture. 'My work is all about the "Future" and China is a country undergoing insanely rapid development – even the most basic fundamentals of infrastructure, being built for the first time in China, demand the latest technology,' he proclaims. Like an enormous sponge, the country's capacity to absorb and, more importantly, accept new ideas is unprecedented.

All things being equal, some might argue that, as a Hong Kong architect, Law's foot is not only already in the door, but on the boardroom table. However, he believes this is no longer the case. 'There's a wide range of international architects now working in China. No particular place has a "head start" over another, it's all about ideas and how much energy you have to promote them in a budding field of opportunity like China,' he maintains. Law's repertoire of cybertecture ticks all the right boxes to win work there, partly due to the above, but in a general sense he feels that architectural design in China is predominantly obsessed with the hardware of the built environment.

## 'My work tries to blend the software aspect of life and events into architecture, and this is sometimes very different when our proposal is presented – Chinese clients have to learn to appreciate this balance.'

'My work tries to blend the software aspect of life and events into architecture, and this is sometimes very different when our proposal is presented – Chinese clients have to learn to appreciate this balance,' he says.

Technology has been a convenient hook, not only introducing Law to unexpected domains such as cinema, but improving his probability of fielding the broadest possible range of commissions, from city planning and infrastructure in Sri Lanka to prototypical intelligent furniture that supports a range of interface technologies. The latter emerged in the process of Law designing his own apartment. The project became a test bed for many of his ideas. Where possible, domestic functions are not fixed, but fulfilled by a generous, if not unexpected, quotient of sliding walls and ambiguous reflective surfaces. The ultimate plaything is the electronic wallpaper – a series of drop-down projection screens that line two adjoining walls of the apartment.

By its very nature, much of Law's work can be transitory and non-tangible, and almost always transcends typological categories. 'My perception of the world and that of spaces can now be designed through a language much wider than conventional concrete, stone, steel and glass by using technology as part of the materiality of the work,' he explains. 'The ways in which a human interfaces with the world are now on a much wider bandwidth than anything ever achieved in the past.' He illustrates this with the idea of 'personal space', physically contained by conventional architecture yet far more fluid and complex because of mobile phones, international travel, memory storage and global Internet communities.

A similar spirit defines the mechanism of his practice. At one time, Law was able to pursue the notion of 'no fixed office address'. James Law Cybertecture International began life at home with a laptop, but now Law oversees three studios dotted around Hong Kong. 'I see myself as the centre of a neuro net – I am the key neuron that sends out visionary guidelines for each project and I find and attach on to myself like-minded experts in their particular fields … they in turn do the same.' It is a two-way relationship that sees any person within this neuro-nexus including Law, feeding off others and vice versa. Operating at its peak under Law's solo helming, the net contained up to 20 people at any one time.

However, over the last year the sheer volume of work has meant a shift in direction. Law explains that in order to parallel process a number of projects simultaneously, he has found it necessary to build a core team of 15 people 'who understand me intimately in terms of my philosophy of design and cybertecture'. This team helps keep the rest of the neuro net – up to 50 people dotted around the world – coordinated and on track. With everyone moving in and out of different spheres and time

**Electronic Arts Experience, Peak Tower, Hong Kong, 2006**
At the heart of the building is a virtual stadium in the form of an 8-metre (26-foot) high 'egg' containing an 'animatronic' stage that can adapt its configurations according to the event inside. Computer-games shopping at the Electronic Arts Experience enables customers to immerse themselves in different game environments through the merging of real and virtual materialities.

zones, the studio's intranet system is crucial. At 9.30 am every morning, the three studios are linked by video conference and every team member delivers a five-minute progress report which invites an instant response from Law. 'Everything is said in front of everyone else, so everyone is learning about the organisation, like a neuro net, beyond their individual work.'

One obvious link into the cybertecture 'bandwidth' is the computer games industry. Opened in July this year in Terry Farrell's recently rejuvenated Peak Tower at the top of Hong Kong's Peak Tram, the game design company is launching its first Electronic Arts Experience retail showroom worldwide. Law has devised 'a building inside a building' to create a freestanding retail cybertecture that uses the concept of the game itself to form the space inhabited by customers. The result is a hybrid environment that combines the materiality of the real and the digital of the virtual.

There's a touch of theatrics, but Law's work is not all wow factor and special effects. Much is about harnessing technology to generate the most cost-effective and utterly simple solutions. While Hong Kong's tallest tower and retail project, the International Finance Centre (IFC), was under construction, Law was asked to design a temporary hoarding that would enable commuters and shoppers to short-cut through the complex without lengthy diversions whilst disguising the surrounding site works. He made a twisted tunnel of stretched gauze fabric washed with a changing programme of coloured light.

Scroll down Law's roster of clients and perhaps the most surprising aspect is the number of government-related organisations that pop up. Whether it is automated postal systems for the Hong Kong Post Office, retail stores for Pacific Century Cyberworks (the telecommunications company that acquired Hong Kong Telecom) or a media lab for Radio Television Hong Kong, these are companies that would

## Shanghai IFC Commercial Showsuite Building, Pudong, Shanghai, 2006

Mounted on a complex web of splayed steel trusses, the spiral building forms the launch pad for Shanghai IFC, a multi-use mega-project in Pudong, Shanghai. The initial part of the journey along this ribbon development provides a general taster of Shanghai, orienting guests to the city geographically, historically and economically through a panoply of interactive technology tools. The loop-the-loop architecture of the IFC Commercial Showsuite Building is designed to propel prospective clients on an upward journey of six floors with the least discomfort.

Wallpaper*

OCTOBER 2006

*INTERNATIONAL DESIGN INTERIORS LIFESTYLE

# looping space

James Law Cybertecture has designed a showsuite building like no other for Sun Hung Kai Properties for their Lujiazui Development in Pudong, Shanghai

World's Most Amazing Showsuite building - Shanghai 2006

normally be perceived as conservative. On the contrary, to Law they are among the most innovative, 'because they know how much inertia is generated by bureaucracy and the difficulty for ideas to be generated, permeated and matured through their organisations'.

One concept that repeatedly emerges from this welding of spatial and technology realms is the process of exaggerating reality to create a hyper-reality. It is a theory that is perfectly played out by a project Law is currently engaged in. At 108 storeys, the next skyscraper to grace Hong Kong's skyline, the International Commerce Centre (ICC) Tower, will rank as the third tallest worldwide. Not a clear-cut winner in height, but floors 100 and 101 will grab the prestigious honour of being the world's tallest public observation deck in a commercial building. In a city that has a fixation with verticality and likes to quote superlatives whenever the opportunity arises, this is big news. Law has been invited to propose ideas for the interior of its observation deck, focusing his concept on the need to fulfil two key functions: viewing and eating, logically enough. The sensible strategy would be to split each function between the two

floors, but Law's scheme intermingles the two activities and, in the process, secures the ambition of a double-height space. The two functions can be envisaged as tilted 'halos' that intersect each other and encircle the building core. The restaurant 'halo' is not only on a ramp, but also rotates. Vision-enhancing and info-tainment systems will no doubt add to the already earth-defying experience. The underside of the halos will be illuminated so that from a distance the top of the building will project a double ring of light suspended over the city.

The same client, Sun Hung Kai Properties, has also asked Law to design a show building to launch a new commercial megaproject called Shanghai IFC. In China, and Hong Kong, huge efforts are expended in marketing and promoting future building ventures to the extent that show suites and sales offices are as much a mainstream design typology as restaurants or shops. The show venue for Shanghai IFC, located in Pudong (Shanghai's financial hub), is more fairground roller coaster than conventional building; a continuous ramp looping back on itself in an overlaid figure-of-eight allows prospective tenants and buyers to climb

six floors effortlessly. Variously themed electronic show suites are latched on to the DNA-like strand, highlighting different programmes within the multiuse Shanghai IFC complex, such as retail, residential and office accommodation. Law will be incorporating technology that will generate a life-size optical illusion of the completed building in its precise site context.

While some argue that technology has lost its sex appeal and made our lives more programmed, Law insists that it is engaging our physical and emotional needs on new levels. 'Our technology is like the caveman's flintstone – it keeps us warm, keeps us fed, keeps us safe and allows us to learn,' he enthuses. Luddite is one thing he will never be accused of being. And at the youthful age of 35, he also has a long way to go before the hyperdynamic leaps of technology threaten to leave him behind – as if that's likely. ⧊

Anna Koor is a design and architecture editor and journalist whose industry experience stems from 12 years working and living among practitioners and academics in Asia, particularly Hong Kong.

## Resumé

James Law

**2000**
James Law Cybertecture International founded. Dickson Cyber Express, Bricks & Clicks shopping mall, Kowloon Station, Hong Kong

**2001**
Hong Kong Government RTHK Media Broadcasting Laboratory

**2003**
Palace IFC Cinema, Hong Kong
Pacific Century Cyberworks Multimedia Stores, Tsuen Wan, Hong Kong
Hong Kong Cyber Post Office, Cyberport
Television Broadcast Limited, TV-City, Hong Kong

**2004**
China Telecom Cybertecture Centre, Shantou, China
Broadway Kwai Fong Cinema, Kowloon, Hong Kong
Zheijiang Cybertecture Automobile HQ Building, Hangzhou, China
Tolvanen Morphable House, Denmark (in partnership with IBM)

**2005**
Cybertecture City, Sri Lanka

Palace APM Cinema, Hong Kong
Samsung METRO Cybertecture Retail Stores, Seoul, Korea

**2006**
The Visual Building, New Town Plaza, Hong Kong
Electronic Arts Experience, Peak Tower, Hong Kong
Hong Kong ICC Tower Observation Deck
Shanghai IFC Commercial Showsuite Building, Pudong, Shanghai, China

**Awards**

2004 Asian Innovation Award (awarded by Singaporean president)

2005 Perspective Design Recognition Award (Best Residential Category & Best Overall)

2005 HKDA Award

2005 REDS (UK Retail Entertainment Design Award)

2005 Microsoft Digital Liftestyle Award

# Idea Store, Whitechapel

**Jeremy Melvin** visits David Adjaye and Associates'
second Idea Store in London, on the Whitechapel
Road, and discovers how, through a confluence of
'image, purpose and experience', Adjaye
has been able to advance on the
library as a conventional
building type.

David Adjaye's Idea Store in Whitechapel revives a long and honourable tradition of weaving the cultural practice of architecture into the cultural, social and educational purposes of a library. Its disciplined facade of coloured and clear glass picks up just enough of the tints and shapes of the market stalls in front of it, holding it on the intriguing, rather than the alien, part of the spectrum. And the ease of entry turns intrigue into the possibility of an internal exploration, up its escalators, around its serpentine book shelves and through its various floors. As well as books, magazines and Internet access points are classrooms, a dance studio and café. What starts as a metaphor for autodidactic education appears to merge seamlessly into it, and it is this quality, where image, purpose and experience work together, that distinguishes Adjaye's work from his predecessors in this tradition.

A century ago, the printer Passmore Edwards used his cash to pay for some striking libraries in London's East End, as well as what became the Mary Ward Centre in more salubrious Bloomsbury. The idea of a library then was considerably less fraught than it is now. Its offerings were limited to printed books and magazines, and its social purposes fitted with the overall aims of philanthropy: reduce the temptations of alcohol and incest – for which supervised, panoptical spaces are very suitable – and foster a self-motivated thirst for knowledge. That popularising reading increased the market for Edwards' commercial products was probably not entirely lost on him. Even if the architecture used to achieve these ends was in those free and inventive idioms that even merely competent Edwardian architects could make so attractive, it almost always depended on reference to established tradition to create its effects. Although the formula worked well because architectural and social agendas could be tightly defined

The Idea Store sits serenely in its context, adjacent to a converted brewery and with Foster's 30 St Mary Axe looming in the distance.

and dovetailed, its more than occasional lapses into architectural cliché intensify how it echoes those faintly mechanistic social goals. Without those certainties to provide a static frame of reference, cliché is only cliché.

Fortunately, Adjaye's range of reference is broad enough to cope with the far wider scope of what we would now consider to be culture's raw material and means of delivery, and all these are reflected in the Idea Store's programme and design. Grounded in a late Modernist tradition, his architecture uses tactile and sensory experience that may be related to one or several cultural traditions, but does not entirely depend on them to be meaningful. Two fundamental elements drive this aspect of Adjaye's work. One is his knowledge of Africa and other parts of the developing world, which takes his experience of deprivation beyond anything found in Whitechapel, just as it expands his visual repertoire; the other is his association with leading contemporary artists with whom he has collaborated on homes, studios and installations, including two memorable ones for Chris Ofili's work – the Upper

Room at the Victoria Miro Gallery and the British Pavilion at the Venice Art Biennale of 2003. Both strived for a unification of sense, image and intellect that anyone but Richard Wagner might have accepted as an attempt at the *Gesamtkunstwerk*.

Like many of his artist collaborators, Adjaye is interested in exploring how the experiences and sensations of everyday life can be transformed into a work of art. His approach depends on allusion rather than dogma; it opens a range of visual and physical experiences, rather than using them to induce a predetermined end. As an architect, Adjaye can add the hopes and aspirations that come from a building's function to the visual and sensory qualities of an object itself that all visual artists use to create effect. In a building with as broad a social impact as the Idea Store, in an area as culturally diverse as Whitechapel, such hopes and aspirations reach right into the community and might even be latent and potential connective tissue to give it some cohesion. If his collaborations with Ofili might be considered as some form of *Gesamtkunstwerk*, then the Idea Store

---

**David Adjaye and Associates, Idea Store, Whitechapel, London, 2005**
By reflecting and distorting images of the surrounding buildings and allowing partial views to the inside, the glass facade relates to function, image and context.

Ground-floor plan: the glass facade overhangs, but does not enclose, the street.

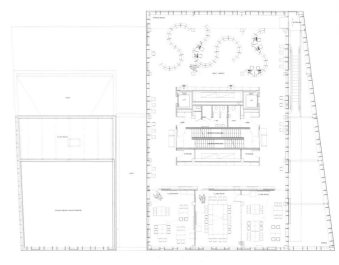

*Mens sana in corpore sano*: to the rear on the first floor is a dance studio.

First-floor plan: at this level are the dance studio and treatment room.

Second-floor plan: the external escalator terminates at this level.

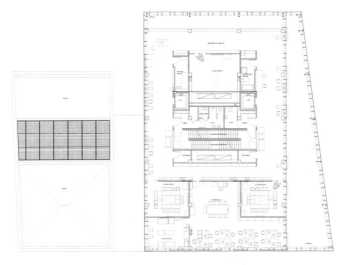

Third-floor plan: a balcony overlooks the second floor.

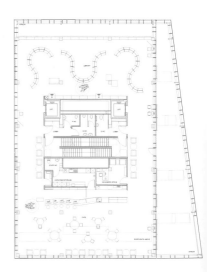

Fourth-floor plan: the architectural promenade concludes in the café, with views back towards the City of London.

Through Adjaye's frame, even the disorder of a busy urban street assumes the qualities of a composition.

might delicately hint at what the Greeks called a Gymnasium, a place where mind and body were developed together. It certainly seeks to make a civic statement.

Its five-storey height and glass facade in an area where brick predominates immediately give the Idea Store prominence and can carry information. With the entrance the flat sign turns into a four-dimensional experience. The first floor cantilevers over the pavement, forming an open atrium that offers its own shelter to shoppers in the street market or pedestrians making their way to the London Hospital on the other side of the Whitechapel Road.

The ground floor is easy and inviting to penetrate. It leads to a seating area with a CD department on one side and a children's library on the other – though the robust, almost industrial nature of construction means that departments can be moved. A more intriguing entrance is the escalator that runs straight up from the street. As it rises, the space narrows and the bustle

of the market is left behind. Turning around opens a prospect towards the City of London, and the narrow atrium-like space frames Foster's Swiss Re tower. A simple ride on an escalator begins to reveal some of London's contradictions before you are plunged straight into the realm of reading.

In keeping with Adjaye's aim of demystifying the idea of a library and learning, the building's basic form is a simple stacked rectangle of five floors. Though there is a clearly implied route up the building to the top floor café, itself a draw through its various spaces, the flow of movement is not coercive. Whether going to a specific department, to take part in an adult education class or to use the dance studio at the rear of the first floor, each visitor can choose from a variety of routes. Concentrating the services in the centre leaves the perimeters free for desks, seats and views. Similarly, though the surfaces are robust and self-finished where appropriate, including

the underside of the floor slabs whose deep ribs and thermal mass help with the heating and cooling strategy, effects like the modulated light prevent the interiors from feeling harsh. Luckily too, Adjaye designed the fittings, devising a simply constructed book-shelf system that can be moved and combined in various configurations to divide space according to need and give each floor a distinct layout.

Helped by the unusual patterns of light, the limited range of materials and forms never becomes monotonous, but nor does it demand attention to usurp the books themselves. In Adjaye's world, architecture can invite and intrigue; it can establish possibilities, allude and make suggestions, and within the ebb and flow of such effects can allow individuals to choose how they engage with cultural activities. Δ

# Adelaide Court

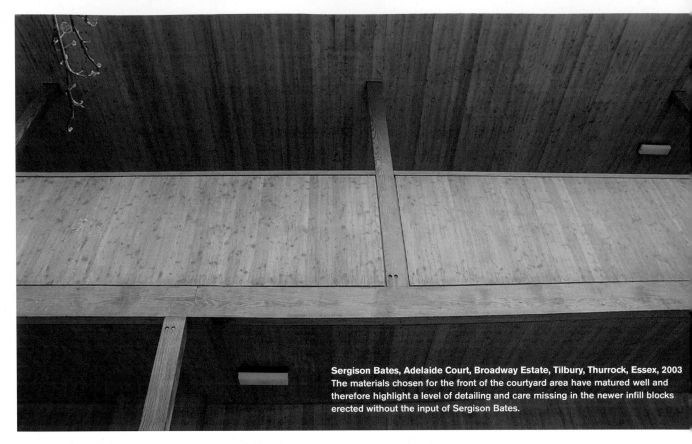

Sergison Bates, Adelaide Court, Broadway Estate, Tilbury, Thurrock, Essex, 2003
The materials chosen for the front of the courtyard area have matured well and
therefore highlight a level of detailing and care missing in the newer infill blocks
erected without the input of Sergison Bates.

**A modest housing block for a run-down estate in Essex presented London-based Sergison Bates Architects with the opportunity to explore the cohesive effects of an assisted self-build scheme for a group of young tenants. Bruce Stewart describes the practice's strategic thinking behind the project and how the design intentions were, to some extent, frustrated by external forces.**

The Broadway Estate in Tilbury, near Thurrock, Essex, is typical of many council housing estates built by local authorities during the 1960s and 1970s. Consisting of largely two-storey, flat-roofed terraces of family homes placed around a large, open, green space, the estate is bounded on its northern edge by three medium-rise tower blocks. As is the case with very many of these large-scale, postwar housing developments, time has not been kind to the Broadway Estate, and the initial street layout has proven to be less than successful. The Modernist ideas of space and light, thought to be the saviour of mass

housing, have been shoddily implemented and have led to the abandonment of the public spaces, such as the large green and the wide footpaths and alleys, and to residents feeling no sense of ownership. Alongside the failure of the design of the estate is the again very familiar tale of increasing unemployment and benefit dependency.

It was within this rather inhospitable environment that architectural firm Sergison Bates was asked to provide a small intervention that would transform a particularly tricky plot into a safer, better-loved space. A young firm

founded in 1996, Sergison Bates has won several awards for its work. A kee[n] interest in the quality of the spaces it designs is matched by a thorough and innovative interest in the nature of the materials used. The range of scale of th[e] practice's projects – from modest singl[e] family dwellings to large-scale urban planning solutions – is always approached with care and sensitivity f[or] the end user and the environment in which the architects find themselves.

The site within the estate was a sm[all] area that, due to the layout of the surrounding streets, was well hidden from outside observers and as such wa[s]

From the upper-level access of the 2003 building, views out across the industrial landscape that surrounds the estate are quite striking. The wooden cladding of this elevation has matured well, as has a sparse amount of planting. It can only be hoped that the newer blocks, one of which can be seen here in the near background, will mature as well.

a prime area for drug taking and underage drinking. Working with the New Islington and Hackney, and the New Essex, housing associations (now known as Mosaic Housing), the scheme was the first phase of a larger regeneration programme envisaged for the community. After discussions with the agencies involved, and as part of the 'New Deal for Communities' initiative, it was thought most appropriate that the scheme should focus on the very disenfranchised youth of the estate for whom there were little or no amenities or targeted housing units – a deficiency that was leading to a migration of the young out of the area.

Once the end users had been identified it was then a natural progression for the architects to consider how the process of architecture could further help the targeted group and give them skills and, hopefully, the confidence to try to break free from the despondency that being young and unemployed can create. The scheme was therefore designed around the idea of the prospective residents

being heavily involved in the construction of the new flats – a process known as assisted self-build – alongside attendance at a local community college to gain skills and qualifications. In order to keep their benefits, those who signed up had to commit to attending college and to working alongside the main contractor on the building of the flats.

It was the hope of both the architects and the housing associations that allowing the residents to physically contribute to the creation of their own homes would encourage a sense of pride, independence and community. But the process was difficult. Of the original 12 people who agreed to help build the scheme, only four managed to complete the project. Several fell by the wayside, due to the realisation that, in order to end up with their own new flat, a great deal of hard work was needed not only in the relative comfort of a college classroom, but also in the much more uncomfortable conditions of a building site in winter. Others left the scheme because they had found full-time

employment or, in one or two cases, because they were sent to prison.

Although this was the first plot that Sergison Bates was asked to look at, two further plots within the estate were brought on board. Though in the end these were developed by other agencies, at the outset they helped form the strategic thinking of the Sergison Bates scheme. The inclusion of more buildings, and the fact that there was to be a large element of unskilled labour (the new residents), dictated the construction technology for the site. The choice of prefabricated panels within a frame structure was greatly influenced by the increased number of buildings, creating an economy of scale particularly suited to an assisted self-build project. The size of the plot was such that, in order to maximise its potential, two levels of small units would be provided with a courtyard space for the tenants to inhabit and develop. Although the existing buildings surrounding the site are of very little architectural merit, the planning requirements of the local authority meant the existing height and building lines had to be replicated in the new building, it effectively becoming the termination of an existing terrace.

While the planners had imposed constraints on height and so on, the choice of a timber-framed structure allowed the architects to engage with the materials that would define the nature of the building. It is one of the practice's primary philosophical goals to handle materials with clarity and rigour alongside well thought out construction processes. The orientation of the west-facing site, along with the interest in materials, defined the site layout, the new building lying on the eastern edge in order to leave space for the courtyard. The basic structure of the new building is a stiff box, slightly raised from ground level, with piles rather than traditional foundations due to the very marshy nature of the area. The western face of the building was then formed from a wood-clad veranda that shelters the entrances to the individual flats, with the vertical

The new block on Adelaide Road has been shoehorned into a small space overlooking one of the unloved public green spaces that are scattered throughout the estate. The echoes of Adelaide Court are clear, but care in the site planning is missing, with the stairs to the upper level abutting a harsh metal fence.

While the new blocks, which were taken to planning approval stage by Sergison Bates but then handed over to other agencies, have traces of the original – seen in the background – they lack its detailing and attention to materials. Lights and television aerials are rather thoughtlessly tacked on.

circulation attached to the front of it. The overhanging roof provides some weather screening. The remaining three sides of the building were then clad in an unfinished cement weatherboard. This was originally left untreated to provide a strong identity for the new intervention – a positive visual reminder that change can be for the better. The slight differences in colour and how the board would weather were also intended to add to this identity.

The fact that the two extra plots were not in the end part of Sergison Bates' project drastically reduced the viability of having a completely prefabricated system, and partially prefabricated panels that had then to be finished on site were used instead. This shift from the original plan had several knock-on effects, adding to the cost of the building and reducing its thermal integrity. And changes due to the differing perspectives of the housing

association client and the designers also altered the internal layout of the units. Initially, Sergison Bates had wanted to leave the internal space free of partitioning to create a loft-like space that the new residents could adapt and use according to their individual needs. However, the client disagreed on the grounds that since the tenure of the units was to be 100 per cent rental, it was likely that the original occupants would move on, and thus a more traditional plan layout with separate kitchen and bedroom spaces was preferred – a pity, as the opportunity for young people to experiment with domestic space has been lost to the pragmatics of what a landlord thinks is easiest for itself.

It was hoped that the creation of the courtyard would enable the young residents to take ownership of the external element of the site and, through doing so, create a small community. Unfortunately, this has not been as successful as hoped for, due in part to the lack of money to plant the space in such a way as to encourage its use. In addition, the insertion of the new housing block, which is gated to prevent casual passers-by using what is to all intents and purposes a private courtyard space, has meant the removal of a short cut through the site, from the

| ADELAIDE COURT A | G<br>0-29% | F<br>30–39% | E<br>40% | D<br>41–49% | C<br>50–59% | B<br>60–69% | A<br>70–100% |
|---|---|---|---|---|---|---|---|
| QUALITATIVE | | | | | | | |
| Space-Interior | | | | | C | | |
| Space-Exterior | | | | | | B | |
| Location | | | | D | | | |
| Community | | | | D | | | |
| QUANTITATIVE | | | | | | | |
| Construction Cost | | | | | C | | |
| Cost-rental/purchase | | | | | C | | |
| Cost in use | | | | D | | | |
| Sustainability | | | | D | | | |
| AESTHETICS | | | | | | | |
| Good Design? | | | | | | | A |
| Appeal | | | | | | B | |
| Innovative? | | | | | C | | |

This table is based on an analytical method of success in contributing to a solution to housing need. The criteria are: Quality of life – does the project maintain or improve good basic standards? Quantitative factors – has the budget achieved the best it can? Aesthetics – does the building work visually?

The original finish to the building was unpainted grey cement board, with individual variations that would have become more explicit with weathering. The housing association has taken the unfortunate decision to paint over this boarding, not only adding to the maintenance costs of the building, but actually making it stand out from its neighbours more than was previously the case.

The assisted self-build scheme of 2003 was to help young people into their first homes. The scheme was 100 per cent rental with no equity for the residents. Having gained planning approval for the remaining sites, the end-user base has changed, along with the quality. These units are now being presented as a shared-ownership scheme by the housing association.

estate to the nearby mainline railway station. Many of the residents have taken exception to this and vandalised the gates and fences.

And in another move, which could almost be an act of vandalism also, the landlords have painted over the exposed cement weatherboarding that clad the back and sides of the building, removing the individuality of the project and leaving an anonymous magnolia block, while also adding to the maintenance costs for the building.

Nevertheless, Adelaide Court is a very attractive and well-designed project that has tried to engage with how architecture and construction can help to mend fractured communities. Had Sergison Bates developed the other two plots alongside it, the benefit for the estate would have been much more apparent. Though these sites were investigated by the architects and taken to planning approval stage, they were given to other agencies to develop and are currently being completed. Almost three years after the completion of the initial project, in 2003, it is sad to say that, while the original building by Sergison Bates has been used as a template for the new infill buildings, they are very poor imitations. Whilst Adelaide Court dealt with ideas of densification and the sensitive handling of materials, the new dwellings have been poorly detailed and their positioning on the sites available to them is awkward to say the least. The increased availability of affordable housing is, of course, something to be welcomed, especially in run-down and neglected areas such as the Broadway Estate, but it is a great shame that such a good model should be undermined by a lack of sensitivity. Here, the ideas explored by Sergison Bates have been misinterpreted at best, and ignored at worst. ⊿

Bruce Stewart is currently researching and writing *The Architects' Navigation Guide to New Housing*, to be published in early 2007 by Wiley-Academy. He trained as an architect and is currently a college teacher at the Bartlett School of Architecture, UCL London.

| ADELAIDE COURT B | G 0-29% | F 30–39% | E 40% | D 41–49% | C 50–59% | B 60–69% | A 70–100% |
|---|---|---|---|---|---|---|---|
| QUALITATIVE | | | | | | | |
| Space-Interior | | | | | C | | |
| Space-Exterior | | | E | | | | |
| Location | | | E | | | | |
| Community | | | | D | | | |
| QUANTITATIVE | | | | | | | |
| Construction Cost | | | | D | | | |
| Cost-rental/purchase | | | | | C | | |
| Cost in use | | | | D | | | |
| Sustainability | | | E | | | | |
| AESTHETICS | | | | | | | |
| Good Design? | | | E | | | | |
| Appeal | | F | | | | | |
| Innovative? | | F | | | | | |

This table is based on an analytical method of success in contributing to a solution to housing need. The criteria are: Quality of life – does the project maintain or improve good basic standards? Quantitative factors – has the budget achieved the best it can? Aesthetics – does the building work visually?

## CLOUDS AND CLOUDBUSTING

A cloud can be described as a volume of water held in a gaseous state, neither liquid nor solid. It may also describe a four-dimensional arrangement of sonic grains, which composer and Le Corbusier collaborator Iannis Xenakis described as 'Sound Clouds'.[1] The delicately balanced state of the saturated ether of a water cloud may also be useful for selective climatic conditioning. German environmental engineering consultant Transsolar has developed a cloud-producing, air cleansing and cooling system, exhibited in Frankfurt in 2002 and currently being developed as the New Souk project, a climate-conditioning scheme for a Qatar office building.

Another type of climate-influencing artificial cloud is the condensation trail, or contrail, produced by the turbine of a jet engine as the cool, low-pressure air of our upper atmosphere is mixed with the hot exhaust air of the engine. These route-marking clouds are not uniformly popular with some observers, such as Professor Andrew Carleton of Penn State University, who argues that cirrus clouds (artificially produced or not) 'tend to warm the earth's surface overall because they trap heat more than they reflect the sun's radiation ... This is a concern to climate scientists because it could mean that a lot more contrails would make global warming worse.'[2] This 'atmospheric graffiti' could be avoided by reducing or increasing the flight altitude, but would cause alternative environmental problems.

Perhaps it is time to revisit the ideas or, more specifically, the pioneering yet enduringly contested inventions of psychoanalyst Wilhelm Reich. Reich began his professional career as one of Sigmund Freud's anointed pupils and went on to identify a new physical energy, which he called orgone. Orgone energy may simultaneously exist in the weather and human emotion. It was (he

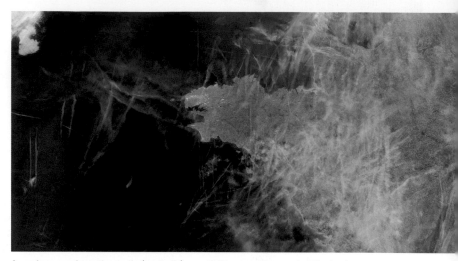

Aeroplane condensation trails (contrails) over Brittany and the west of England, from the *Terra* satellite, 25 April 2005.

attested) tangible and measurable with the aid of a Geiger-Müller counter, and its powerful force could, like all energy, be used for good or ill. He developed the orgone accumulator, a dielectrical capacitor healing box, and his cloudbuster. The latter, when focused on clouds, would draw out orgone energy and remove the clouds. Reich's orgone-accumulator therapy for terminally ill patients attracted much interest and scorn from sections of the scientific community and popular press. In 1947 the US government's Food and Drug Administration (FDA) took out an injunction preventing Reich's use of his technology as a medical treatment. He was put in prison for an alleged violation of the injunction, and died there two years later in 1957. His will stated that his private papers, accumulated at his work place Orgonom in Rangely, Maine, be sealed and stored for 50 years. This archive is due to be opened on 5 November 2007, and is causing a good deal of fantastical speculation (good and bad) about what the contents may reveal, which the Orgone Institute (www.wilhelmreichmuseum.org) is keen to play down.

In 2005, the organisers of the Glastonbury Festival were said to have reprised a Reichian cloudbuster first used at the event in 1971 to guarantee a rain-free event. In May 2005, the Russian president Vladimir Putin ordered the Russian air force to deploy a procedure known as 'cloud seeding' to keep the skies clear for the May Day parade. The process uses dry ice and silver iodide flares dropped into clouds to trigger precipitation and cloud removal. This type of technology has been in existence for about 50 years and is increasingly available from commercial operators selling good weather.

This year has seen the launch of two NASA satellites specifically designed to study clouds, their properties and their cumulative effect on climate. *Calipso* and *Cloudsat*, reported in the *New York Times* (20 April 2006), have now joined three other satellites in a constellation called the 'A-Train' which looks at clouds and climate. The aggregation of data across this array, which will expand to accommodate a sixth satellite, the Orbiting Carbon Observatory (OCO), in 2008, should enable more accurate weather forecasting and prove to be a valuable source of climate-change data.

## A LIGHT PLEASE

A USB 'glow in the dark' information storage duck.

*Much time and energy – not to mention money – are wasted on the design of light fixtures rather than on the required illumination of objects. Should one now propose the 'shining room', the 'glowing book' or the 'shimmering roadway'.*[3]

Some recently noted examples of the self-illuminating object include Rosanna Kilfedder's solar-powered electroluminescent handbag 'Suntrap' whose interior lights up for the swift location of one's keys, and the Forest of Dean's 'glow in the dark' painted sheep who were previously run over at the rate of one a week. Both these items were reported in the same *Guardian* news column (23 September 2005). If you do happen to be out in the dark and do not want your handicraft production to be held up, then buy yourself some Knit Lite knitting needles, illuminated with LED tips. Other glowing products include Veluna from Nippon Electric Glass (NEG), a cast-glass block that glows after exposure to light, although I have yet to see any thoughtful application of this product. And finally the self-illuminating hair gel from Voltage, to go with your high-visibility site clothing one supposes?

## WATER, WATER

Viktor Schauberger pictured with his 'domestic power station' (1955), from Olof Alexandersson's *Living Water.*

With much talk of England's drought, accompanied by a well-timed and sustained deluge, the focus on water and water supply in the not recognisably arid region of the UK turns serious, or perhaps not. Thames Water, one of the UK's privatised water companies, has recently revealed that in the case of an emergency drought one possible solution considered, but subsequently rejected, was the floating of an Arctic iceberg up the river Thames. Whilst one must applaud the theatrical gesture of such a proposal, this comes from a firm that the UK's water regulator Ofwat has estimated loses 915 million litres of potable $H_2O$ a day through the leaking infrastructure of its ageing distribution network. Iceberg refreshments are surely a diversionary wheeze to distract from Thames Water's proposed desalination plant at Beckton in east London, much resisted by London's mayor. Mike Stanger, writing in the *Scotsman* newspaper (18 January 2006), suggests the usefulness and inevitability of a national grid for water, as there is no shortage of water aggregated across the country and only lack of infrastructure is stopping Scotland exporting one of its most abundant natural resources to the rest of Europe and beyond. Viktor Schauberger, the Austrian naturalist and inventor, was widely derided when he claimed in the 1930s that it would not be long before a bottle of mineral water was a more valuable commodity than a bottle of wine. He was convinced of the life-giving properties of this 'earth blood', but only if properly handled. Through his early life and work as a junior forest warden he learnt and studied tree types, rivers, fish and their behaviour, and was increasingly interested in the properties and potential of the water that sustained them. Fish, he said, might be swum by the river as much as they swim in the river. He became convinced that the temperature and geometric motion of the water controlled the very success of a natural habitat, in particular the 'cycloid spiral motion'. Schauberger was, or became, another heretical figure who, like Wilhelm Reich ('Clouds and Cloudbusting') was praised for his early work – in his case on fluid dynamics – then damned for his far-out thinking, which takes in the Trout engine (an implosion engine as opposed to an explosion engine, which utilised his vortex technology), flying-saucer propulsion systems and the 'Golden Plough'. For further information visit www.pks.or.at and Olof Alexandersson's account of Schauberger and his work in *Living Water.*[4]

**Notes**
1. GD Poli, A Piccialli and C Roads, *Representations of Musical Signals*, MIT Press (Cambridge, MA), 1990.
2. http://www.rps.psu.edu/probing/contrails.html.
3. Cedric Price, *Pegasus*, Mobil Services Co Ltd (London), 1972.
4. Olof Alexandersson, *Living Water: Viktor Schauberger and the Secrets of Natural Energy*, Gill & Macmillan (Dublin), 2002.

# Subscribe Now

As an influential and prestigious architectural publication, *Architectural Design* has an almost unrivalled reputation worldwide. Published bimonthly, it successfully combines the currency and topicality of a newsstand journal with the editorial rigour and design qualities of a book. Consistently at the forefront of cultural thought and design since the 1960s, it has time and again proved provocative and inspirational – inspiring theoretical, creative and technological advances. Prominent in the 1980s and 1990s for the part it played in Postmodernism and then in Deconstruction, in the 2000s ⅄ has leveraged a depth and level of scrutiny not currently offered elsewhere in the design press. Topics pursued question the outcomes of technical innovations as well as the far-reaching social, cultural and environmental challenges that present themselves today in a period of increasing global uncertainty. ⅄

SUBSCRIPTION RATES 2006
Institutional Rate (Print only
or Online only): UK£175/US$290
Institutional Rate (Combined Print
and Online): UK£193/US$320
Personal Rate (Print only):
UK £99/US$155
Discount Student* Rate
(Print only): UK£70/US$110

*Proof of studentship will be required when placing an order. Prices reflect rates for a 2006 subscription and are subject to change without notice.

**TO SUBSCRIBE**
Phone your credit card order:
+44 (0)1243 843 828

Fax your credit card order to:
+44 (0)1243 770 432

Email your credit card order to:
cs-journals@wiley.co.uk

Post your credit card or
cheque order to:
John Wiley & Sons Ltd.
Journals Administration Department
1 Oldlands Way
Bognor Regis
West Sussex PO22 9SA
UK

Please include your postal
delivery address with your order.

All ⅄ volumes are available individually.
To place an order please write to:
John Wiley & Sons Ltd
Customer Services
1 Oldlands Way
Bognor Regis
West Sussex PO22 9SA

Please quote the ISBN number of the issue(s) you are ordering.

⅄ is available to purchase on both a subscription basis and as individual volumes

○ I wish to subscribe to ⅄ *Architectural Design* at the **Institutional rate of** (Print only or Online only *(delete as applicable)* £175/US$290.

○ I wish to subscribe to ⅄ *Architectural Design* at the **Institutional rate of** (Combined Print and Online) £193/US$320.

○ I wish to subscribe to ⅄ *Architectural Design* at the **Personal rate of £99/US$155.**

○ I wish to subscribe to ⅄ *Architectural Design* at the **Student rate of £70/US$110.**

○ ⅄ *Architectural Design* is available to individuals on either a calendar year or rolling annual basis; Institutional subscriptions are only available on a calendar year basis. Tick this box if you would like your Personal or Student subscription on a rolling annual basis.

Payment enclosed by Cheque/Money order/Drafts.
Value/Currency £/US$ _____

○ Please charge £/US$ _____
to my credit card.
Account number:

| | | | | | | | | | | | | | | | | | |
|--|--|--|--|--|--|--|--|--|--|--|--|--|--|--|--|--|--|

Expiry date:

| | | | | | |
|--|--|--|--|--|--|

Card: Visa/Amex/Mastercard/Eurocard *(delete as applicable)*

Cardholder's signature _____
Cardholder's name _____
Address _____
_____
_____ Post/Zip Code _____

Recipient's name _____
Address _____
_____
_____ Post/Zip Code _____

**I would like to buy the following issues at £22.99 each:**

○ ⅄ 183 *Collective Intelligence in Design,* Christopher Hight + Chris Perry

○ ⅄ 182 *Programming Cultures: Art and Architecture in the Age of Software,* Mike Silver

○ ⅄ 181 *The New Europe,* Valentina Croci

○ ⅄ 180 *Techniques and Technologies in Morphogenetic Design,* Michael Hensel, Achim Menges + Michael Weinstock

○ ⅄ 179 *Manmade Modular Megastructures,* Ian Abley + Jonathan Schwinge

○ ⅄ 178 *Sensing the 21st-Century City,* Brian McGrath + Grahame Shane

○ ⅄ 177 *The New Mix,* Sara Caples and Everardo Jefferson

○ ⅄ 176 *Design Through Making,* Bob Sheil

○ ⅄ 175 *Food + The City,* Karen A Franck

○ ⅄ 174 *The 1970s Is Here and Now,* Samantha Hardingham

○ ⅄ 173 *4dspace: Interactive Architecture,* Lucy Bullivant

○ ⅄ 172 *Islam + Architecture,* Sabiha Foster

○ ⅄ 171 *Back To School,* Michael Chadwick

○ ⅄ 170 *The Challenge of Suburbia,* Ilka + Andreas Ruby

○ ⅄ 169 *Emergence,* Michael Hensel, Achim Menges + Michael Weinstock

○ ⅄ 168 *Extreme Sites,* Deborah Gans + Claire Weisz

○ ⅄ 167 *Property Development,* David Sokol

○ ⅄ 166 *Club Culture,* Eleanor Curtis

○ ⅄ 165 *Urban Flashes Asia,* Nicholas Boyarsky + Peter Lang

○ ⅄ 164 *Home Front: New Developments in Housing,* Lucy Bullivant

○ ⅄ 163 *Art + Architecture,* Ivan Margolius

○ ⅄ 162 *Surface Consciousness,* Mark Taylor

○ ⅄ 161 *Off the Radar,* Brian Carter + Annette LeCuyer

○ ⅄ 160 *Food + Architecture,* Karen A Franck